Best Wishes,

Kathleen Garvey

YOUR MONEY PERSONALITY

YOUR MONEY PERSONALITY

What It Is and How
You Can Profit from It

Kathleen Gurney, Ph.D.

Doubleday

NEW YORK
1988

Library of Congress Cataloging-in-Publication Data
Gurney, Kathleen.
Your money personality.

Includes index.
1. Money—Psychological aspects.   I. Title.
HG222.3.G87   1988   332.4'01'9   87-24449
ISBN 0-385-24254-9

Money is like a sixth sense—and you can't make use of the other five without it.

—Somerset Maugham

ACKNOWLEDGMENTS

I want to thank Carol Orsag Madigan, my colleague and friend, for the high level of professionalism and exceptional dedication that she gave to this book. She was generous with her ideas, time, and energy, and contributed significantly to the translation of the message for the reader. I feel very fortunate that we are continuing to work together.

And to Bob Newell, I wish to express my sincere appreciation and gratitude for always being there for me, whether as caring critic, reading and rereading the manuscript, or as constant supporter. His keen insight, analytical skills, and professional expertise were an immeasurable asset throughout the various stages of this book.

In addition, I feel deeply grateful to Florence Ollstein for giving her wisdom as well as her support. Her encouragement of my work and this book has been invaluable.

I am also grateful to Jerry Baesel, my former professor and now friend, who introduced me to the world of finance and economics. And to Jannie Mackay, who has pitched in more than her fair share as a friend and a colleague. And to David Grossman, whose professional opinions I value, as well as Elliot Gordon and Roger Angle, who have always believed in this book. And special thanks to my parents as well as the numerous friends and colleagues who have been a continual source of support.

And finally, I am grateful to a great many people who cannot be thanked by name—the men and women whose experiences appear in this book and whose privacy I have promised to protect. *Your Money Personality* would not exist without them.

Contents

Contents

Introduction

Money. Thoughts of the almighty dollar evoke the strongest of emotions—happiness, depression, greed, envy, fear, excitement. For Americans, money is an identifiable benchmark, our most valid measure of success. It symbolizes power, security, love, freedom, and self-respect.

Money is much more than an economic necessity. It is one of the most powerful motivators of human behavior. It taps into the deepest layers of our personalities and sets off powerful emotional charges. Who you are and how you relate to money make the difference between working hard or working smart, struggling financially or living comfortably, making ends meet or feeling enriched, between poverty and wealth.

Why does money seem to work so well in some people's lives yet act as a destructive force in others? Do only the rich enjoy a sense of money satisfaction? Are the wealthy the only group that has learned to use money as a tool for happiness and contentment? Do you have to be a power seeker and a risk-taker in order to be financially successful? Why do some talented, creative, educated people end up on the bottom rung of the money ladder? How do men and women differ in their attitudes about money?

These questions have never been fully addressed. Amazingly, the psychological and financial arenas have never joined forces. We know so very little about our money selves and the potent force that money has on all aspects of our lives. We live in an age of increasing self-awareness, yet our otherwise liberated selves remain perplexed about the role that money plays in our everyday lives. Our confusing and paradoxical attitudes about money have set up a number of money traps from which we are unable to escape. At the same time we both condemn and worship money. These double messages are entrenched in every lifestyle, every profession, every personal relationship.

Nothing stirs the imagination like the thrill of money, yet its meaning eludes our intellectual grasp. Those of us trapped in unfulfilling money personalities have been unable to cross over into a better money world because we haven't a clue as to how to do it. There are an overabundance of books, seminars, and conferences on money strategies for getting rich, seeking money and power, climbing the corporate ladder. Yet none of the advice givers get to the root of the dilemma—making your emotional self work in harmony with your money self.

Your Money Personality is designed to make you a winner in the money game. To begin the game it is necessary to discover how you fit into America's financial picture. Are you a money participant or a money spectator? Do your attitudes and feelings about money foster economic health or economic deprivation? Do you understand and implement the rules of the money game or are you playing by an old set of standards that sabotage financial liberation?

My pioneering work in "financial psychology" dates back to the fall of 1981 when I became my first client. I had just received my doctorate degree from the University of Southern California and had accepted the university's offer to lecture on psychology for the Department of Defense at American military bases in Holland, Germany, Belgium, and Spain. Per my request, my paychecks were to be deposited into my checking account every month.

As I moved about Europe, I wrote checks at the PXs and banks on the military bases to cover my living expenses and sent checks back to Los Angeles to cover my home mortgage payment and other bills. At the end of six weeks abroad, I tried to cash a check for fifty dollars at a PX in Belgium and was told that the check was no good. Soon afterward, bounced checks from all over Europe began to catch up with me. I called the payroll department at USC to find out what had happened and was told that due to an administrative oversight my contract had not been processed and I was not on the payroll. They would look into the matter and rectify the situation immediately. I had enough money in a savings account to cover my bills for two months, but two months later my checks were still bouncing because the payroll error had still not been corrected. As a result, I called my parents to borrow money from them.

As the weeks passed and USC failed to untangle the bureaucratic red tape, my money anxiety began to grow. I kept a logbook of every dollar I spent and all the checks that had bounced. I was blacklisted, had no credit line in Europe or the United States, and felt powerless. Since I had very little cash, I rarely went out in the evenings and spent a lot of time wondering how I had allowed myself to get into such a financial fix. While I kept telling myself that the problem was only temporary and I would laugh about it someday, I was anxious and depressed. I lost ten pounds and began to suffer bouts of insomnia. One of my journal entries at the time read: "My world has fallen off its axis. I have felt frightened and lonely before but never like this. What has happened to the sense of well-being I've had all of my life? Everything stable and certain in my life is in flux. Without money, how vulnerable am I? What does money mean to me? I will never let money do this to me again."

The university finally straightened out its financial error, but I knew that I would never forget the financial and psychological impact of that year in Europe. When I returned to Los Angeles, I began to take graduate courses in finance and to read books about money. Although I found countless books about money and investing, there was very little information about how people feel about money and how feelings and attitudes influence the way people handle their money. I felt there should be information and services available to others who might be experiencing money problems individually as well as in relationships.

My money problems in Europe were due to the fact that while I was solvent on paper, I was cash poor. For years I had invested all of my money in real estate and had no liquidity for any emergencies. After taking a number of financial courses, I was ready to diversify my investments and sought out an investment adviser with a major financial institution. Throughout my first meeting with him, I felt he was only trying to persuade me to buy the products he was selling. I walked away certain that he really didn't understand how I felt about my money—the kind of investments that would not only reap profits but would leave me content, secure, and comfortable. He appeared very well intentioned but placed my money into investments that left me anxious and unhappy. At first, I attributed my uncomfortable feelings to the new experience of investing in unknown areas. In retrospect, I realized my discomfort was due to the fact that he had not really taken the time to get to know me—what I was all about, what investments would give me peace of mind. He was not able to match my money style with suitable investments because he did not have a tool that enabled him to understand my money style.

Subsequently, I developed the Moneymax Profile, the cornerstone of financial psychology. The one-page questionnaire determines attitudes on thirteen financial traits that influence money behavior and investment decisions. Using the Moneymax Profile, I surveyed a large segment of the American population to determine how people think about money and how they deal with money. The results of that national survey divide Americans into nine distinct money styles, and those styles are the basis of this book.

Today my company, Financial Psychology Corporation, markets the Moneymax Profile for use in major corporations and financial service companies. I have also used the profile in my private practice to help clients change self-sabotaging money styles into styles that are more productive and enriching.

The Moneymax national survey will be updated every year. In addition, new information on each of the nine Moneymax personalities will be available: the cars they drive and the credit cards they use, the magazines they read and the breakfast cereals they eat, the television shows they watch, where they live, and where they go on vacation.

Your Money Personality is divided into three sections. Part One, "Let's Talk Money," looks at our generation's growing obsession with money and the enormous changes that obsession is bringing into our everyday lives. This section also looks at money relationships, both at home and at work. Part Two, "Discovering Your Money Personality," explores how each of us has developed a money style and examines the thirteen traits which are the key to our money style. In addition, this section devotes one chapter to each of the nine Moneymax Profile groups—The Entrepreneurs, the Hunters, the High Rollers, the Safety Players, the Achievers, the Perfectionists, the Money Masters, the Producers, and the Optimists. Finally, Part Three, "Attaining Mental Wealth," presents in-depth interviews with successful businessmen and businesswomen from a variety of professional arenas, and concludes with the chapter, "Maximizing Your Money Personality."

Your Money Personality is a guidebook to help you find the "you" in your money. It will help you to understand how to become more financially successful by learning about the financial traits which affect how you earn, spend, save, and invest money. It will help you to develop insight into how you react to money, why you have those reactions, and how your attitudes affect financial success or failure. *Your Money Personality* will help you to achieve financial excellence, freedom, and peace of mind, and reduce the debilitating effects of stress and confusion.

You are a winner with money when you understand how it works for you: when you control money instead of money controlling you; when your investments give you peace of mind as well as a piece of the action; when you learn to work smart as well as work hard; when you enjoy money whether you are making it, investing it, or spending it; when money becomes a vehicle to assist in realizing goals and dreams. *Your Money Personality* is designed to allow you to tap your inner financial wealth and narrow the gap between the vision of you—as you are with money—and you, as you would like to be.

PART ONE

LET'S TALK
MONEY

1

〰️

Har-Money
Where Money Meets the Mind

It was 9 A.M. Saturday on a bright summer day in Los Angeles and Sam was unlocking the door to Clancy's ("Clancy Can't Say No") car dealership. The weekend promised to be a busy one since it was their biggest car sale of the year. Ads on television and radio had been running all week assuring customers that "No reasonable offer will be refused."

Sam had been selling cars for twelve years and he knew all the tricks of the trade—he had even invented a few of them. Today he was planning to sell a lot of cars, particularly since he and his wife had just put down a deposit on a two-week family vacation to Hawaii. Sam planned to have a good time and some extra cash would certainly guarantee a good time. The car to move was the Majestic, a model that had been selling well for the last six months. Rated high for performance and dependability by most car magazines, the Majestic had a nice sleek look and overall was a very handsome car. A new shipment of Majestics had just arrived two days ago and Sam was ready to wheel and deal.

One of the first customers in the door was a Moneymax Hunter. She was tall, very attractive, very well dressed, and seemed to be in her mid-thirties. Accompanied by a female friend, the Hunter was immediately attracted to the flashy red, deluxe model of the Majestic. As

Sam approached the two women, he could smell a sale. The Hunter said to Sam, "I really wasn't planning to buy a car today. My friend and I are on our way shopping but as we drove by, we saw this car in the window and we just had to stop in. What a beautiful car! How much does it cost?"

Sam walked the Hunter over to the other side of the car and showed her the sticker price, which was just over $15,000. The Hunter said, "Oh, I had no idea it would cost that much. Can't you give me a better price?" Putting on his most sincere look of helplessness, Sam told the Hunter that the price was firm—the Majestic was a car in great demand and, as a matter of fact, the car she was looking at was the only deluxe model, in red, that he had in stock. Perhaps she would like to look at the standard model, which cost less?

As Sam and the two women moved toward a standard model Majestic, he knew the Hunter would never settle for less than a red, deluxe model. Showing her the standard model would only help to convince her that she should buy the deluxe edition. The sticker price on the standard model—Sam showed her a dull, gray model—was $12,041. Of course, he pointed out that the standard model didn't have an air conditioner, cruise control, a rear window defroster, a stereo radio/cassette player—none of the options found on the deluxe. The Hunter then asked how much it would cost to add some options —and she listed them—to the standard model, and Sam went to his desk to get pencil and paper.

While he was away, the Hunter said to her friend, "My high school class reunion—dinner dance and picnic—is coming up next weekend. I would love to drive up in that fabulous red car. My best friend from high school would just fall over. Still, I probably shouldn't make such a big purchase now; I have so many bills to pay. But there are so many ways these days to finance a car. I bet I could figure out a way to afford the monthly payments. My down payment would have to be pretty small since I'm short of cash. But can't you just see me behind the wheel of that car?"

When Sam returned, he showed the Hunter that when he added up all the options she wanted to the price of the standard model, the price was coming very close to the deluxe model. In addition, he had checked his inventory list and there were no red, standard model

Majestics in stock. He could, however, get one for her, add the options, and promise her delivery in about eight weeks.

The Hunter became a bit agitated. She needed the car for next
weekend. What good would it do to get it after the reunion? She
looked at the numbers and saw that the salesman had a point—all in
all, she might as well go for the deluxe model, since the difference in
price was not that much. As she looked at her watch, she noticed that
she had been in the car dealership for over an hour. She had a lot of
shopping to do that day and had an early dinner date at six. She knew
that salespeople could come down on the price of a car, so she boldly
said, "You just have to give me a better deal."

Sam said, "What would it take to get you to write out a check
today? Tell me what you are prepared to pay for this car and I will
talk to my manager and see what I can do." The Hunter thought for a
moment and said, "I think $14,500 is reasonable—for the red, deluxe
model." Sam said, "I'll do my best," and walked away. The Hunter
said to her friend, "I knocked $500 from the price of the car; do you
think the manager will go for it?"

When Sam returned, he had a big smile on his face and he shook his
head and said, "I didn't think the manager would approve that price,
but we are out to sell cars this weekend. Madam, you just bought
yourself a fabulous car—the only one like it on the lot. I know you
will be happy with it."

After the two women left, Sam thought, "If I can keep this up, I
might be able to stay in Hawaii for an extra week or two." What the
Hunter did not know was that the difference between the dealer's cost
for her deluxe Majestic and the sticker price was $2,200. Her $500
savings was a mere drop in the bucket to Sam. If pressed to the wall,
he would have come down lower on the price of the car. As a matter
of fact, he had sold Majestics for as little as $400 over the sticker price.
If the Hunter had had that knowledge, she might have paid $13,200
for the car instead of $14,500.

By midafternoon Sam had sold three cars. None of his sales had
been as profitable as the Hunter deal but all in all he was having a very
good day. Across the room he spotted a man standing beside the gray
standard model Majestic he had tried to sell to the Hunter. This man,
a Moneymax Achiever, looked deadly serious as he wrote down numbers on a tablet attached to a clipboard he carried. Sam put on a big

smile and said, "Great little car there; you couldn't have picked a
nicer one. Can I answer any questions you might have? As you probably know, this is the best weekend of the year to buy a car here at
Clancy's." The Achiever looked directly at Sam and said, "I'm not
planning on buying a car today. I'm just doing some comparison shopping."

"What do you want to pay for this car?" Sam inquired. Once again
the Achiever said, "I'm not planning on buying a car today." Sam
thought to himself, "This guy is going to be a tough sale but I feel it in
my bones that he wants to buy a car—this car." For a few minutes
Sam chatted about the wonderful features of the Majestic—nice style,
good gas mileage, great reliability. Then he gently returned to the
question of price, "Now, what are you prepared to pay for this car?
Give me a number and I'll take it to my manager." For the third time,
the Achiever said, "I'm not planning on buying a car today, and
besides that, why don't you quote me a price?" Sam was getting edgy.
He retorted, "Look, I can't go in and talk to the manager until I have
a price commitment from you." The Achiever shot back, "You mean,
you sell these cars every day and you don't know what to charge for
them?"

Sam was getting nowhere so he walked away from the Achiever to
take a phone call. Finally, he decided to give it a final try and approached the Achiever, who was still taking notes beside the gray
Majestic. "I'm sure we can come to an agreement, so tell me what you
are prepared to pay for this great little car?" implored Sam. At that
point, the Achiever handed Sam a note card:

	DEALER COST	STICKER PRICE
Majestic standard model	$10,400	$12,041
Air conditioner (option)	680	798
Rear defroster (option)	130	160
Destination charge	440	440
Totals	$11,650	$13,439

Sam started to get angry. Who did this guy think he was—some
Wall Street hot shot? He didn't get too many customers who did this

much homework when buying a car and it put Sam in a bad negotiating position.

The Achiever asked, "Including your profit and overhead, what are you willing to sell this car for?" Sam started to mumble something about the high cost of advertising for the big weekend sale and said the Achiever's numbers didn't include "things" that needed to be added into the dealer's price of the car. Then Sam said, "How much profit do you think is reasonable?" The Achiever said, "You tell me."

Sam was getting tired of this bickering. He said, "Would you buy the car right now for $12,250?" The Achiever said, "As I told you, I was not planning to buy a car today." "How about $12,150?" asked Sam. For the next twenty minutes the price jumped back and forth. Finally the seller and the buyer agreed on a price of $12,000—$350 above dealer cost but $1,439 below sticker price. The Achiever had taken the $1,789 difference between dealer and sticker price and trimmed it down by $1,439. The Hunter, on the other hand, had taken her difference of $2,200 and trimmed it down by $500.

With two hours to go before Clancy's closed up for the day, a Moneymax Perfectionist entered the showroom. Carrying a couple of magazines and a handful of papers, he seemed nervous and dropped all of his papers as he bumped into Sam. After a few minutes of chitchat, the Perfectionist said that he was interested in the standard model Majestic—no options, just a radio. Sam told him that he should at least consider an air conditioner but the Perfectionist said he didn't need an air conditioner or any other of the unnecessary options that bumped up the price of a car.

As they started to talk money, Sam became aware that the Perfectionist had definitely been to a few other dealerships, checking out the price of the standard Majestic. "Hell," thought Sam, "this guy has done some comparison shopping and he really wants to buy a car today. I'll give him a decent deal." Sam started out at $700 over the dealer cost of the car. The Perfectionist said, "No, that is way above what I'm willing to pay for this car." Then Sam moved down to $600 above dealer cost. The Perfectionist did not budge. Another forty-five minutes went by and Sam was down to $450 above dealer cost.

The Perfectionist said, "Look, I know how you sales people take advantage of customers. Either you give me a fair price or I'll take my business elsewhere." Looking at his watch, Sam saw that closing time was only thirty minutes away and he made one last attempt to sell the Majestic—$350 over cost. Except for the sale to the Achiever, Sam hadn't sold a car all week for that small a profit.

The Perfectionist turned toward the door and finally stated what he was willing to pay for the car. The price he offered was $100 below dealer cost. Sam was astonished. This man had done some comparison shopping but he really didn't know how all the numbers stacked up. Obviously, the Perfectionist didn't know a good deal when it was handed to him on a silver platter. Sam said the price was so unacceptable that he couldn't talk to his manager. The Perfectionist strode out of the showroom, saying, "And your ad said you would accept any reasonable offer."

WHAT IS THE MONEYMAX PROFILE AND HOW DOES IT WORK?

There are many different theories about personality, but to date none have looked at personality in terms of money. Do Americans differentiate themselves from one another by the ways they think and act with money?

How do Americans feel about money and how do those attitudes and feelings affect the way Americans earn, invest, and enjoy their money? The Moneymax Profile, a questionnaire designed to address those issues, was used in a nationwide survey to determine for the first time how psychological factors influence money management. The people included in the survey were representative of the American population, according to U.S. Census data.

The Moneymax national survey asked Americans to respond to a variety of questions which measured attitudes on thirteen financial traits: involvement, pride, emotionality, altruism, anxiety, power, work ethic, contentment, risk-taking, self-determination, spending, reflectivity, and trust. In addition, participants were asked to provide demographic information including age, sex, income and asset levels, education, geographic location, marital status, and occupation. Finally, participants were asked to provide comprehensive investment data—including what investment and saving vehicles they use, the degree of risk they perceive in those vehicles, how satisfied they are with those investments, and how they would rank financial goals and objectives (current income, growth and appreciation, tax advantage, safety).

When the scores were tabulated, using sophisticated statistical techniques, Americans were clustered into nine groups, each with a distinct money style or personality. Not only do the people in each group share similar attitudes about money, but they have similar investment preferences and financial goals. The nine groups, or money styles, determined by the Moneymax national survey are the Entrepreneurs, the Hunters, the High Rollers, the Safety Players, the Achievers, the Perfectionists, the Money Masters, the Producers, and the Optimists.

It is very important to point out that membership in a group was determined solely by money attitudes—not by how much money was earned or accumulated or by any other demographic factor. That single criterion—attitudes about money—is what makes the Moneymax survey unique. When the thirteen trait scores of any group are analyzed as a whole, it is possible to learn how that combination of attitudes affects the way that group deals with money.

Does the combination of traits enable one to earn and accumulate money and get pleasure and security from money? Or do the traits sabotage financial opportunities and success? Part Two of this book, "Discovering Your Money Personality," will explain the significance of all thirteen traits and examine each of the nine Moneymax groups.

While *Your Money Personality* is not intended to give investment advice, it does present investment preferences and satisfaction levels as stated by each of the Moneymax groups. While the Moneymax survey was able to ascertain a trend in the investment preferences and satisfaction levels for the various groups, it did not determine whether a particular group used and liked an investment because the group profited financially from it. While one may assume that a group prefers and is satisfied with an investment because it makes money or because of economic and market conditions, that is not necessarily the case. People choose and like particular investments for a number of reasons outside of anticipated or realized profits—including the amount of involvement and control they want with an investment; how safe or risky the investment is perceived; how comfortable or anxious they feel about an investment. Many of those reasons will be discussed in this book. In other words, if you feel, after reading this book, that you are an Entrepreneur (they use and like common stock), I am not suggesting that you start making investments in the stock market. Before investing your money, you need to be thoroughly aware of your money personality and educated about a variety of investments. You should also consult with a professional financial adviser if you are not inclined to do your own investment analysis.

In all forms of human behavior there is a relationship between how you think and feel about a situation and how you act upon that situation. Money is no exception. Your money attitudes determine the amount of money you earn and accumulate, the way you invest your money, and the happiness that money brings into your life. If your money style is positive and healthy, then money is a useful tool to enhance personal and financial growth. If your money style is self-sabotaging and unproductive, then money is a nemesis that fosters insecurity and misery. Before you can manage money successfully, you need to understand how and why you act and react to money. That insight will help you to become your greatest financial asset.

THE MEANINGS OF MONEY

Simply put, money is a medium of exchange. We go to work, perform our required duties, and get paid with money. That money has a certain value and we exchange it for goods and services necessary for our everyday life. We spend money to buy necessities like food, clothing, and shelter, and we spend it on items that give us pleasure and enjoyment like cars, vacations, televisions, motorboats.

Throughout history, hundreds of different objects have been used as a medium of exchange. Among them are brass rods, salt, gunpowder, woodpecker scalps, and the jawbones of pigs. Today, the natives of Yap, an island in western Micronesia, still use large doughnut-shaped stones (some as large as twelve feet across) as a medium of exchange, while on Rossel Island in the Pacific the natives use shell money—ndap shells are men's money and nko shells are women's money.

In actuality, money is not real wealth but a device to measure wealth. Somehow the distinction has become blurred. Today money is less of a commodity and more of an idol. Its definition has expanded to such an extent that it is impossible to differentiate wealth from money from material goods. Or as John Ruskin said, "What right have you to take the word wealth, which originally meant 'well-being,' and degrade and narrow it by confining it to certain sorts of material objects measured by money?"

Psychologists contend that money has many values beyond the goods and services it will buy. Attitudes about money are intrinsically tied into everyone's personality framework. Money is emotional currency that symbolizes many of our unconscious needs and desires. Among the most prominent:

Security. If I have enough money, I will always be safe. No person and no catastrophe can ever harm me. Money is a protective shield that guards against all danger.

Freedom. If I have enough money, I can buy financial independence. I can freely choose my jobs or choose not to work. My options are open, my life is in my hands, and I can tell anybody to "go to hell."

Love. If I have enough money, more people will care about me. In this society, it's easier to love a rich person than a poor person. Money makes relationships a lot easier. Who wants to fight over money all the time?

Respect. If I have enough money, everyone will recognize that I have merit, that I accomplished what I set out to do. I worked hard and earned the money, earned the respect.

Power. If I have enough money, nobody will ever push me around. If life is divided into winners and losers, I will come out on top. I will be strong and have total control over my life. People will recognize my importance and no one will try to manipulate me.

Happiness. If I have enough money, I would truly be happy. I'm tired of scraping by from paycheck to paycheck. I'm tired of fighting with my husband (or wife) and kids about money. Maybe I'll never be able to relax and enjoy life. Most of my problems concern money. If I didn't have to worry about money, my whole life would turn around.

We have lived with our money attitudes and habits for so long that we rarely stop to take a look at our behavior. We may spend a full day shopping at various grocery stores to get the best bargains and go out the next day and impulsively buy a new car. We may continually complain about a lowly job and a lowly salary yet never seriously take action to seek out a new position. We may help friends move into a new home or generously offer to paint their garage, yet refuse to lend them even a small sum of money. We may buy designer jeans for our children, yet turn down their request for a raise in allowance. We may have loving relationships with brothers and sisters, yet find ourselves in the middle of a bitter feud when parents die and the estate has to be settled.

It's easy to snicker and gossip about the money paradoxes of others —your spouse, your neighbor, your relative, your boss. And it's particularly enticing to look at the money styles of the rich and famous. Oil tycoon J. Paul Getty installed pay telephones in his seventy-two-room mansion. Hetty Green, once the richest woman on Wall Street, wore the same black dress every day and had pockets sewn into her petticoats where she stashed cash and stock certificates. When her son Ned injured his knee, Hetty dressed him in rags and tried to get him treated as a charity patient; Ned's leg was amputated due to neglect. Mark Twain, one of America's preeminent authors, invested in so many investment schemes—a self-pasting scrapbook, a bed clamp to keep children from kicking off blankets, a fire extinguisher that worked like a hand grenade, a granulated high protein food concentrate—that he was forced into bankruptcy. Albert Einstein was so ambivalent about money that when he came to the United States just before World War II to work at Princeton University, he asked for $3,000 a year in salary, but university officials insisted upon paying him $16,000.

One doesn't have to turn the pages of a history book or tune the television in to "Lifestyles of the Rich and Famous," to build up a repertoire of money paradoxes, money hypocrisies, and money manipulations. The stories abound everywhere and among every income group. The following is just a small sampling of stories which have been told to me by clients, people I interviewed for this book, and people I have met in financial seminars and workshops:

Arthur and Ruth are in their mid-sixties and have amassed a sizable fortune. They inherited an electronics company from Ruth's father and over twenty years built it into a multimillion-dollar business. The couple live in a small mobile home, never go on vacation, don't own a car, and take the bus to work six days a week. Since they got married in 1942, they have kept a yearly journal of every dollar they have spent. More than forty-five ledger books are neatly arranged on a bookshelf in their bedroom.

Kevin sends long-stemmed red roses to women he has never met but who have been recommended as "good date material" by friends. After sending two or three dozen roses, Kevin calls and invites the women to the most expensive restaurant in town. According to Kevin, "It always works. Money and romance is an irresistible combination." Kevin estimates that his florist bills exceed $2,500 a year.

Eileen, a corporate vice president, earns $85,000 a year and has just completed plans to start her own business. When asked what financial accomplishment gave her the most pride and satisfaction, she replied, "Every year I save around $1,000 by clipping coupons."

Jessica, a secretary for a public relations firm, is attractive, popular, and gregarious. Always in attendance at office gatherings and dinner parties, she has never invited any of her coworkers to her apartment. For years her friends have speculated why Jessica is so social at everyone else's home and yet so antisocial when anyone suggests having a party at her home. What was she hiding? The truth was simple but sad: Jessica was ashamed of her studio apartment and vowed not to have friends over until she could afford a nicer place and a good set of china and crystal to entertain properly.

Bert is on welfare and has a wife and five children to support. In one year he spent $2,000 on lottery tickets and his winnings totaled $15. Undaunted, Bert says that his ship is coming in any day.

Craig, a salesman who earns $60,000 a year, always brings a six-pack of beer to a party. As soon as he arrives, he puts the beer in the back of the refrigerator or at the back of the bar. One of the first guests to leave, Craig will fetch his beer, put it into a paper bag, and say to the host, "I had a wonderful time. Hope you don't mind but since nobody drank the beer, I think I'll take it home."

Larry is an accountant for a large insurance company. A financial whiz at work, Larry refuses to have anything to do with managing his own money. All purchasing decisions as well as investment decisions are left to his wife Nancy. When she makes a mistake that results in a financial loss, Larry is upset and belligerent. Nancy is more than willing to turn over the financial reins to her husband but Larry says he has to deal with money all day at work and he's not about to deal with it at home.

Earl is a self-made millionaire who retired at age fifty-three. He says that all four of his children—a writer, a musician, a car salesman, a restaurant manager—are failures. "None of them," says Earl, "has the smarts or the guts to start up a business and make it work—like I did." Every year at least one of Earl's children comes to him with a plan for a new business and a request for a start-up loan. While Earl admits that some of the ideas are "damn good," he withholds the money because "lots of good ideas go down the tubes. I'm not sure the kids can cut it." "Besides," he adds, "I give each of them $500 a year at Christmas."

Laura is in her late thirties and has been separated from her husband for three years. An ardent feminist, she is eloquent when talking about her favorite subject—how women can be independent from men. However, Laura is a spendthrift and her husband pays for all of her shopping binges. At least once a month she spends an entire day at the department stores, arriving home late at night with her car stuffed with purchases. On one trip she bought twelve pairs of shoes, three sets of china, four tape recorders, five watches, eight bathing suits, fourteen dresses, and a large box of assorted jewelry. When asked why she doesn't divorce her husband, Laura replied, "I still love him and he would be lost without me."

Regarding money, miscommunication is not the primary problem. No communication is the culprit. While thoughts of money fill our minds everyday, we rarely talk money—personal money. It is perfectly acceptable to talk about money in general—the state of the economy, taxes and inflation, what Sylvester Stallone or Lee Iacocca or Oprah Winfrey earns in a year, whether real estate is a good investment. However, a conversation comes to an abrupt end when someone asks, "How much money do you earn?" or "What did you pay for this house?" or "How much money did you make in the stock market last year?" Personal money matters are a social taboo. Like any taboo subject, money is cloaked in secrecy and fear. When someone asks about our money, we are shocked and defensive because someone has dared to invade our privacy. It's a lot easier to talk intimately about sex than to talk intimately about money.

Studies have shown that: Most people do not reveal their income to family and friends. Most parents do not reveal their incomes to their children. The more money you make, the less likely you are to reveal your income to anyone. Nowhere is the communication gap greater than in a marriage. Prior to a marriage a couple rarely discuss money. During a marriage all they do is fight about money. When a marriage ends in divorce, too frequently the partners try to destroy each other, using money as ammunition. For many of us, money is a dark little area of incompetence and the last frontier of self-disclosure.

2

⊂•⊃

Money in
the Casino Society

That's the American way. If little kids don't aspire to make money
like I did, what the hell good is this country?

—Lee Iacocca (on his $20
million-plus in salary, bonuses,
and stock options in 1986)

THE AMERICAN RELIGION OF MONEY

In our society, money is everything. For Americans, it is how we keep
score. In the absence of an inherited class structure, we use money to
differentiate ourselves from one another. In our Horatio Alger, rags-
to-riches society, *anyone can.* Get rich, that is.

Americans worship money. We crave material possessions and idol-
ize the wealthy. Getting rich is a chief goal of all red-blooded Americans, our great national obsession. It has always been this way. As the
French traveler and social critic Alexis de Tocqueville commented
during his travels in the United States 150 years ago, "The love of
wealth is at the bottom of everything that the Americans do."

We even have a quasi-religious rationale for seeking wealth. According to the Protestant ethic on which our country was founded, work is
a virtue and we can expect it to be rewarded—especially when great
Yankee shrewdness and strength in the face of adversity are required.

Most religions preach the virtues of poverty. The American religion of money questions only that which is too easily gotten, as by gambling, or (in the past) too promiscuously displayed.

What's more, Americans honor rather than scorn the person who rises from humble origins (Abe Lincoln's proverbial log cabin), to win a fortune with no other advantages but courage and wits. According to one millionaire businessman and politician who was born poor, W. Michael Blumenthal, "One of the unique things about this country is that it's just as much of an honor to say, 'My father came steerage from Sicily,' as to say, 'My father's family has been here for twelve generations.' "

Americans particularly admire the maverick, the lone wolf who takes great and daring risks. This is something distinctively American. Europeans are more afraid to risk loss of prestige than loss of money; they scorn as nouveau riche anyone avidly pursuing wealth. And in the Orient, where the world is but an illusion anyway, why try to circumvent your fate?

MONEY MAGIC ON WALL STREET

Everyone would like to believe in a money benefactor—someone or something—to bestow financial security and freedom. This is especially true for the generations of Americans who have never lived through tough economic times like the Great Depression. For these generations of Americans, the stock market was a great benefactor—a source of money magic—until the stock market crash of October 1987.

On October 19, 1987, known as Black Monday on Wall Street, the Dow Jones industrial average plummeted 508 points, an amazing drop of 22.6 percent. Approximately $500 billion in paper value was lost. Even though only 20 percent of Americans invest in the stock market, the crash had a rippling effect that impacted on everything from consumer spending to pension plans.

Americans seemed remarkably calm and showed surprising unconcern. According to a *Newsweek* poll taken right after the crash, 61 percent of those surveyed said the crash did not necessarily indicate a serious downward economic trend, and 63 percent said the decline in stock prices might help the economy in the long run by forcing the government to face up to economic problems.

Likewise, a Los Angeles *Times* poll found that 64 percent of Americans thought the odds were better than fifty-fifty against a recession. The *Times* poll also found that stockholders who lost money in the crash were not discouraged about the stock market. According to the poll: 69 percent of the stock market losers said they do not plan to change the level of their stock investing, 17 percent plan to increase their stock investing, and only 12 percent plan to cut back.

Why such confidence in the face of loss? Psychologically, when we make a commitment to something—e.g., the stock market—we tend to rationalize any conflicting information and avoid behavior that would alter that commitment. We are all creatures of habit. In addition, some of the investors—those who did not sell their stocks—may have felt a psychological loss but not a financial loss. As a result, the stock market, which had such allure for many Americans, continues to hold its magical luster even in the face of an economic crisis.

CONSPICUOUS CONSUMPTION

Amassing wealth has always been a chief motive in U.S. society. And with our money, we indulge in a national feast of conspicuous consumption.

Writer Tom Wolfe has called the 1980s the age of plutography, or reverence for riches. Consider the spectacle of the Duchess of Windsor's jewels, appraised at $7.5 million but sold for $50 million at a glitzy celebrity auction in Switzerland. Then there are the upscale TV soaps, "Dallas," "Dynasty," and their offspring, which have been called visual celebrations of the good life, adult fairy tales about having it all.

Or for sheer crass, one can tune in to another TV celebration of wealth, "Lifestyles of the Rich and Famous," which is almost obscene in its display of immense homes and expensive toys. One program featured a rich dentist who spent twelve years and millions of dollars to build his very own medieval castle, complete with a sixteen-foot waterfall/fireplace and a replica of King Arthur's sword. The dentist was followed by a San Francisco jeweler, purveyor to the rich of such items as jeweled tennis rackets ($8,500), jeweled frisbees ($18,000), and his pièce de résistance, a gold and platinum garbage can (only $150,000). "One man's trash is another man's class," quipped host Robin Leach.

Americans have always been conspicuous consumers, and never more so than in the post-hippie era of the Yuppie (sometimes Yumpie), or young, upwardly mobile professional. Demographers also call them baby boomers. Born between 1946 and 1964, their numbers are variously estimated at from 50 to 75 million, or about a third of the population. Their influence is felt everywhere.

In the 1960s, hippies protested against materialism as well as war. In the 1970s, teenagers wanted to be rock stars; the more enterprising among them sold marijuana or scalped tickets to rock concerts. Today, kids just want to be rich. The *Wall Street Journal* recently featured a teenage Wunderkind who had recruited 135 classmates to invest in a mutual fund.

As a measure of how far we have come from hippiedom, consider the story of Mitchell D. Kapor, featured in a 1984 *Business Week* success profile. Born in 1951, Kapor was a Beatles' fan in adolescence, wearing long hair and protesting against the war in Vietnam. In his early twenties he dabbled in transcendental meditation, earned a master's degree in psychology, worked as a radio DJ. In the 1980s he went into the computer business and became a millionaire.

According to an annual study conducted by UCLA's graduate school of education, 73.2 percent of college freshmen in 1986 said that getting rich was an essential or very important goal in life—compared with 63.3 percent who believed this in 1980 and 49.5 percent in 1975.

And whereas hippies ranked "a meaningful philosophy of life" very highly, some one-third fewer of today's freshmen consider this important. Or, as one observer put it, the Yuppie philosophy of life is simply to make lots of money.

MAJORING IN MONEY

One measure of our current obsession with wealth is the distribution of college students by major. A recent study by researchers at UCLA compared career choices of freshmen at U.S. colleges and universities over the last twenty years. In 1966, 18 percent of freshmen chose arts and sciences while 14 percent chose business; by 1985 those choosing arts and sciences had dropped to 7 percent while those choosing business had escalated to 25 percent. The UCLA study also looked at student attitudes over the past two decades and concluded: "There is greater interest in material and power goals, coupled with decreased social concern and altruism. These changes exactly parallel the changes in college major and career preferences." The University of Illinois reports that only 19 percent of humanities students have jobs lined up after graduation, compared with 90 percent of business students.

The big push now is for an MBA. Business schools report applications increasing 20 to 30 percent yearly. In 1986 UCLA had 3,487 applicants for 370 openings. To get these coveted spots, some applicants are paying consultants $100 an hour to help complete admission forms, filling in the proper answers and the right buzz words.

The payoff is high. A "brand-name" MBA entitles you to a slot in investment banking, the hot money arena of the 1980s, where median starting salaries are nearly $60,000 plus bonuses and where one can expect $200,000 annually not far down the line. By way of comparison, law and medicine, the former big-money professions, look relatively less appealing. The New York *Times* recently ran an article about lawyers quitting $80,000 jobs to become investment bankers. A senior partner at a top law firm can make a million dollars annually, but a Wall Street merger and acquisition expert can double that—or more.

ME/NOW WORKAHOLICS, IMPATIENT FOR SUCCESS

For baby boomers, work is an obsession, and the thrill of acquiring material wealth something like an addiction. New York *Times Maga-*

zine editor Bruce Weber toured the United States in spring 1987 to interview sixty recent college graduates aged twenty-two to twenty-six. He found them to be cynical and materialistic, career planners with firm priorities—"their life equations already written" and "doubt banished." Weber concluded sadly: "Young people are older than they used to be."

One Yuppie explained: "I feel entitled to have everything I want. Why? I am well educated, well credentialed. I feel I am successful in what I am doing . . . I can have the best."

Some say this Me/Now generation is hedonistic and narcissistic. No down payment and no personal entanglement—they want it all NOW. Workaholics, they take greater risks but expect immediate payoff. "Post-war affluence gave them a feeling of entitlement," explains *Business Week.* "Television, jet travel and the sexual revolution accustomed them to instant gratification."

Yuppies reportedly have difficulty adjusting to the corporate world where the big money lies. Management researchers say this group has little if any organizational loyalty or people skills. (Business school, after all, teaches you to be president of the corporation, not one of the subordinates.) They are optimistic, impatient, and change jobs frequently. And when they move on, Yuppies tend to splurge rather than reinvest what benefits they have accumulated. As a Tampa real estate salesman explained to *Business Week,* he wasn't interested in saving for retirement: "If I do spend my old age in an undershirt eating dog food, I don't want to have some sort of a bleak past to look back on."

But there are signs of malaise in Yuppie-dom. Boomers seem to be suffering their midlife crises beginning at about twenty-eight. Consider the case of a thirty-three-year-old vice president of a manufacturing firm, owner of his own home in the right suburb and of two expensive cars. Unfortunately, he is sniffing four grams of coke a day, cheating on his wife, and increasingly failing to meet his business obligations.

According to Dr. Steven Berglas, clinical psychologist at Harvard and head of the Executive Stress Clinic in Boston, "success is a disappointment, an ending for many people." Berglas has written a book on what he calls *The Success Syndrome.* It is not a new problem. Remember King Midas, who was granted his wish that everything he touched would become gold? Then he found himself near death, because he could not eat or drink gold.

Early in our country's history, Benjamin Franklin warned that money could never bring happiness. "The more a man has, the more he wants," Franklin said wisely. "Instead of its filling a vacuum, it makes one."

Previous generations of Americans may not have liked their jobs, or not found them fulfilling, even after reaching the top. But Yuppies just expect more, and success can come too easily for many of them. Depression can set in when the thrill wears off, followed by anxiety about what to do for a second act.

DOWNWARD MOBILITY?

Yuppies are at a distinct demographic disadvantage. Their numbers are great; they came of age at a time of economic stagnation; competition will keep their incomes down; and there simply isn't enough room at the top. Consequently, all is not well in Yuppie suburbia.

A thirty-year-old fast-tracker today should be earning about $62,000, and $132,000 by forty, according to *Business Week.* Some do, but the Census Bureau reports that average wages of thirty- and forty-year-olds are only $18,000 to $24,500.

Relatively speaking, Yuppies may be worse off than their parents were at the same age. Given inflation, a thirty-year-old is earning an average of 10 percent less in real money than his father did, according to a report prepared for the Joint Economic Committee of Congress. The report concluded that the American economy has been in a "quiet depression in which neither wages nor family income has grown."

Whether they are living only for the here and now, or because their salaries are bottoming out, not to mention the tremendous inflation in real estate values, Yuppies are postponing home ownership. This leaves them with more of what is called "discretionary income," or spending money, and they are spending it: on flashy cars, scuba diving in Bora Bora, skiing in Utah, gourmet dining.

But such affluence is only skin-deep. Yuppies seem unable to attain the solid achievements of their parents, who made far less money. One unmarried advertising saleswoman, for example, makes $42,000 a year and takes Club Med vacations. Her parents consider her rich, but her $675 rent is twice their mortgage payment, and she can't seem to save enough for a down payment to buy her own home.

Less affluent boomers are spending their entire incomes just to stay afloat. In fact, more and more of them are going home to live at their parents' expense. In 1987 the Census Bureau reported that 59 percent of men and 47 percent of women aged eighteen to twenty-four were dependent on their parents for housing (up 6 percent since 1970), as are 14 percent of men and 8 percent of women aged twenty-five to thirty-four. These may include live-in college students, divorced people, or young people staying at home with their parents until they can afford to leave.

One twenty-five-year-old technician making $20,000 annually prefers to live in his parents' comfortable midwestern home so he can use the money he saves on rent to buy a new car, an $800 stereo, an expensive wardrobe. Yuppies are above all conspicuous consumers of gadgets, clothing, cars. They wear Burberry raincoats and Gucci loafers, walk Labrador dogs, and write with $200 Mont Blanc fountain pens. Food is especially important—"not everybody can live like a Rockefeller, but most can eat like one."

"But," warns *Forbes* magazine, "keeping up with the rich is no way to get rich." It also contributes to this country's record high consumer debt.

POSTPONING PARENTHOOD

Just as with home ownership and other symbols of permanence, Yuppies are also postponing parenthood—again, out of convenience as well as financial necessity. In the 1980s, the cost of raising a child to age eighteen is variously estimated at up to $250,000, not counting college. By way of comparison, it cost only $35,000 to raise a child born in 1960, exclusive of college.

Some Yuppies are postponing parenthood indefinitely. One of four women aged twenty-five to thirty-four has never had a child, and demographers predict that one in three born in the 1950s will never have any children. As a result, the one group staying ahead of the game financially today is the double-income/no-kids family, called DINKs. Simply put, without the financial burden of raising children, DINKs can devote their entire earnings to lifestyle.

But are they happy? There are growing signs that women especially are frustrated with their newfound careers and freedom, that DINKdom leaves them basically unfulfilled, that the "career mystique" of the 1970s is no more fulfilling than the "feminine mystique" of the 1950s.

Fortune magazine reports that some 30 percent of females earning MBAs from top schools in 1976 had left the management track ten years later (compared with 21 percent of their male classmates). One possible explanation is that, as the biological clock begins to run down, these women are opting out to have children.

There is probably more to this phenomenon than frustrated maternity. First of all, women are not paid as well as men. According to a Columbia Business School survey, they start at the same salary, but ten years later male MBAs are earning 25 percent more. Women are also less likely to get to the top, and only 2 percent become senior executives with a rank of vice president and above. And they are also less tolerant than men of organizational rigidity.

In fact, women are discovering that working is *work*—often boring, tiring, unfulfilling. "I thought a career was supposed to be an escape from the humdrum life of a housewife," a twenty-eight-year-old professional told *Working Woman* magazine. "Instead, I sometimes find myself trying to escape from the humdrum of work." Maternity may be one such avenue of escape.

Working Woman warns that "liberated" women may be retreating into "the cocoons of domesticity from which their mothers came." Certainly the bookstores are full of best-sellers about such "reactionary" concerns as how to get and keep a man (*Too Smart for Her Own Good; Women Who Love Too Much; Smart Women, Foolish Choices*). Social commentator Anne Taylor Fleming reports that there is no discernable woman's movement left, and that sales of sexy underwear are up again. . . .

The baby boomer population is aging, inevitably, but remains devoted to youth. There is a breakdown of age barriers due to "youth maintenance"—compulsive attention to diet, exercise, looks. Consider the fact that rock stars Mick Jagger and Tina Turner, in their mid- to late-forties, are still going strong. Twenty years ago, they would have been considered beyond the pale, ancient, by traditional standards. "Plastic surgery will be the orthodontics of the 1990s," predicts Kenneth Dychtwald in a *Money* magazine article on youth maintenance.

GET-RICH-QUICK

Boomers caught by the demographic squeeze, and other Americans whose expectations have exceeded their achievements are increasingly attracted to get-rich-quick schemes. Currently one popular example is the one-day seminar on making a fortune in real estate without investing a penny. Or the lottery, which gives everyone an equal chance; there is no ego to be risked in failure, because you win only by chance. In a 1985 *Money* magazine survey, 39 percent said the best route to riches was the lottery.

Another apparent avenue to instant wealth is the TV game show, which has the same appeal as the lottery—the lure of the lucky strike. The Los Angeles *Times* is full of ads for contestants: "Win over $50,000 a day"—"Win $100,000"—"Appear with major celebrities." But these shows use only about 10,000 contestants annually, and not all of them win. Still, to improve the odds of being one of these lucky few, several companies will tutor you for a commission on any winnings.

Actually, the quickest route to wealth in our society, but only for a very few, is show business. You don't have to be educated, you don't have to be smart, you don't necessarily even have to be attractive, as long as you've got some kind of a *look*. Consider Vanna White, game show hostess (described by *Newsweek* as "Mary Poppins in Joan Collins' clothing"), who has made a fortune in product endorsements, posters, an exercise video, even an autobiography.

If you have made some genuine but unremunerative achievement, you may be able to convert your celebrity into cash. Mark Spitz cashed in on his gold medals for swimming at the Munich Olympics and collected $5 million in advertising contracts. And many of the astronauts parlayed their space flights into lucrative new careers.

Failing achievement, some try a stunt. One of the most memorable in recent times was that by D. B. Cooper, the hijacker who parachuted to freedom $200,000 richer without hurting anything but the airline's bank account. Or Clifford Irving, author of the bogus Howard Hughes biography; Irving actually did some prison time, but has found since his release that notoriety has its own value.

Nothing seems sacred anymore. Mark Hofmann, who forged documents of his Mormon faith, earned a very handsome sum of money. His so-called "Salamander Letter," suggesting that a fish rather than an angel, as previously believed, led Mormon founder Joseph Smith to the sacred scriptures, brought Hofmann $40,000. Hofmann also killed two people to cover up his fraud, for which he received a five-year-to-life prison sentence in 1987.

In one of the most glaring of several recent treason-for-profit cases, a former Navy warrant officer was arrested in 1985 for selling top military secrets to the Soviets for nearly two decades. John A. Walker had recruited a spy ring that included, among others, his brother and his son. It is impossible to calculate how much Walker earned, but just before his capture the spy emeritus was planning to ask the Soviets for a stipend of $1 million yearly.

THE CASINO SOCIETY: DEEPER IN DEBT

Whatever it takes to get rich quick, Americans are trying it. The United States seems awash in fraud and scam. *Business Week* calls it the "casino society," where everything rides on a roll of the dice. Individually and collectively, we are going for it, risking it all.

Harvard economist Robert Reich agrees. The U.S. economy in the 1980s, Reich says, is about "the rearrangement of money. . . . Doing deals. Making it quickly, then getting out. You don't read about new products, new inventions, new processes. . . . Our economy is a house of cards, a sophisticated chain letter, a casino."

Meanwhile, we are falling deeper into debt, individually and collectively. The United States ranks as a debtor nation ahead of such banana republics as Brazil and Argentina. On an individual level, mortgage delinquencies reached an all-time high in 1985, and personal bankruptcies a postwar high in 1987. In the 1960s, Americans saved 8 percent of their incomes; now we save less than 4 percent. In 1980 our personal debt, excluding mortgages, was 15 percent of our personal income after taxes; by 1986 personal debt had risen to 19 percent.

A group called Debtors Anonymous, patterned after Alcoholics Anonymous, has arisen to help compulsive debtors. DA meetings begin with the same prayer as AA (". . . grant me the serenity to accept the things I cannot change . . ."). According to DA literature, warning signs on the road to compulsive debt include "an inordinate feeling of euphoria on opening a charge account," and frequently asking to "borrow" things (cigarettes, pens, etc.) when you have no intention of returning them.

"Shopaholics," according to *New Women* magazine, "have poor impulse control and use their addiction to cover up feelings of inadequacy." According to the National Foundation for Consumer Debt, the typical shopaholic is thirty-five years old with an after-tax monthly income of $1,437 and an average debt of nearly $10,000 (not including home mortgages).

CORPORATE CRIME

Corporate debt is also at record highs in the United States, primarily due to finance mergers and buyouts, not to purchase of capital equipment or aids to productivity. And we are seeing new forms of what used to be called "white collar crime," now involving huge sums of money.

"They put handcuffs on them?" This refrain echoed throughout Wall Street in February 1987, when four prominent investment bankers were arrested in their offices and taken away like common criminals to face charges of insider trading. Some tried to attribute this rash of illicit stock market activity to Yuppie amorality or impatience for instant wealth. But in fact, only one of the major culprits was of the Yuppie generation. The remainder were highly respected principals in Wall Street's most prestigious investment banking firms. These pedigreed and pin-striped members of the most exclusive old guard clubs, according to the evidence, had been making assignations to hand over suitcases full of cash, payoffs for the tips that brought them millions on the stock market. The general consensus, according to the New York *Times,* is that these white collar criminals, working with pencils instead of guns, are motivated by greed and the belief they won't get caught.

In a recent poll, only 52 percent of Americans said they considered corporate executives honest. Ironically, at about the same time as the insider trading scandals, Harvard Business School received a $30 million gift to create a program in business ethics. Previously, the subject had been strictly elective, and its only two teachers had recently been denied tenure—at a time when professors specializing in entrepreneuring earn $150,000 a year plus consulting and expert witness fees, not to mention lucrative royalties on textbooks.

Given this epidemic of lawlessness and cynicism, some people are revolting. Complaints against stockbrokers, for example, have trebled since 1982: for trading without knowledge or permission, for misinformation, or for excessive trading (called "churning") merely for the purpose of generating commissions.

Stockholders are also rebelling, suing directors of corporations when they disagree with corporate decisions. General Motors is the target of one such suit, for its $700 million payment to depose former director H. Ross Perot, and People Express is the target of another involving its merger with Texas Air. Since a 1985 court ruling against a corporation's directors for approving a takeover without lengthy consideration (called "due diligence"), the cost of insurance (board-of-directors malpractice) has skyrocketed 900 percent in two years.

How widespread is dishonesty in American life? In 1981 *Psychology Today* asked Americans what they would do if a clerk gave them too much change (26 percent said they would keep it), or if they accidently scratched a parked car while driving (nearly half would leave without writing a note). The survey found that one third cut in line, over one third admitted to some falsification of tax returns, and 93 percent exceed the speed limit. The most troubling moral dilemma was and is adultery, the editors of *Psychology Today* reported. The survey concluded that the most "honorable" Americans are those who consider themselves very religious. As a group, these people were less likely to bend the rules: to cheat on their expense accounts, park illegally, or deceive their spouses.

THE ALMIGHTY DOLLAR

According to the Bible, the root of all evil is the love of money. Most world religions preach the virtue of poverty and the value of sacrifice. Yet some American religious leaders have been inclined to a somewhat idolatrous worship of the "almighty dollar," reversing the biblical dictum that it is better to give than to receive.

This is not a recent phenomenon. At the turn of the century, Russell Herman Conwell, an American Baptist, toured the United States preaching the gospel of money. "Money is power," he exhorted. "I say, get rich, get rich." Another American religious plutocrat was the Reverend Ike (Frederick J. Eikerenkoetter), who had limousines and villas all over the world. Ike joyfully admitted to the worship of money: "Money loves me. . . . I see a mountain of money piling into my arms . . . I see myself on shopping sprees . . . taking fabulous vacations . . . Oh bless you, money, you're wonderful stuff."

In the age of mass communications, there has arisen a lucrative alliance of religion, TV, and marketing. Scores of celebrity preachers compete on television for some 13.3 million regular viewers and an estimated $1 to $2 billion in annual contributions.

This competition erupted in scandal in spring 1987. In the leading role was the Reverend Jim Bakker, founder of the PTL (Praise the Lord) Club, a TV preacher garnering $179 million in annual revenue. PTL also owns some other very tangible assets, including a 2,300-acre theme park in North Carolina, the third most popular park in the United States.

Amid newspaper exposés and a barrage of charges by rival preachers, Bakker admitted to committing adultery once seven years earlier with a church secretary. The secretary and her "legal representatives" subsequently received some $265,000 in what was called hush money and were to have received considerably more had the story not become public.

There were further charges against Bakker: innuendos of wife-swapping, even homosexuality, not to mention financial wrongdoing. These charges came from rival preachers, themselves suffering from sagging Nielsen ratings, who were suspected of aspiring to an unfriendly takeover of the PTL empire. There were also extensive audits of PTL finances.

The Bakker "shakeout" opened a titillating window onto the lifestyles of the rich and pious. Bakker and his wife, Tammy Faye, were reported to own $700,000 in real estate, including a $400,000 retreat in the Southern California desert, two other homes, even a houseboat. Since 1984 the couple apparently received $4.8 million, largely in bonuses, from their church.

Bakker resigned and was succeeded as head of PTL by Jerry Falwell, self-proclaimed head of the Moral Majority, himself reported to be suffering financial embarrassment because his own TV broadcast had recently been suspended for nonpayment of bills. Another contender for the PTL succession was Oral Roberts, founder of a midwestern university and hospital bearing his name. In the midst of the PTL scandal, Roberts resorted to a little spiritual fund-raising of his own.

Claiming to need $8 million, Roberts retreated to his "prayer tower" to fast until the money was forthcoming, warning that God would call him home unless the money arrived soon. During his fast, Roberts reported a visit from the prince of darkness himself, who tried to choke the preacher to death. But Roberts was rescued from the devil by his loyal followers and by a Florida dog-track owner, who contributed $1.3 million.

Despite current financial embarrassments, religion is still apparently a possible route to the American dream of getting rich. Various celebrity preachers, when asked, admitted to yearly earnings of from $75,000 to $200,000. To these sums must be added uncounted gifts and perquisites, making possible a very affluent lifestyle.

MILLIONS OF MILLIONAIRES

The IRS reported in 1985 that there are more millionaires than ever: some 410,000 with a net worth of $1 million or more, increasing at the rate of 8 percent a year, more than double the number of millionaires a decade earlier. The Federal Reserve Board disagrees and states the number of millionaires is much higher; it counted 1.3 million American millionaires in 1987. There were 26 billionaires in 1986. The Joint Economic Committee reports that our national wealth is increasingly concentrated in the hands of the rich. The richest 1 percent of Americans now have more assets than the bottom 90 percent.

In a 1985 survey by *Money* magazine, 59 percent (including 64 percent of the most affluent Americans) said hard work was the surest route to wealth; 39 percent (including half of the female respondents) thought winning the lottery was the best bet. Among those surveyed, 33 percent of women favored marrying wealth, and 31 percent (men and women) stressed the importance of the right personal connections.

Horatio Alger and the Protestant ethic notwithstanding, hard work alone will not make you rich. Nobody in the United States gets rich on a salary, unless he founded the company or is named Lee Iacocca (whose 1986 compensation was $20.5 million). However, the CEO of a large American corporation averages $700,000 to $800,000 in annual salary and bonuses. In general, money begets money. Most wealth comes from unearned income. To be truly rich, you must inherit wealth, be successful in the investment world, or be an exceptionally daring entrepreneur.

Daring contemporary entrepreneurs like H. Ross Perot, who started Electronic Data Systems, take enormous risks but strike it very rich. Another example is Ted Turner, who defied all the experts to establish an independent television network. Both Perot and Turner are very much in the tradition of the lone-wolf entrepreneur, succeeding against the odds, cut from the same mold as Henry Ford or John D. Rockefeller.

The converse of the rags-to-riches story is frequently played out by sports and entertainment personalities. Some come into wealth suddenly, as if by a windfall, but lack the self-discipline and financial skills to handle money. So they spend it quickly, as if to test whether it is real. For example, Joe Louis, after retiring as heavyweight champion of the world, owed the IRS alone more than he could ever repay.

According to Carole Hyatt and Linda Gottlieb, authors of *Why Smart People Fail,* there is no great and permanent shame attached to failure in our society. "Since status does not depend on birth," they write, "there is always the possibility of remaking yourself. This is the land where you can go from rags to riches to rags and still hope to go back to riches. Second only in popularity to the saga of the self-made man is the saga of the comeback."

There may be more millionaires today, but a million dollars isn't what it used to be. It takes an estimated $20 million today to keep up with the Colbys. *U.S. News & World Report* described a few years ago what inflation has done to the price tag of the good life: A full-length sable coat, for example, which cost $25,000 in 1940, trebled in price in forty years; a Fifth Avenue townhouse, available for $55,000 before World War II, sold for $2.5 million in 1980 and would sell for a great deal more today.

Lewis Lapham, former editor of *Harper's* magazine, makes a clear distinction between new money and old. "New money is more fun to be around," Lapham writes. The new rich "will send a limousine across town at 3 a.m. for a chicken sandwich and two bottles of champagne. . . . Cash has been acquired recently enough to provide an element of magic surprise." Old money, on the other hand, is "niggardly and defensive . . . besieged . . . inclined to understatement and the color beige." (The credit card in an old-rich wallet is more likely to be for Sears than for Saks Fifth Avenue.) "The old rich," Lapham continues, "recognize one another by faint and subtle signals —a tone of voice, a name. . . . The new rich recognize one another by comparing possessions, like children matching Christmas presents."

The lives of the old rich are discretely managed by private bankers, old family retainers (including physicians, not just butlers; even the vet makes house calls), personal secretaries, and a car and driver. For these people, life is a work of art, with just the right homes, summer and winter (not displayed on TV's "Lifestyles," but possibly featured in *Architectural Digest,* the right wives and children, even the right dogs. These people know cuts of diamonds and the difference between male and female sable. *Forbes* magazine calls them the truly filthy rich, estimating their numbers at 70,000 households with incomes of $10 million and more.

It is the nouveau riche who are more likely to attract our attention and sympathetic envy. They feel less guilty about enjoying their money; they may even flaunt it. One wealthy music aficionado hired the entire American Symphony Orchestra so he could conduct his own performance. A rich divorce lawyer buys three copies of every hardback book he reads: one for the bedside table, one for the bathroom, and a walking-around copy. In Southern California there are rich sports buffs who consult a psychologist at $250 an hour for conflicts that interfered with their golf or tennis game. The American South is also in the running for conspicuous display. One Southern heiress recently threw a $500,000 wedding for her daughter, who went to the altar in a silk gown trimmed with ermine.

THE DISAPPEARING MIDDLE CLASS AND THE NEW UNDERCLASS

What about the rest of us? Demographers report that the middle class is shrinking and the traditional family is disintegrating. Fewer Americans are getting married, fewer are having children, about half of all marriages currently end in divorce, and the family as Norman Rockwell idealized it is nearly extinct.

In fact, according to the Census Bureau, single people account for almost 25 percent of all households, while couples with children under eighteen numbered only 28 percent in 1985. In the last fifteen years, single-parent households have doubled, and childless couples have increased 75 percent.

In 1987, the *Wall Street Journal* sent reporters into a formerly middle class suburbia where they found "no more Ozzie and Harriet." Instead, suburbia now encloses a great diversity of lifestyles, reflecting a fragmentation of values. In one house, the wife was the breadwinner, working night shifts to support her husband, who enrolled in law school after he got laid off. Next door were three unmarried housemates. Down the street was an unmarried traveling saleswoman.

The blue collar worker, once one third of the U.S. labor force, now constitutes only 20 percent. In the auto industry alone, the number of workers has fallen 40 percent in the last decade. There has been a shift from unionized factory work to service professions that pay no benefits and offer no job security. In one typical example of downward mobility, a former steelworker who once brought home $30,000 now earns only $13,000 as a maintenance worker. This is the roll of the dice in the casino society: one man loses his job, and another sees the value of his home double due to inflation. The result: great anxiety about the future.

Economists are currently engaged in a great debate over the shape of our national economic future. They point out that there are virtually no new high-paying jobs in manufacturing. And, of the new jobs being created, those paying a middle-level wage fell by 30 percent in the 1980s. There has also been a great expansion of part-time jobs (employers thereby save on benefits). As *Forbes* magazine put it, the new job openings are at McDonald's.

In 1985, middle class families earning $15,000 to $35,000 a year fell to 39 percent of the total, from 46 percent in 1970. Katherine Bradbury in the *New England Economic Review* reports that four times as many families dropped out of the middle class than rose above it from 1973–84. Some economists call this a temporary industrial shakedown. Others say the "alleged" shrinking of the middle class is "statistical mythmaking designed to advance a political [i.e., anti-Reagan] agenda."

Overall, the U.S. economy has grown since 1970 but the gains are unevenly distributed. Since 1973, productivity and real wage growth have fallen behind, creating a greater polarity between haves and have-nots: on the one hand, the old rich and the new affluent of well-educated, two-paycheck families; on the other, deepening poverty and a new underclass living off welfare and crime.

Divorced or unmarried mothers supporting children constitute a great proportion of the new poor. With no-fault divorce, the husband's standard of living rises, while that of his wife and children falls. Two thirds of divorced mothers receive no alimony, so they are struggling along on paychecks that average only sixty-five cents to each dollar earned by men.

According to Marvin Harris, an anthropologist, working women first entered the economy in droves during the great inflation of the 1960s, in an effort to help maintain their families' middle class standard of living. These women, "trained to be unaggressive and to take orders from men," were willing to take jobs that were neither permanent nor secure—boring jobs with no future—because their husbands were still the primary breadwinners.

One side effect of the great increase in working wives was a falling birthrate. "Day care has to be paid in cash, while home care was paid for with sentiment," Harris remarks. Also, greater numbers of women in the economy drove down wages. And at about the same time, well-paid manufacturing employment was declining. In its place arose a service economy in which white women were replacing black men.

The new underclass is regrettably real. According to *Fortune* magazine, this new underclass includes some 5 million of 33 million Americans under the poverty line, predominantly blacks and Hispanics—5 million people mired in chronic failure, lawlessness, drugs, illegitimacy, and welfare dependency, in the middle of the most affluent society in world history.

A FINAL WORD: IF YOU ARE SO SMART, WHY AREN'T YOU RICH?

You don't have to be a genius to strike it rich. In fact, studies show that not-so-smarts sometimes fare better financially than highly intelligent people. In 1972, *McCall's* magazine reported that some high school dropouts live better than Ph.D.s, even though the Ph.D.s may earn more, because the dropouts are better money managers.

Money-making ability is unrelated to IQ, according to the head of Mensa, whose members score among the top 20 percent on intelligence tests but rank only at median levels financially. "They could probably make more," Mensa's executive director told *Money* magazine, "but they tend to work at what they like, not what pays best."

3

Money Relationships

Money is the most powerful and subtle (if need be) weapon of dominance available to us. We use it to achieve power over others, and also to avoid falling into others' power.

—Thomas Wiseman,
The Money Motive

Money permeates every relationship in life. This is not only true on the job, where we go expressly to earn money. Money also affects every interpersonal interaction: friendship and courtship, living together and marriage, divorce and death. It is a primary interactive force between parent and child, men and women, friends and lovers, and is passed down from generation to generation.

Curiously, in the United States at least, money is the last taboo. Researchers have found that Americans, men more than women, are more likely to discuss sex (formerly, also a taboo subject) than money. Just ask someone how much he earns, or what his house cost; even an incurable braggart will probably not tell you, possibly fearing to arouse your envy or contempt.

"Never talk about money, and think about it as little as possible," recommended nineteenth-century American society novelist Edith Wharton. It is a carryover from our class-bound British heritage, the notion that doing things for money is somehow suspect. In colonial America, for example, a lawyer had to be a gentleman of means to survive, because accepting a fee was thought to prejudice his fairness.

In other times and places, the bride price or dowry and the suitor's financial capability to marry have been matters of extensive negotiation and careful consideration. But in the era of romantic love (from the late nineteenth century on), we have felt that it somehow tarnished the purity of love to discuss it in the same context as money. As a result, the importance of money is often utterly ignored during courtship, yet it becomes a primary focus of contention during marriage.

GENDER DIFFERENCES

There are significant differences in how men and women relate to money. American women are often raised to think of money as a reward instead of something earned (and a reward is, of course, controlled by the giver). Men, on the other hand, expect to spend their whole lives paying the bills and supporting the family. To men, money represents identity and power; to women, security and autonomy.

Warren Farrell, author of *The Liberated Man,* argues in his book *Why Men Are the Way They Are* that men have traditionally used money and power to get sex and love, whereas women use sex and love to get money and power. If women have traditionally been denigrated as sex objects, Farrell writes, then men have been seen as "success objects," forbidden love until they could pay for it.

Another gender difference relates to financial planning. A 1972 study of family finance for *McCall's* magazine revealed that women take a short-term view, worrying primarily about the here-and-now priorities such as dentist bills and food prices. Men, on the other hand, are forced by their traditional role as family provider to consider the long term—getting the kids through college, possibly having to support elderly parents, providing for retirement, death, or disability. *McCall's* also reported that husbands tended to call their wives spendthrifts, while wives usually thought their husbands were too stingy.

Linda T. Sanford and Mary Ellen Donovan, authors of *Women & Self-Esteem,* found that money was a constant source of worry and unhappiness to women, a significant burden to their happiness in life. But, Farrell would object: what of the lifelong financial burden that a man faces, day in and day out, in his commitment to marriage and parenthood?

According to a 1981 survey in *Psychology Today,* even more women than men relate money to negative emotions such as fear, panic, spite, anger. And fewer women than men associate money with love and happiness. Finally, relating money to another of the great taboos, sex, *Money* magazine found some curious gender differences. Of female respondents to a 1985 *Money* survey, 51 percent think about money more often than about sex, and nearly one third enjoy money more than sex. Only 27 percent of men thought about money more than sex, and only 16 percent found it more satisfying.

MONEY BETWEEN FRIENDS

How does money actually work in relationships? Starting with friendship, it is often said that money should not come between friends, but it can and does. Everybody has had the experience of dining out with someone who orders the most expensive item on the menu, then wants to split the bill in half. Or the people who habitually give cheap gifts, although they can afford better.

These occasional, aggravating experiences are rarely enough in themselves to disrupt a friendship, but what happens when a friend asks for a loan? In actual fact, according to the *Wall Street Journal,* personal loans have a high default rate. The newspaper advises that when making a personal loan, you should get a promissory note, payment schedule, even collateral and interest. Only with such documentation can you, if worse comes to worse, and it often does, write off an uncollectible debt on your taxes. As Mark Twain warned, "The holy passion of friendship is of so sweet and steady and loyal and enduring a nature that it will last through a whole lifetime, if not asked to lend money."

Most of us resent cheapness, but generosity can also be a problem among friends. Consider the case of a college friend who strikes it rich, or at least becomes relatively more affluent than you. If he or she were to invite you out to the same cheap restaurant where you ate as students, you might resent such cheapness. Yet if your friend took you to an elegant place, you might feel he or she was lording it over you. Money has the power to arouse envy, anger, and resentment. Within families, these destructive emotions may be expected to be fought out to the bitter end, but friendships are supposed to be somehow exempt.

COURTSHIP

Courtship is a time-honored tradition allowing one to shower the object of one's desire with gifts, flowers, candy. "A girl who is being wooed," Thomas Wiseman writes in *The Money Motive*, "expects to have money spent on her, and there is no doubt that an expensive dinner has more erotic value than a hamburger." Wiseman considers money a definite aphrodisiac, and cheapness "sexual anathema." Wiseman's views might be called traditional, even old-fashioned now. In the United States today, courtship is an entirely new game, with confusing, sometimes contradictory customs, the old and the new rules overlapping.

The rules of modern courtship, according to *Cosmopolitan* magazine, a woman's manual for getting and enjoying it all, provide that a woman may and should pay or contribute to dating expenses some of the time. This is more than a matter of basic reciprocity or fairness, because you don't want him to feel you owe him anything, *Cosmo* warns. But you don't want to be insulting or threatening either, so read your man's signals carefully. Old-fashioned provider types may be hurt if you offer to pay. But generally, unless a man is "loaded" (*Cosmo*'s word), he should not have to pay the whole tab all the time. *Cosmo* suggests that a woman chip in on the tip, treat her date to after-dinner drinks, pay the cab fare. And if she really likes him, invite him over to her house for dinner.

In the world of courtship, as in all other worlds, one thing is certain: he (or she) who pays all the time usually controls the relationship. It is true in almost all relationships, at almost all times, that money is power. In *American Couples,* a study by Philip Blumstein and Pepper Schwartz, research showed that the amount of money a person has establishes his or her relative power in the relationship (with one notable exception, which will be discussed later).

LIVING TOGETHER

According to the 1982 census, there were 3 million Americans sharing living quarters with unrelated members of the opposite sex. Some couples choose this arrangement because they are unwilling or unable to make a greater commitment; others, because they have been hurt emotionally or financially by marriage.

In cohabitation, as the researchers call it, neither partner usually plays the role of sole provider. Women work therefore out of necessity rather than choice. There are any number of possible ways to divide expenditures and responsibilities, but most couples adopt a pay-as-you-go style, sharing expenses equally or according to the ability to pay. But rarely do cohabitors go so far as to establish joint accounts.

Keeping money separate, according to Blumstein and Schwartz in *American Couples,* reduces overall conflict. It is also one less bond, an "escape hatch," allowing the relationship to be more easily dissolved. This is not to say that cohabitors do not argue about money; who gets what/when and how is a source of contention in any relationship. Money arguments between cohabitors are often really arguments about commitment.

Farrell, crusading to free men from the stigmas of women's lib, believes that the more money a woman has, the less willing she is to remain totally committed to a relationship. She may also be less likely to consult about money decisions. A single woman who supports herself is called a career woman, Farrell points out, and is considered mature and enterprising, whereas a man who supports himself and nobody else is inclined to be called a playboy.

Although cohabitation is generally based on egalitarian ideals, the fact that women do not earn as much as men is often a source of conflict. Should the higher-paid male subsidize a more expensive lifestyle, or should the couple scale down to a level the female can afford? In general, cohabitors are wary of dependence. Neither will write a blank check for the other. Should one of the parties in such a relationship become unemployed, an impossible, and sometimes terminal, strain on the relationship may be imposed.

HOMOSEXUAL RELATIONSHIPS

The extent to which money represents power in relationships is nowhere more graphically clear than in Blumstein and Schwartz's findings on gay cohabitors. Gay men, they report, share with heterosexual men the belief that financial power conveys the right to dominate decision-making. Since male cohabitors are both likely to work, there will be two incomes in the household—meaning a lot of discretionary spending power, and also two opinions very likely to come in conflict.

Lesbians, on the other hand, seem to have deliberately sought to avoid the dominant-submissive characteristics of American heterosexuality. Blumstein and Schwartz report that lesbians make an extra effort to prevent money from affecting their relationship. They are the only American couples for whom money is not a measurement of power. Women are not accustomed to judging their own worth by the size of their paychecks, the researchers suggest, so they do not subject women partners to this standard either.

Gay cohabitors have one characteristic in common with heterosexual cohabitors. Lacking the institutionalized union of marriage, homosexuals (like other cohabitors) usually do not pool their money together—unless they deliberately make a lifelong commitment to each other.

CHOOSING PARTNERS; THE PRENUPTIAL AGREEMENT

"Money can't buy you love," the Beatles sang in a more innocent era. But as the universal American yardstick of value, money can most definitely help you acquire a more desirable partner.

Formerly, as Thorstein Veblen first theorized in *The Theory of the Leisure Class* (1899), the main criterion of a wife's desirability was usefulness. But when machines took over most of women's work (laundry, food preparation, cleaning), beauty and sexual skills became more highly valued assets than usefulness. A desirable wife is usually expensive, a living proof of her husband's success—"of the fact that their husbands can afford them," according to Thomas Wiseman. He adds, "So these symbols of success are hung with jewels and furs and sent off to the hairdressers so they may reflect credit on their husbands."

Women are not immune to crass monetary considerations. Marrying up has been the goal of many women, but women are not alone in marrying for money. "Remember," advised Thackeray, the Victorian novelist, "it is as easy to marry a rich woman as a poor woman."

As women become more financially independent and practical-minded, marriage may appear to be less attractive. A recent New York *Times* study found that instead of romantic partners, women want husbands with college degrees and a significant annual income.

One sign of new and more practical attitudes toward marriage is the prenuptial agreement. Writing such an agreement is about as romantic as taking a lawyer into your honeymoon bed, someone once quipped. But with more money at stake these days, and a one-in-two probability of divorce, marriages are taking on aspects of financial mergers.

Where there is no appreciable money at stake, the prenuptial agreement is more likely to focus on who does what rather than who gets what. *Time* magazine recently published a parody about a couple that prenegotiated everything from responsibility for picking up the doggie poo to feeding the kids and doing the dishes. In the end, *Time* concluded, delinquency in the doggie-poo removal department might be grounds for divorce.

TRADITIONAL MARRIAGE

Only three in ten American families now fit the traditional model of the male breadwinner/female homemaker-and-mother, the Norman Rockwell image of the American family. Traditional marriage is not usually democratic. Generally, the breadwinner wants and demands discretion over spending. But the power of the wife as chief purchasing agent and sometimes budget manager may be considerable. So there is great leeway for manipulation via money in traditional marriage, with money serving as a means of reward and punishment, caring and control—the ultimate way to get to one another.

Blumstein and Schwartz found that married couples fight more about money than cohabitors, who suppress conflicts that might threaten the future of their relationship. But within the greater security of the institution of marriage, such conflicts are often played out to the bitter end. Money may become, in effect, a battleground where financial as well as surrogate issues are won and lost.

No matter how high the family income, there are still daily decisions to be made about the allocation of money. Among low income families, money is a constant source of irritation because of its short supply, but it may also be a chief irritant among the more affluent. Actually, a shortage of money is not usually the real problem in a money fight; rather, the problem may be differences in attitudes, pre-existing grievances, any number of factors. Of marriages ostensibly threatened by money arguments, according to the Family Service Association, only 6 percent of the couples were actually short of money. The most ferocious marital money conflicts occur when there are irreconcilable differences in money personalities—for example, when a saver marries a spender.

The higher the husband's income and the more successful he is, per Veblen's theory of the leisure class, the less likely that his wife works. Today, 87 percent of the wives of executives in large corporations are not employed. In addition to status considerations, some husbands prefer their wives to be financially dependent because they are afraid of losing them.

Breadwinning males often make their own financial decisions without consulting homemaking wives. They are also inclined to self-indulgence around the home, as their reward for being the chief income earner. "They became accustomed to doing no housework unless they wished to be magnanimous, and it was unquestionably their right to have their sexual needs and desires shape the couple's sex life. Although times are changing, it is still difficult for men to give up these privileges," write Blumstein and Schwartz.

There are various ways a homemaking wife may get revenge for the disparity of money and power in her marriage. One very common means is the spending splurge. The more parsimonious the husband, the more the wife is aroused to extravagance. Such wives are expressing hostility, wasting their husbands' "most vital capacities," indulging in a kind of promiscuity and freedom from customary inhibition that has sexual as well as financial undertones.

For some women, spending is a temporary means of overcoming feelings of inner emptiness and worthlessness. And if funds are short, it also represents a denial of reality. Men, on the other hand, are more likely to get revenge by getting drunk or committing infidelity.

Another means of feminine revenge is to secrete funds, putting a little away on the sly. *Working Woman* magazine reported in 1985 that almost 20 percent of wives (and 25 percent of cohabiting women) keep a secret cash fund. Even happily married homemakers say they do this so they won't have to ask their husband's permission to spend money or justify every expenditure.

CHILDREN: TO HAVE OR HAVE NOT

Today we have a growing phenomenon of women postponing or fore-going motherhood altogether in order to pursue careers or other goals. One in four women between the ages of twenty-five and thirty-four has never had a child. And up to 39 percent of all married couples in 1982 had undergone voluntary sterilization, compared with 16 percent in 1965.

This brings us to the DINKs: double-income/no-kids couples. *Newsweek* described one such marriage: "No time to cook at the end of the day, they usually meet for dinner at a trendy restaurant or . . . pick up gourmet takeout on the way home. Their car is an expensive sporty two-seater—just right for weekend getaways. Their white living room rug has never known the muddy footprints of little feet. . . ."

These two-income families are staying ahead of the game financially. UCLA researcher Bonnie Burman also concluded that intentionally childless DINKs are more happily married than couples with children. They have more time together and less stress (although prospective grandparents are inclined to complain about "all that love wasted on a dog"), more money for pleasure and luxury.

Childless women also do better professionally. Harvard economist David Bloom says women with children earn 20 percent less. The differential grows with each additional child, according to a Stanford University study.

If a couple decide to have children, in most cases the wife will have to work anyway. *"Leave It to Beaver* is no longer the norm," one DINK told *Newsweek,* "because now two people gotta bust their butts for Beaver." Raising a child in the 1980s has been variously estimated to cost from $80,000 to $250,000 to age eighteen, plus another $50,000 for four years of private college education.

For most mothers, work is a financial necessity, and not a very remunerative one at that. The average woman earns $9,300, and over half of working wives' husbands earn $20,000 or less—not enough to afford a very luxurious lifestyle these days, even with two paychecks.

In any case, the extra paycheck has its effect on the marriage. Among more traditionally minded couples, there is a tendency to downplay the importance of the wife's financial contribution, to treat her paycheck as auxiliary, as if her work were voluntary rather than necessary.

Caroline Bird in *The Two Paycheck Family* reports that working wives have more say in family financial matters. They may also make greater demands on their husbands, who formerly "bought out" of household responsibilities. And generally the more affluent women rely heavily on personalized, time-saving convenience services, from dog walking and gourmet microwave dinners to catalogue buying and even personal shoppers.

Dual-income families have various ways of handling their finances. Rosanna Hertz, a sociologist who studied two-paycheck families, discovered that they were as likely to pool their money as not, or to pool some and keep separate allowances for personal expenditures. Pooling money, however, may be complicated in a yuppie marriage because both bride and groom are already experienced consumers, with their own cars, stereos, credit cards, insurance. Once married, they must decide not only how to divide expenses, but also how to set priorities and negotiate different preferences.

WHEN THE WIFE EARNS MORE

What happens when the wife earns more than her husband? According to the Blumstein and Schwartz paradigm, the money should allow her to have greater power. What happens, in fact, is often a subtle but troublesome shift in the marital power balance.

In 1985 the Census Bureau reported that 5 million American women were earning more than their husbands. Few of those couples have been willing to discuss their financial arrangements, and then only anonymously.

Joan Gallas, a management professor who studied eleven such couples, found that nine of the eleven used the husband's paycheck for basic support and kept the wife's earnings for extras. Thus, they promoted the belief that the husband was the chief provider.

Since earning money is intimately bound up with self-respect, men may suffer feelings of inadequacy when they are not the primary breadwinners. And if the wife is not particularly deferential, her paycheck may take an even greater toll psychologically. One divorcée who earned more than her ex-husband put the matter very bluntly: "The person who is in charge of money is in charge of sex too." Undoubtedly many husbands find this emotionally and sexually troublesome. Ironically, some men are reported to be taking out their resentment in exactly the way dependent wives have always gotten back at their more powerful husbands: by withholding sex.

Psychology Today reported in 1981 that couples argue more when the wife earns more. In the short run, if the wife's larger paycheck underwrites a higher standard of living, the husband is likely to be more accommodating. But in the long run, such marriages may not be very stable. Women earning high salaries are more likely to be honest in their marriages because they are not afraid of being left penniless. Thus, these marriages might be more likely to end in divorce. A wife who can support herself without any help no longer needs marriage for security. Money can be her ticket to independence.

DIVORCE

Half of all American marriages now end in divorce. The rate might be even higher were it not for money considerations. Some unhappily married couples undoubtedly stay married rather than face the financial upheaval of divorce—unless of course one spouse falls in love with someone else. In that case, the expense of divorce may prove extremely onerous. Some studies report that a contested divorce may cost as much as $60,000 to $70,000.

Before no-fault divorce, separations usually revolved around who did what to whom. Nowadays, money is the major issue. "Money becomes the focus for the residue of affection that remains," writes Carole Phillips, author of *Money Talk*. Alimony may play the role of reparations, or it may be used for punishment. A man who left his wife at midlife for a younger women told Phillips that "money isn't much of a substitute, but it's the only thing I can give her." In this case, a generous settlement was motivated by guilt. More often, divorces are bitter affairs and the settlements punitive.

Families at the bottom end of the financial ladder may have no choice but to remain married. Almost 40 percent of women polled recently by *Woman's Day* magazine said they would not marry their husbands again. But they remain married—sometimes out of inertia, it is true, but often for financial reasons. In a 1981 *Psychology Today* survey, 23 percent of separated couples were postponing divorce because of money.

Generally, it is the wives who suffer the financial consequences of divorce these days. A divorced husband's standard of living rises 42 percent while that of his wife and children falls 73 percent. Alimony is now paid in only 5 to 10 percent of divorces, and two thirds of divorced mothers receive no child support at all. As a result, women and children now constitute 77 percent of the nation's poor.

SECOND MARRIAGES

Are money issues more easily resolved during second marriages (which someone once called the "triumph of hope over experience")? The second time around, couples are usually better prepared to handle sex and in-law problems, but money may continue to bedevil them, particularly if there are financial obligations to former wives and children. In these cases, money is not only a problem in itself; it is also a surrogate for feelings of jealousy and insecurity. The second wife may be jealous of her predecessor, for example, or if she has no children, may focus her resentment on her husband's child support payments.

PARENT-CHILD-PARENT MONEY RELATIONS

Money poses problems at both ends of the generation gap. Indeed, the seeds of our individual money attitudes are planted in childhood by our parents, by their example as well as their instruction. Lessons learned in childhood can help us to grow up secure or dependent financially, sensible or irresponsible. For example, a child whose whims are always indulged may become accustomed to instant gratification and unable to tolerate money frustration.

Within the family, as between husband and wife, money is power. And between parent and child, it is an instrument of authority. "No, you can't have that" is a refrain echoed many times in every child's day. At the opposite extreme is giving young children money instead of love, literally buying their love. Particularly in affluent families, there is a tendency to solve problems with money, which in turn becomes a substitute for parental responsibility.

Children and young adults may follow or rebel against their parents' financial example. Women whose mothers were not allowed to spend money without their husbands' permission may strive for financial independence. And men who saw their fathers as hopelessly burdened with debt may actively seek partners to share financial responsibility.

INHERITANCE: EVENING THE SCORE
BEYOND THE GRAVE

At the other end of the generation gap, we are often called upon to help support aged parents. Many people respond in a manner motivated by long-standing grievances, real or imagined. And when it comes to questions of inheritance, the most intense family, and sibling, conflicts may surface.

Nearly all wills are written in favor of family members—sometimes a distant relative rather than a friend or institution. Whether relationships are good or bad, most of us believe that money should be kept within the family. Even wealthy men who in principle consider it harmful to leave money to their children may still do so as a means of binding them beyond the grave, continuing to "pull the strings."

But this may be changing. Louis Auchincloss, lawyer and novelist, believes that the "dynastic impulse" is dying out in the United States. This is borne out by a 1986 *Fortune* magazine feature on how the rich handle inheritance issues. For example, the chairman of a billion-dollar holding company says he plans to leave most of his money to charity, because he believes it harmful to children to guarantee them "a lifetime of food stamps." Other superrich fathers worry about how to keep their hard-earned millions from destroying their children, considering wealth to be "certain death to ambition." ("No country so readily celebrates the self-made man," *Fortune* said, and "no culture is more suspicious that the silver spoon contains something vaguely narcotic.")

According to a New York probate lawyer for the affluent, sixteen of the twenty wills he has drawn up recently have stipulated that at least half of the fortune be left to charity. Some wealthy fathers give their children just enough to get them started; others provide a down payment on the first home. The current rule of thumb seems to be that a few hundred thousand dollars each won't entirely ruin the children, but there is general agreement that twenty-one is too young for anyone to inherit a windfall.

Disinheritance, on the other hand, may lead to intense feelings of anger and rejection. Christina Crawford, author of *Mommie Dearest,* a tell-all biography of her mother Joan, seems to have forgiven the years of cruelty and abuse she suffered at her actress mother's hands. But what still disturbs her, years after her mother's death, is the fact that she was disinherited. This grim memoir of celebrity childhood closes with a phrase from her mother's will, final chilling words disinheriting Christina and her brother ". . . for reasons which are well known to them . . ."

Parents may use their wills to get even. "Dear Abby" once published a letter from a mother distressed over her son's failure to remember special occasions or give her gifts. Sometimes she even bought expensive presents for herself and her husband and told everyone the gifts were from her son. But, she wrote to Abby, the son would pay in the end, for she was keeping a tab that would be subtracted from his inheritance.

Ted Turner, maverick broadcast millionaire, got his first stake out of a painful family tragedy. In 1963 his father committed suicide, just after selling his advertising business so that Ted, then twenty-four, could not squander it. But Ted was persuasive enough to get the buyer to cancel the deal, which became the foundation of his own very successful enterprise. On a happier note, an Arizona lawyer, successful in his own right, was raised to expect nothing from his rich father. He was thus surprised and gratified to receive a $1.5 million bequest in his father's will—"I think my father was saying from the grave that he approved."

REVENGE OF THE CHILDREN

Financial independence is the major threshold of adulthood. But at this crucial point, as earlier in childhood, some parents use money to keep their children dependent, clingers instead of autonomous adults. And some children take every advantage of this understandable parental desire to hold on.

Such was the case with the Franklin Bradshaw family of Salt Lake City. Bradshaw, a self-made man from an old Mormon family, lived frugally, almost as if he were poor. Actually, he had a profitable auto parts business, with thirty-one stores, and extensive oil and gas leases (200,000 acres, the legal limit, in Utah alone, and more acreage elsewhere). After his murder, his net worth was estimated at anywhere from $60 to $400 million.

Bradshaw was so stingy that his wife Berenice, the family bookkeeper, signed his name on checks to get extra household and spending money. Berenice had a special weakness for her youngest child, strong-willed Frances, who was very adept at manipulating her mother and anyone else in order to get whatever she wanted. Frances married twice, divorced twice, and had two sons. Constantly strapped for money, and unable to squeeze enough out of her mother, she finally turned from "parasite to parricide," in the words of author Shana Alexander in *Nutcracker*, a fascinating tale of family money madness.

In the summer of 1977, Frances Schreuder, who lived in New York City, sent her teenaged sons, Marc and Larry, home to Salt Lake City to work in their grandfather's warehouse. First, she instructed them to look for stocks, bonds, checks—anything that could be cashed, forged, negotiated. The summer's haul was $200,000. But that didn't last Frances very long, and the next summer, she sent her sons west with instructions to murder their grandfather. Marc, the younger son, always desperately eager to win his mother's approval, committed the murder.

For three generations this family was dominated, and ultimately ruined, by the struggle for money. Like old Franklin and his covetous daughter Frances, Frances' two sons also cared passionately for money. Before his arrest and conviction for second-degree murder, Marc Schreuder, not yet twenty-one, had a stockbroker who made $10,000 transactions for him at a time.

Before her conviction for first-degree murder in 1983, Frances Schreuder used over $1 million of her father's hard-earned money to fulfill a lifelong fantasy of becoming a benefactress to the New York City Ballet (hence the title of Alexander's book, *Nutcracker*).

Berenice Bradshaw, heartbroken after the murder trials of her grandson and daughter, changed her will. She disinherited her other two daughters, leaving the entire family fortune to the convicted murderess serving a life term in prison.

PART TWO

DISCOVERING YOUR
MONEY PERSONALITY

4

The Making of Your Money Personality

Man is not the sum of what he has but the totality of what he does not yet have, of what he might have.

—Jean-Paul Sartre

You are at a party.

Martin, your best friend, takes you aside toward the end of the evening and tells you that he is about to start up a new business—one that is guaranteed to make a fortune. Over the past ten years, you have watched Martin launch three enterprises; two have been successful and one crumbled to ruin in less than a year. Still, Martin has a beautiful home, a new Mercedes, and seems to have plenty of money in the bank.

In a hushed but excited tone, Martin asks if you would like to be a partner in his business. He is looking for five investors, each to contribute $20,000. On Monday morning he is having a meeting at his office to discuss all the details. Can you come?

You have the $20,000 but would have to liquidate most of your investments to get the cash. Should you call in sick at work on Monday and attend the meeting to learn more about the offer? Should you talk to your spouse, who isn't particularly impressed with Martin or his business savvy? If you do take the plunge and end up losing some, or all, of your money, how will the loss affect your financial situation? As the questions overlap each other, you try to decide what to do.

Your answer—how you would handle the situation—tells a great deal about the way you feel about your money and the control or lack of control you have, or you think you have, over your financial life.

For most of us, money—and our feelings toward it—are not static but fluid, dynamic, and intense. We love money, or we hate it, or we fear it, or we worship it, or we enjoy it—but we certainly never ignore it. And yet, we know so little about why we experience these emotions toward money and the effects they have on our very existence.

As a financial psychologist, I have confronted these money emotions every day of my practice. I have worked with hundreds of men and women from all kinds of backgrounds and income levels: company presidents who make million-dollar decisions in the boardroom but can barely balance their own checkbooks and make disastrous personal financial decisions; divorced housewives who spent years watching their husbands control the money but must now join the work force and negotiate new financial lives; couples who never retreat from the financial battleground as they argue over "my" money, "your" money, and "our" money.

HOW WELL DO YOU KNOW YOUR MONEY SELF?

Not only do we have a physical self, an emotional self, and a social self, but we have a financial, or money, self. This money self is an integral part of our behavioral repertoire and influences the way we interact with our money. In other words, your money personality is a major factor in how you utilize your money. Most of us fail to realize the extent to which our money personality impacts our financial habits and affects the degree of satisfaction we get from what money we have. There is an inseparable link between our unconscious feelings about money and the way in which we earn it, spend it, save it, and invest it.

Some of the basic needs we try to satisfy with money instead of using our own sense of self are survival (safety and security), power (being in control of ourselves as well as others), love (the need to be cared for, personally and/or financially), respect (being admired and recognized). In the long run we cannot satisfy something inside with something outside—one of the big misconceptions in our society that gets us into a lot of trouble in areas other than money.

Using money as a vehicle to try to work out our basic inner needs doesn't work. We cannot work out a basic inner need externally. For example, if you are fired or laid off from a job, you might head straight to a shopping mall to ward off anxiety and fear. However, going on a buying spree will not relieve insecure feelings; it is only a temporary solution. All too often, our personal problems get projected into money, the concrete object we try to use as a solution. Money becomes the emotional football people kick around to get satisfaction for some inner need. Unfortunately, money is not a miraculous cure. While it may be an effective short-term antidote, money can never alleviate insecurity, loneliness, or dependency.

What does money mean to you? Does it make you nervous or provide you with a sense of well-being? For most of us, money is far more than a simple medium of exchange. It also represents our emotions in many human transactions. Therefore, when money becomes enmeshed with our emotions, it is sometimes difficult to get a clear picture of how it fits into our lives. In a sense, how you use your money is a statement of how you see yourself. So making decisions about how to deal with money—how to spend it, save it, invest it, and even earn it— can be complicated.

Money attitudes influence our behavior, aspirations, and emotional reactions to ourselves, our families, and friends. Understanding your money style will help you gain insight into how and why you react emotionally to money—why you have those reactions and how they affect your financial success or lack of success. If you don't know your money strengths, you can't use them. If you don't know what's preventing you from getting money, you will remain a money victim. If you don't know what you want from money, you will never reach your financial goals. If you aren't willing to change your money attitudes and habits, you will stay in financial status quo.

You have a healthy money self-concept when you know yourself well and how you affect money and how money affects you. You have a healthy money self-concept when you like how you deal with money more than you dislike how you deal with money. If you fall at the other end of the spectrum and have a negative money self-concept, you can alter your attitudes and formulate a new money style that will provide richness instead of deprivation.

The money style you have developed defines the amount of money you are earning now, the amount of money you save, the pleasure you get in using money, and the success of your investment plan. These unconscious money patterns will remain static until you consciously develop a plan to change them. Your income and personal wealth rarely exceed more than who you are. Money only exaggerates who you are. Poor thinking habits keep people poor. As you think, so you become.

Once you are aware of your money style, you can learn what financial traits are assets and which ones are liabilities. You can reinforce those feelings and actions which are your financial assets and stop letting your emotions sabotage your financial success. You can determine what part of you may be holding back your potential for greater financial and personal success. You can bring your attitudes about money into congruent harmony with the way you handle your financial affairs. This interaction is what determines the ability to accumulate wealth and enjoy it at the same time.

By itself, money has no value. We project meaning into it. The way we use money reveals a lot about how we see the world—as fearful and threatening or challenging and adventuresome. There is nothing wrong with making money, nothing wrong with having or enjoying money. Money is neither inherently good or evil.

Whether we like it or not, money is a very significant part of our lives and we must recognize its importance. Unless we have control over our money and accept full responsibility for it, we will have no power over it. Beware of the person who denies the importance of money. When people emphatically tell you that money doesn't mean a thing to them, they are either pretending or lying. However, it's a painful cover-up that has complex psychological meaning.

The money drive is unlike many other drives because there is no biological reason to explain it. Getting rich, having more money than you need or can spend, serves no fundamental purpose. Yet it is a powerful drive in a society where human worth is often measured in dollars and cents. Money can enhance or destroy friendships, marriages, careers, and family unity. In short, it brings out the best, and the worst, in us.

The symbolic meaning of our money is determined by our cultural background, religion, attitudes of parents and teachers, our life experiences, and our short- and long-range goals. Our money background predetermines the exact way we invest money, save money, squander money, lose money, live for money. Thus, we need to uncover our financial past to better understand our feelings and views of money today.

MY MOTHER, MY FATHER, MY MONEY

Most of us never stop and think about how our early childhood experiences impact our money self today. Our money attitudes were molded as we watched our parents struggle with the dollar. We watched them rejoice over money, get depressed over money, and fight over money. Even when the attitudes and actions were confusing and paradoxical, one thing was very clear—money was an important thing to have. As a result, the meaning and value of money got blown out of proportion. Our parents weren't fighting about vacations or clothes or power or love—they were fighting about money. Those early money lessons are heavily imprinted in our money styles.

The following questions are designed to trigger some of your childhood memories. They should elicit at least a few new money revelations. They may also provoke a little anxiety. Thinking about money, in the present or the past, can be uncomfortable.

—Did you get everything you asked for when you were growing up? Or were you often disappointed because your parents' pocketbook couldn't accommodate your desires and fantasies?

—What was your family's financial status? As a child, did you think your parents were wealthy or poor or middle of the road? Did your friends have more or less money?

—Did you get an allowance? Was it adequate or were you always asking for more money?

—How much did your parents argue about money? Can you remember what the arguments were about?

—What world events were taking place when you were a child? And how did they influence your family's financial status? Were you a Depression baby, a baby boomer, or did you arrive much later?

—Did one or both of your parents attempt to control you with money? If so, did you rebel or were you an obedient child who followed all of the money rules? If your parents were controlling, do you find yourself today with a spouse who tries to control you with money?

—Do you deprive yourself of enjoying money because one or both of your parents was so security conscious that money was rarely spent on pleasure? If so, what would you do for yourself now if you had all the money you might ever need?

—Was one or both of your parents particularly destructive with money? What fears were evoked in you as a result?

—Did you find yourself feeling there was never enough money while you were growing up? Is that feeling alive in you today? Per your financial status, is that fear realistic?

Family money scripts are powerful motivators of our unconscious money patterns and styles. How we have been conditioned in the past significantly influences our money and self-esteem, our money and personal freedom, and our money and our financial freedom. You may be living according to money rules from the past that are unconsciously motivated and may be inappropriate for your money life today. We receive mixed messages from our parents and we have to sort them out to find those that work to our benefit and those that are detrimental.

Your money self-concept is a learned process. Its development in the early formative years is most critical. As we grow up, the set of feelings we develop about money becomes a filter for the rest of our life experiences. This money filter, or money screen, greatly influences your approach to life's money situations and your interpretation of them.

Our attitudes and our emotional reactions to money are governed and guided by our family money styles. By the time you are an adult, your money responses and style of making financial decisions have already been programmed. If money has meant security to your family, you probably save more money than you spend. If your parents grew up during the Depression, saving for a rainy day may have been necessary and prudent, but your repetition of that style may serve as a barrier to your financial success. On the other hand, if you grew up during baby boomer days when money represented prestige and status, you may find yourself determined to buy a Porsche when all you can afford is a Honda.

We are more influenced by what parents do rather than by what they say. For example, a client of mine told me a story about a weekend outing to Tijuana, Mexico. When she and her husband were crossing the U.S. border, the guard asked her husband if they had any liquor to declare. He promptly replied "no" despite the fact that they had three bottles of tequila in the trunk of their car. Her ten-year-old son asked his father why he had lied to the guard and repeated the saying taught to him by his father—"the truth always pays." The son had just experienced a contradiction between his father's words and his father's actions.

Nowhere are the contradictions more apparent than in the money equation. If parents consistently say that "money can't buy happiness," what does a child think when Mother is depressed because she can't afford a new dress, when Father is angry because he lost money in the stock market, when parents quarrel about whether or not to buy new dining room furniture? And why are they so happy when Mother gets a raise in salary or Father wins the lottery?

Most children are never taught the meaning, or the limitations, of money. Money somehow magically appears to pay for school clothes, gifts at Christmas, and summer vacations. Since the supply of money seems somewhat unlimited, children get angry and confused when they are denied money. One client of mine told me about an argument she had with her eight-year-old son. After telling him that she could not afford to buy him an expensive toy laser gun, he yelled, "I don't care if you don't have any money. Write out a check."

Children learn quickly how money can be used to reward or punish them. If they bring home a good report card, they get paid for each A. If they behave well at the dentist or doctor, a trip to the toy store will follow. Even the loss of a tooth can be good news because putting it under the pillow will signal the tooth fairy to replace the tooth with shiny pieces of money. But when children neglect to clean up their rooms, forget to do other chores, or misbehave in some way, money is taken away—allowances are docked and the planned trip to the pizza parlor is canceled.

This system of money rewards and punishments often leads children to make a connection between money and love. Too often parents use money to bestow or withhold affection and approval: Do something right and you get a present or some money; do something wrong and you get nothing or something will be taken away. It is, therefore, not surprising that when parents refuse to dole out money to a child, the child's instant reaction is, "You don't love me anymore."

Without an understanding of the mechanics and the meaning of money, children tend to think of money in the extreme—you either have it or you don't. If parents buy a new car, why can't they buy a new television set or new stereo equipment? On the other hand, if children overhear parents talk about money cutbacks—no vacation this year, fewer dinners out at restaurants, the possible sale one of the family cars—they may think that the family is headed for the poorhouse. Like any complex and misunderstood entity, money takes on a mystical, sometimes frightening, significance.

When parents exhibit unhealthy, uptight attitudes about money, children adopt those attitudes as their own. When parents deal with money constructively and get the most out of their financial lives, children likewise view money as positive not negative. Those attitudes are formed regardless of the amount of money a family has. Sally, a woman I met at a financial seminar, told me this story: "I grew up in a small town outside of Pittsburgh. I remember thinking that my family was pretty well off. Every year my sister and I got a couple of new outfits for school, we went on summer vacations to Lake Erie, and we always had cookies and ice cream in the house. We seemed to have more money than most of the kids in my school. And I was particularly proud of the fact that we had two telephones in my house—none of my friends had two telephones. Anyway, after I graduated from high school I went to Penn State University, on a scholarship. It was the first time I had ever really been away from home. I took this introductory sociology class and I remember the day the professor was talking about different income levels in the United States. In our textbook was this chart of income levels. I knew how much my dad earned and I quickly looked at the chart. I was shocked to see that his salary was in the "lower middle class" bracket. At first I thought the chart must have had some mistakes in it. All the while I grew up, I thought my family was rich and now this book was telling me that we were borderline poor. Funny, I never felt poor at all."

Many of my clients have been profoundly affected by the way their parents handled money. The parent-child relationship is certainly a complex one. We learn our money styles from our families, which pass the patterns and habits down from generation to generation. We may get healthy messages from our families—that money is a commodity to be used for our maximum benefit—or told that it is the root of all evil. We may learn how to budget money wisely or we may learn how to become money hoarders or spendthrifts.

Just as our parents did, we project our problems into our money, making money responsible for our problems, not ourselves. The early parental messages and scripts we learn carry over into adult life, positively or negatively, and affect our attitudes toward our money and our money styles.

As we move from childhood into adulthood, we take our money scripts with us and they ultimately shape the way we live our lives. This doesn't mean that we have to play out these scripts for a lifetime. We can develop our own new money styles which match more appropriately who we are today or who we would like to be.

LETTING GO OF CHILDHOOD MONEY SCRIPTS

At the root of the common money complaint—"there's never enough" —is the tendency to settle for whatever is dished out to you. Many people have self-images which don't do justice to their potential. Because of that, they tend to settle for very little and don't believe that they can have much more. Self-esteem or self-image and the amount of money you earn generally go hand in hand. If you have a poor self-image, you're apt to have a low income. And if you have a good self-image, you're apt to have a better income. Money is a baffling commodity because our psychological needs are intertwined with our money. We have difficulty dealing with money openly and directly because we seldom understood money issues when we were growing up, and money was not something we were allowed to discuss openly.

I've had clients who were so angry about their childhoods that they unconsciously became financial failures in order to retaliate against their parents. If you want to prove to your parents what a lousy job they did in raising you, becoming a financial failure is a powerful weapon. However, in the end the act of retaliation backfires because money, or lack of money, cannot resolve emotional problems.

Using money to rebel against one's parents is a complicated issue. The outcome can hurt the child as much as, or more than, it hurts the parents. The reasons for rebellion are varied:

1. Children want to turn away from a lifestyle which was forced upon them. The underlying thought is: "I don't like the way you chose to live so I'll make my own kind of life."

2. They are getting back at parents who were very critical. The underlying thought is: "You tried to make me perfect but I'm not and trying to be perfect got me nowhere."

3. They want to assert their independence. The underlying thought is: "I'm different; I don't have to act as my parents did."

4. They were pushed to be overachievers and they are now pushing back. The underlying thought is: "You tried to make me a success but it didn't work. I'm a failure and it's your own fault that you are disappointed in me."

A major disadvantage of rebellion is that it takes a lot of energy to keep up the fight. That energy could be put to better use by pursuing happiness instead of misery. It should be pointed out that rebellious acts do not necessarily lead to financial failure. Asserting independence and developing a lifestyle different from your parents can be a very positive and necessary goal. The rationale and examples listed above relate to my clients who have had self-sabotaging, and unproductive, money styles.

The clients I've worked with who have been able to differentiate themselves from their family money habits have had high self-determination—the Moneymax trait which measures the extent to which you feel in control of your financial destiny. Their high rate of success was directly and positively correlated with their ability to motivate themselves financially and to resist outside pressure from family and friends. Being open, courageous, and assertive allowed them to discover what it means to be powerful in the quest for ultimate financial control, independence, and contentment.

Changing a money style often requires forgiving our parents; otherwise we keep alive the image of an unhappy child and maintain a money victim mentality. If we don't forgive our parents, we remain hooked into their style even if we try desperately to alter it.

Many of my clients say, "But how can I be like my parents when I have tried so hard to be different?" Often, the more we try to be different from someone who had a significant role in our development, like our parents, the more the behavior unconsciously persists. I've heard many a client say, "That's impossible. I couldn't have married someone like my mother [or father]. In fact, I looked for someone who was not like her [or him]. I didn't want someone that cheap [or that much of a spendthrift]."

In many cases a spouse might not appear to be like a parental figure, but a closer inspection might turn up some interesting similarities. Even if a person is successful in picking someone directly opposite from a parent, the difference in money styles might cause a great deal of conflict. I had a client who married a spendthrift because he was trying to avoid another penny-pinching woman like his mother. He wanted to live with someone who had a free and easy spending style. In reality the difference in the styles made him so uncomfortable that he began to assimilate his mother's style into his own. He scrutinized his wife's every expenditure, tried to put her on a budget, and became angry when she didn't consult him on any purchase over twenty dollars. Obviously, he had not been successful in finding a good match for his own money personality and money management style. Choosing a wife with an extravagant money style was an overreaction to his need to avoid his mother's strict and overly frugal money patterns.

When our unconscious links with our family money styles have not been resolved, we maintain a parent-child money pattern that bonds into our other money relationships. Anger toward a parent can easily be projected into another relationship without our conscious knowledge. Barbara, a female client I worked with, was so angry that her father didn't give her what she needed—namely love—that she turned it into a need for a husband who would give her what she desired— namely money, or a financially secure life. When she finally found and married a man who wanted to take care of her, she lost interest in him sexually. Barbara finally had what she always thought she wanted but she was frustrated and bored. She spent money wildly but got no lasting enjoyment or sense of fulfillment from money. She didn't realize that it was hard to fuse sexually with her spouse when she had unconsciously projected all of her unresolved anger for her father onto her husband. No matter how many material objects her husband's money could buy, she was never satisfied. In the end, it was not really the money she desired but the love she never got from her father.

At a very young age, Barbara didn't get any affection from her father and she projected that need onto the most handy object at the time—money. Barbara always heard her mother complaining that her father didn't earn enough money to buy the children what they needed. The anger Barbara felt toward her father for not taking care of her properly, for not loving her, was transferred to his inability to provide financially for his family. The helplessness she felt in dealing with an issue from childhood was resurrected in adulthood and pinned on her spouse. Until she resolved the anger and resentment about her father, Barbara would never have a rational style of money management but would indulge in emotional spending sprees. In addition, she would remain powerless and childlike, always financially dependent on the man in her life. This style was so much a part of her money self that she wasn't aware of what she was doing. She only knew that she was not happy even though she had found a man and the financial security that was supposed to bring her contentment.

If we think of ourselves as coming into the world with a *tabula rasa* (a clean slate) with all the potential and self-esteem necessary to achieve all of our goals, we can then see how our parents intervene and imprint their messages on that slate and teach us how to model their behavior regarding money. In most cases, we are never given the opportunity to develop our own unique money style because our money conditioning is so strong and so one-sided. The money slate is not only filled with the beliefs of our parents. Other important people in our lives make contributions—a favorite grandmother, grandfather, uncle, aunt, cousin, teacher, neighbor. We are fortunate if the messages we receive are sound and beneficial but some of us are not so lucky. We have to overcome negative messages and role modeling as well. Some of us never take the opportunity to change and continue to live out money scripts that we inherited but did not choose.

MONEY—A REFLECTION OF SELF-ESTEEM

The set of thoughts and beliefs you have about yourself is your self-concept. How you evaluate those beliefs, or the amount of pride you have in your self-concept, is your self-esteem. If you like and approve of your self-concept, then you have high self-esteem. Also called self-respect or self-worth, self-esteem is the core of our personality, the sum of all the parts that determine how we relate to the world. Generally speaking, the higher your self-esteem, the better equipped you are to cope with life's challenges and adversities and the better chance you have of finding happiness and security.

The amount of self-esteem you have affects everything you think and every action you take. It affects every personal and business relationship—how you view others and how you think other people assess you. It influences every decision you make—whether you step out into the world with confidence or step backward with fear and apprehension. In addition, self-esteem has a profound relationship to how you deal with money issues. Nothing is more important than self-esteem when measuring psychological and financial well-being.

Self-esteem is not black or white; we don't either have it or don't have it. It is much more a matter of degree. Everyone is born with high self-esteem. It gets ground down and reshaped, and its final form and value depend greatly upon family upbringing and cultural conditioning. If you think of it in those terms, you can understand why self-esteem is not something you can go out and get. Rather, self-esteem is more an acknowledgment and acceptance of who you are and the pride you attain from knowing yourself. In terms of money, self-esteem is achieving a more positive image of yourself and your money. It is finally coming to terms with your money self.

The most effective counseling is aimed at raising self-esteem. The aim of my work with clients is to raise their awareness of themselves, to realize their financial assets and liabilities, and to determine the gap between where they are with their money and where they want to be.

A high level of self-esteem—knowing and trusting yourself intellectually, emotionally, and financially—leads to the ultimate goal of personal power, security, and contentment.

One way to judge how much confidence you have in yourself is to determine how good you are at taking risks, knowing that you might fail. Do you have the courage to take a risk and know deep inside that if you do fail, you'll have whatever it takes to bounce back? Do you pursue new job opportunities with a sense of optimism and adventure or do you not even apply for a position because the competition may be too tough? If you want a new relationship in your life, do you seek out situations where you can meet new people, or do you stay at home and hope the phone will ring? When frustrated about your financial status, do you consider looking into different investment plans, or is it easier to let your money remain in a savings account because at least you feel safe?

An inner core of strength and positive self-esteem is built by taking risks and finding out that the rules of life—as taught to you by parents, teachers, and peers—can be changed. The money script played out by your parents may have been valid for who they are and when they grew up, but that same script might be totally inappropriate for your life. The most significant ingredient in building self-esteem is to stretch ourselves in order to realize our dreams, to take risks and not settle for comfort. This certainly applies to money and financial aspirations. It takes making a commitment to yourself—a promise to declare what you want and then a willingness to go after it. With commitment, focus, and persistence, it's hard to lose.

Money, and the possessions it will buy, cannot substitute for self-esteem. It's difficult to deny that money commands both attention and respect and is frequently used as a measure of self-worth. In our society people with money often seem special, gifted, even superior. Built into us is the assumption that what you do and what you have is more important than what you are. Money success becomes a form of self-validation: "What am I worth? I don't know. How much money do I make?" However, we can live in the right neighborhood, drive the right car, land the right job, and make the right investment, but doing the "right" things does not necessarily build confidence and self-esteem.

Rewards and reinforcement for human behavior come in two forms

—external and internal. Internal rewards are the positive feelings we get for a job well done—pride, satisfaction, and joy. External rewards are the concrete, tangible measurements of success—trophies, diplomas, medals, gifts, and money. After winning a competition, most children would prefer a new bicycle to words of praise and encouragement. Likewise many adults would gladly trade in a hug and a handshake for a hundred-dollar bill. Since money is quantifiable, easy to measure, it's often difficult to weigh a money reward against something harder to measure like pride and satisfaction. All too often, money is used as the yardstick to compare the accomplishments of human beings. How much money we make and how we use it constitute our "market value." Without much protest, many of us allow our market value to be converted into our "value."

Self-esteem is not a superior attitude. Having it does not mean that you are vain, or egotistical, or selfish. In fact those who act superior are usually people with very low self-esteem. The person who grabs the spotlight, rules the conversation, and lavishly spends money is usually suffering from poor self-esteem. When people have low opinions of themselves, they overcompensate by trying to impress others—trying desperately to establish their value for all to see.

People with high self-esteem don't believe they are perfect but they also don't see themselves as inconsequential creatures who are victims of society. People with high self-esteem know how to take care of themselves. They acknowledge their flaws but don't allow human imperfection to chisel away their self-esteem. No one is absolutely free of self-doubt and bouts of inadequacy, but people who are confident and self-assured don't allow themselves to feel chronically defective. In addition, they don't need to flaunt their accomplishments or their money.

Money acts as a false protector of our self-esteem. We use it to avoid dealing with feelings that cause distress and confusion: if you are depressed, you might spend some money on a vacation to make yourself feel better; if your spouse is angry with you, you might make reservations at an expensive restaurant; if you feel guilty because you haven't visited your mother in weeks, you might send her some flowers; if your children complain that you are never at home, you might buy them a new toy; if you are feeling poor, you might spend some money on lottery tickets; if you secretly feel selfish and self-centered, you might write out a check to a local charity. While money may act as a temporary safeguard against personal and financial problems, it is never a cure-all.

As a result of our upbringing and our past experiences, we have developed a money style which is a reflection of our self-esteem. The dynamics of our personality are revealed through our money behavioral repertoire. Most of our thoughts and actions with money are so deep-rooted that we react automatically when faced with a money decision. Many of us believe that making and accumulating more and more money will gain the admiration of others and build our self-respect. The linkage is only an illusion because money does not engender self-esteem. At best, it is only an outgrowth of self-esteem.

YOUR MONEYMAX PROFILE AND YOUR MONEYMAX FINANCIAL TRAITS

Since 1981, I have been researching which financial traits significantly impact the way we deal with our money—the way we earn it, spend it, save it, and invest it. By learning which traits influence the way we manage our money, it was possible to develop insight into our money personalities and to develop a system to use that knowledge to manage money more effectively. The system is called the Moneymax Profile.

The Moneymax Profile, a questionnaire based on thirteen financial traits, was used in a nationwide survey. By interviewing people across the United States, and through sophisticated statistical techniques, it has been possible to identify groups of people, distinctly different from each other, but groups that have similar attitudes and feelings about money, money management, and investments.

Each of the thirteen financial traits, or money traits—such as comfort level with risk, desired involvement with money, or anxiety experienced in making financial decisions—has a significant impact on a person's money management style. When individuals expressed their feelings about those traits, they formed themselves into congruent, homogeneous groups. Not only did these groups have consistent attitudes about money, but it became apparent that each group also had similar money management styles and investment preferences. From a practical standpoint, Americans divide themselves into nine groups— each one with its own set of financial needs and preferences, each one with its own unique Moneymax personality.

In this book, each of the nine Moneymax groups will be described within the context of their financial traits. Case histories will be used to exemplify the different personalities. The case histories are based upon clients, people I have interviewed for this book, and others I have met in my professional and personal life. All names, locations, occupations, and other identifying information have been changed to protect the privacy of those whose experiences are being discussed. In some cases, stories and/or comments have been combined to form composites.

Unfortunately, it was impossible to include the Moneymax Profile questionnaire in this book because the scoring procedure is a twenty-seven-step computerized formula which could not be adapted to manual scoring. In lieu of the actual questionnaire, I have included "guidelines" at the beginning of each Moneymax Profile chapter. As you read the seven guidelines for each of the nine groups, you should be able to identify with one set of guidelines more than the others.

To further help you identify your money personality, I have included extensive descriptions of the various configurations and blends of financial traits for each of the nine Moneymax groups. The case histories will show how each personality thinks and feels about money and how each uses it. In most instances, the case histories will reflect an extreme characterization of the traits. We all have differing degrees of the thirteen financial traits that comprise the Moneymax Profile. The case histories presented in this book usually reflect a polarized, or extreme, version of the particular Moneymax Profile being discussed. Each of us has a varying degree of each trait, and when all the traits are combined, most of us fall in the middle, between a maladaptive use of money and a good use of money. Polarized examples of the profiles are presented so you can easily understand the essence of each Moneymax Profile and the differences between them. Keep in mind that you may not reflect as extreme a representation of each trait yet still feel that you identify with a particular group. For example, you may be a High Roller even though your traits don't exactly parallel all thirteen traits of the High Roller. In addition, you might identify with parts of several personalities but everyone falls more into one profile than another.

The traits which make up our money personalities are not either black or white but come in a multitude of shades, or degrees. There are low levels of a particular trait as well as high levels. Take, for example, the trait of risk-taking. Some people are extremely cautious and cannot tolerate much risk while others have a moderate comfort level with risk. Then there are those people who seek out risk and thrill with their money. If you think of each trait on a continuum of low to high, most people tend to fall in the middle ranges. People who have taken the Moneymax Profile—through Financial Psychology Corporation, a financial research and consulting company, or their place of employment—have received exact scores: a trait evaluation summary which lists the person's scores and the national profile's scores on the thirteen traits.

There are four criteria by which to judge whether a financial trait is beyond the norm, or the average:

1. Chronicity—the attitude or behavior persists for a long period of time. For instance, many people have, at one time or another, gone on an impulsive buying spree. However, people who find themselves short of cash every month because of their impulsive spending binges would score at the polar end of high emotional money use. That behavior is chronic because it occurs regularly, over a long period of years, and isn't something that happens on occasion—like going on a spending spree after receiving a bonus or while on vacation.

2. Rigidity—the attitude or behavior doesn't stop and start and is not flexible. For example, a person who always has to be the ultimate decision-maker and won't consider anyone else's opinions has a rigid style. This style could cause problems with a spouse, a friend, a business partner, or a financial adviser.

3. Compulsiveness—there is little control over an attitude or behavior. A compulsive gambler is unconsciously driven by the excitement of gambling and has little control over stopping. Another example is the person who has a compulsion to save money for a rainy day when no rainy days are in sight. Those people find themselves running to the bank with money, paralyzed to use it in any other way. Hoarding money is compulsive and they don't stop to think whether it makes sense or not.

4. Overdrawn—there is a lot of emotion involved in a particular attitude or behavior. In terms of money, you are overdrawn when you have an exaggerated response to a financial situation or decision—too much anxiety, too much anger, too much fear. For example, people who experience an enormous amount of stress and tension every time they are reviewed for a raise are overdrawn.

You can match your feelings about each of the financial traits to these four criteria to determine whether your attitudes and behaviors are maladaptive, meaning beyond the usual norm. If you find a match, then you know that change needs to take place before you can alter your money style.

In the following nine chapters you will meet people who have had both successful and unsuccessful experiences with money and money management. Project yourself into each profile and try to determine which Moneymax personality resembles you. The following chart of the thirteen Moneymax financial traits will serve as an additional guide for self-discovery of your Moneymax Profile:

INVOLVEMENT | The degree you desire to be personally responsible and involved in managing and investing your money. *HIGH SCORERS:* You have a need for personally controlling your own money management. *LOW SCORERS:* You display a willingness to relinquish control of your money and investing to others.

PRIDE | An index of the personal satisfaction you have attained in the way you have handled your money. *HIGH SCORERS:* You reflect a feeling of pride. *LOW SCORERS:* You exhibit feelings of disappointment with your money.

EMOTIONALITY | The degree of emotion you feel in dealing with your money. *HIGH SCORERS:* Your feelings often guide your financial decisions. *LOW SCORERS:* You exhibit a practical and rational use of money.

ALTRUISM

The extent to which you believe in the financial generosity of others. *HIGH SCORERS:* You believe that people are basically willing to help others in financial difficulty. *LOW SCORERS:* You tend to believe that financial responsibility is a personal matter to be handled individually.

ANXIETY

The degree of anxiety you feel in making financial decisions. *HIGH SCORERS:* You tend to doubt and worry about your skills in making financial decisions. *LOW SCORERS:* You have confidence and trust in your abilities to make decisions regarding your money.

POWER

The extent that the desire for power drives your behavior. *HIGH SCORERS:* You are motivated by the prestige and status that your money brings you. *LOW SCORERS:* You are uninterested in receiving public recognition with your money.

WORK ETHIC

Your views of how the work ethic relates to your financial success. *HIGH SCORERS:* You believe that hard work brings financial success. *LOW SCORERS:* You question whether financial success can be attributed to hard work.

CONTENTMENT

The degree of personal happiness money contributes to your life. *HIGH SCORERS:* You feel peace of mind with your financial status in life. *LOW SCORERS:* You are discontent with the current financial condition.

RISK-TAKING

The level of comfort you feel in taking risks with your money. *HIGH SCORERS:*

You exhibit a propensity to seek out and assume risk with your money. *LOW SCORERS:* You tend to avoid taking financial risks.

SELF-DETERMINATION The extent to which you feel in control of your financial destiny. *HIGH SCORERS:* You believe that financial success comes primarily from personal effort. *LOW SCORERS:* You tend to attribute financial success primarily to good luck.

SPENDING Reflects your attitudes for spending versus saving your money. *HIGH SCORERS:* You tend to enjoy spending your money. *LOW SCORERS:* You believe saving your money is preferable to spending it.

REFLECTIVITY The extent to which you reflect upon past financial decisions while making current decisions regarding your money. *HIGH SCORERS:* You are reflective in making financial decisions. *LOW SCORERS:* You tend to be impulsive in your decision-making.

TRUST The level of honesty you believe people have in dealing with money. *HIGH SCORERS:* You tend to feel that people are basically honest in financial transactions. *LOW SCORERS:* You hold the belief that people are basically dishonest when it comes to dealing with money.

THE MONEYMAX INTERACTIVE MODEL

There are three ways to look at people according to psychological variables such as the thirteen financial traits:

1. Self-regulation—how you use and regulate your money
2. Self-concept—what you think of yourself and your money
3. Self-expression—how you express yourself with your money

For example, let's look at the trait of risk-taking. What you think of yourself and your money (self-concept) certainly impacts how much risk you feel you can tolerate comfortably. If you have a high self-concept, you will be able to risk more even if the consequences are uncertain because your self-concept can tolerate failure. A person with poor self-concept tends to avoid risk because thought of failure, as a consequence, is too hard to tolerate. How you use and regulate your money (self-regulation) will determine whether you are highly structured and more comfortable with low risk or can tolerate less self-regulation and deal with higher risk. How you express yourself with your money (self-expression) will certainly be indicative of how much risk you will take. There are those individuals who desire a high profile of public expression with their money—the high risk gambler at the casino. On the other hand, there are those who enjoy watching their pot of gold increase in a passbook savings account.

IN CONCLUSION

Before moving to the nine Moneymax groups, it is important to point out once again that the groups are determined according to money attitudes, not income or any other demographic factor. You can be female and earning an average income and belong in the Entrepreneur group, the Moneymax Profile that is the most predominately male and earns the highest income of all nine groups. If that is the case, then you may deduce that you have the mind and attitudes of an Entrepreneur but may not be exercising your talents and potential. Likewise, you can be in your twenties or thirties and may find yourself in the Optimist profile—the Moneymax group that, on the average, is the oldest.

The income and assets rankings for all nine groups are given within the individual chapters to give you some idea of how money attitudes translated into dollars in the survey. However, don't let the income or assets statistics influence your identification with a particular profile.

For example, you may earn in the six figures yet still profile as a Producer, the ninth group in Moneymax income rankings. This simply means that even though your income level is significantly higher than average Producers, you can still relate to most of their money attitudes.

Once you determine which profile you most closely resemble, you must decide if that is where you want to remain or if another profile is more desirable. If you want to change your money profile, then you can closely scrutinize the money attitudes and money management styles of the group you have chosen. If you wanted to learn how to become a good tennis player, you might observe skilled tennis players so that you could model their winning moves. The same is true of the Moneymax Profile groups.

5

Entrepreneurs

People are always blaming their circumstances for what they are. I don't believe in circumstances. The people who get on in this world are the people who get up and look for the circumstances they want, and, if they can't find them, make them.

—George Bernard Shaw

GUIDELINES
Entrepreneurs

. . . Consider career achievements a top priority, even over their financial matters.

. . . Only moderately content with their financial status, even though they earn a good income.

. . . Will take risks in order to achieve a business and financial goal.

. . . Have a significantly high belief that their individual work efforts can bring them financial success.

. . . Believe that good luck will be on their side in attaining their financial goals.

. . . Enjoy the feeling of prestige and fame associated with having financial status and power.

. . . Like to be involved in financial decisions but will delegate money management to someone they trust.

Moneymax Entrepreneurs come in many shapes, sizes, and ages. Some are self-employed and have started large companies with many employees; others are self-employed with small businesses and few, or no, employees. Some, called "intrapreneurs," are salaried workers who have carved out their own entrepreneurial niche within corporations and businesses; some work full time but have second careers outside the office. While their average age is forty-five, some Entrepreneurs are as young as eighteen or as old as seventy. Some typify the public image of "entrepreneur" while others seem unlikely candidates for the label.

The Entrepreneurs are above average risk-takers (second-highest of all nine profiles) and have a strong belief in the work ethic, convinced that their individual energies and efforts contribute significantly to their financial success. The Entrepreneurs are comprised of a significantly high number of professional and managerial people. It is interesting to note that while they are accomplished both professionally and financially (the highest income earners), they have only moderate levels of higher education. The Entrepreneurs appear to have opened the doors of business opportunity with their individual efforts rather than with their diplomas.

They are predominately male. In fact, they are the most male-dominated group of all nine Moneymax Profiles. This is generally true of entrepreneurs in the business world as well. However, since the late 1970s, women have been joining the ranks of this group in much higher numbers than men. In fact, from 1977 to 1983, women started businesses at more than twice the rate of men and now own more than 3.25 million small businesses. Historically, women have not been conditioned to equip themselves with the personality traits and motives necessary to function optimally in the entrepreneurial world. The most significant factor which distinguishes them from their male counterparts is their inability to make an all-consuming commitment to provide for themselves, by themselves, and thus reach financial independence. Women have more conflicting emotions, guilt, and fears to overcome than do men. From a very early age men are taught self-reliance—to venture out into the neighborhood and then into the world. They know that they will be the financial caretakers for themselves and most likely a family.

The women who are stepping out into the entrepreneurial world are doing so for the same reasons that men become entrepreneurs: they want to turn good ideas into profitable companies; they want greater job satisfaction; they want to be leaders instead of followers. Once the business commitment is made, many women do face a difficult issue—how to combine the traditional female, supportive and nurturing, role with the decisive, sometimes tough-minded, role of a successful businesswoman. In addition, some of the women must maneuver in formerly foreign areas—supervising a staff, negotiating deals, securing business loans, creating business and financial plans. However, once women have conquered those arenas and adapted to their new roles, their behaviors, personal as well as financial, tend to alter their attitudes and greatly improve their money prowess.

Some studies show that women make better entrepreneurs than men. They are as ambitious as men, and their management style gives them an extra edge because they are more flexible, less hierarchical, and more progressive when handling employee conflicts between family and career. As one observer commented, "Women don't know the jargon and the rules of the business game as well as men so they develop innovative solutions to problems as they crop up." Others who have studied the growing trend of female entrepreneurs say that in general, women have an advantage over men in that they tend to be more experimental and are good decision-makers because they are not afraid to follow their instincts.

Also, women entrepreneurs usually move out a little slower than men. Many of them start their businesses in their homes and carefully assess the marketplace before they expand. This slower, more calculated approach, according to some experts, seems to make them more successful over the long term. If women continue to outpace men in starting up their own companies, women may own half of all businesses in the United States by the year 2000, according to one business research firm.

The Moneymax Entrepreneur is dominated by individuals driven to excel and win in everything they do. They are driven to compete for concrete, objective goals but also for personal and emotional satisfaction. Some Moneymax Entrepreneurs have never clearly articulated or defined what it is that is driving them or exactly what they are seeking. Is it the opportunity to start their own business? Or, if they already have a business, do they want a 20 percent increase in profits? Or, if they work for someone else, perhaps it is a $10,000 raise and a promotion to vice president?

The people in this profile who have not clearly identified a business vision or goal are still motivated by an internal definition of excellence and success. The clarity of the vision may elude them, but they know that they are driven to perform better and better. They are driven to win. All Entrepreneurs, however, share a unique combination of personality traits which equip them to excel financially and in their chosen careers.

Entrepreneurs are possessed by a business vision. Extraordinary energy and passion are directed at making this vision real. They are confident of success. It is clear to them that what they labor to build is valuable—worthwhile to them and to society at large. Single-minded and self-reliant, they have the power to instill in others their own passion and purpose. The urgency of that purpose and their total commitment to it is what allows them to achieve. Steven Jobs, founder of two computer companies—Apple Computer and NEXT—says, "In the early days of Apple, we built from the heart but didn't use our heads in the process. We're wiser now. We're going to built NEXT from the heart and head. We have a passion about it. We really care about it, but not because we want to make a buck."

Success may bring the Entrepreneurs wealth, yet money is not their primary motive. Not necessarily driven to accumulate wealth, the Entrepreneurs view money as a by-product of achievement—a concrete measure of their progress. Typical of the entrepreneurial attitude toward money is a statement by H. Ross Perot, founder of Electronic Data Systems (EDS): "Money is the most overrated thing in the world. . . . When I came to Dallas, everything I owned was in the trunk of the car and I feel personally that I have always been rich in the things that count. I've had wonderful parents and I have a magnificent wife. I have great children. That's real wealth. Young people who make money their god are inevitably in for a big disappointment."

"Getting rich," the most common measure of success, is not the guiding light for Entrepreneurs. Some say, "I started the company not to make money but to help people." Some say, "Enrichment is more important than being rich." Others say, "Now I have control over my life." For the most part, they seem happy and fulfilled—sometimes frenetically so, since they are people who truly enjoy and thrive on work.

Ron Rice, a ex-lifeguard who founded Tanning Research Laboratories (makers of Hawaiian Tropic suntan lotion), typifies the work ethic of the Moneymax Entrepreneur. In *Winners,* a book about entrepreneurs, author Carter Henderson quotes Rice, "I can remember times when I didn't feel like I worked a day unless I had mixed the product, filled hundreds of bottles by hand, loaded the trucks, done the paperwork, turned off the lights, you name it. I had to kill myself physically and mentally or I didn't feel like I'd done a full day's work. My buddies in the old days used to go out and party and drink while I was home working. I'd never go on dates. I just didn't have a social life at all. For years I'd just eat, sleep, and work. Now my buddies are all working, and I'm going out and having a good time."

RISK—THE BLIND SPOT

The Moneymax Entrepreneurs do, however, sometimes have a blind spot. Risk. They have a penchant for tolerating, even seeking, high levels of risk if it will help them reach a goal. Their comfort level with risk can be, at the same time, a financial asset and liability.

It works to their advantage by allowing them to climb hurdles, real and imagined. It helps them feel confident and assists them in continually outperforming their own standards of excellence. However, the Entrepreneurs' desire for stimulation, their capacity to handle more than the average person, can get them into trouble. They have a tendency to feel they can control situations, often beyond reasonable expectations. It's not that they don't calculate the odds and weigh the risks. They just have a tendency to believe that they will be the recipients of good fortune. For them, lady luck will be on board, assisting them all the way. In some cases, it is a false sense of financial omnipotence. They can do it; they will do it. That may indeed be true but it is misleading and self-sabotaging to believe that you can always win without understanding the reality of the total situation and carefully weighing the odds.

Robert is typical of the Entrepreneur who runs up against this blind spot. At forty-seven he was founder and president of an architectural firm with thirty employees. In business for ten years, he had been very successful. Married and the father of three children, Robert took great pride in his firm and also considered himself very savvy in the investment world.

The stock market was his primary interest. Before investing, Robert analyzed various companies and industries, compared their track records, and looked for undervalued stocks. He made a purchase, watched the company rise to profitability, and sold when he felt that the value of the stock had peaked. He then took his money and invested it in a new stock scenario. This process gave him a real sense of perceived control—important for the Moneymax Entrepreneur. He was confident of his ability to call the right shots and he did profit handsomely.

His business grew; profits from his investments grew; his income soared. Because of the increasing burden of higher income taxes, Robert began searching for alternative investment opportunities that not only would make him money but would also help reduce his income taxes.

That's when he discovered the oil and gas investment. At that time oil and gas investments looked like they couldn't lose. Oil was twenty, twenty-five, thirty dollars per barrel and rising. The price at the gas pump was exploding and some experts predicted an inexorable rise to new heights while at the same time the supply of natural gas was diminishing. New drilling for oil and gas was expanding at a rapid rate as was the price that these precious commodities would bring in the marketplace. Big profits were in the offing and delusions of wealth and grandeur filled the minds of many investors.

Here was an opportunity, Robert thought, to make substantial profits, reduce his extremely high tax bill through big write-offs, and put up only a little capital. The debt he would have to assume didn't worry him because the cash flow from the newfound "black gold" would pay it off in plenty of time.

As is typical with the Entrepreneur, Robert was very analytical and began reading about oil and gas investments, consulted with friends, and then sought out an investment adviser to find a good oil and gas investment. The fact that he would be unable to control the outcome of this investment decision was only an afterthought. Unknown to him, and to the experts as well, was the financial bloodbath that was to follow in the oil and gas industry.

The price of oil took a precipitous drop and natural gas prices declined as well. That calamity, accompanied by a decline in the utilization of natural gas, caused revenues in Robert's investment to slow to a trickle. Finally the gas pipeline was shut down and the bank called in his letter of credit for $250,000. The sudden demand for cash unnerved him. This outcome did not seem possible at the time he made the investment. Anxiety set in as he was forced into raising a quarter of a million dollars to pay off the bank. A resourceful man, Robert came up with the money through a number of sources. He paid off the bank and was left with an investment worth 20 cents for every dollar he paid in and a financial statement reduced by more than $200,000.

What a mistake he had made and how he criticized himself for it. Years of hard work had pushed him far on his performance yardstick, but now he had slipped back to under the one-foot marker. How could he have been so foolish? He knew he was too smart to let this kind of thing happen to him. His emotional distress grew and affected both his business and personal life. His only thought: "I must rebuild my financial position. I'll drive myself even harder in my work and my family will just have to understand."

Preoccupied with righting the wrong he had committed, Robert withdrew from his family. His workdays stretched from ten to fifteen hours. Weekends, usually devoted to family activities, were spent at the office. He became distant, couldn't sleep, and experienced difficulty in making clear and decisive business decisions. His business stopped growing; in fact it began to decline. At the same time, problems at home increased at a rapid pace. His relationship with his wife and children became strained and hardly a day went by when he didn't lose his temper.

Robert's desire always to outperform himself became a trap which led to a poor investment decision. He lost sight of who he was emotionally and what worked best for his money personality. Like most Moneymax Entrepreneurs, Robert was usually a calculated risk-taker but this time he had stepped over the edge. His eagerness to make a big profit and at the same time reap a substantial tax advantage made him lose perspective on the risk that was involved.

Usually Entrepreneurs benefit greatly from the combination of ambition, diligence, and the willingness to take risks. But Robert allowed himself to become overzealous and overconfident. He believed himself to be both smart and lucky because his past investments had always paid off. Since he had such an enviable track record, why shouldn't he reach out a little further? Unfortunately, Robert's one investment mistake was a very costly one. It did, however, lead him to the conclusion that he was most satisfied and successful when he was an active, involved participant, as he was with his stock market investments, and when he carefully counterbalanced potential profit with potential risk. Even though they have a desire for involvement, Entrepreneurs don't necessarily need as much control as the other two Moneymax Profiles with similar levels of affluence (the Achievers, the Money Masters), but Robert had given up too much control and had taken too great a risk.

Interestingly, while the Entrepreneurs are the highest income earners, they rank third of all nine groups in total net assets. This may be due to the fact that they tend to assume significantly more risk than the Money Masters, who were ranked third as income earners yet first in assets. The Money Masters are only two years older, on the average, than the Entrepreneurs. Of all the Moneymax groups, the Entrepreneurs have the largest number of investments in common stock, commodities/options, and futures contracts.

In general, Entrepreneurs are more reflective than impulsive. They do give thought to financial decisions and calculate the odds, but they can get carried away with their own need to excel and the belief that they will be the recipients of good fortune. That combination can, and did, in Robert's case, create financial havoc. His investment in oil and gas didn't complement his financial personality. Even though Entrepreneurs can tolerate risk, they need control. The oil and gas investment didn't allow Robert the degree of control he needed to give him peace of mind.

Even though the Moneymax Entrepreneurs are the second-highest risk-takers of all nine groups, they are not gamblers. They want to win, but they are challenged to win by personal effort, not by luck. They are interested in moderate risks, calculated risks. Even if they gamble, they usually get little satisfaction from their winnings if they don't personally contribute to the effort.

Mark, a Los Angeles restaurant owner, would never buy a lottery ticket, never spend a weekend gambling in Las Vegas. But he loves the racetrack. Within driving distance of three racetracks, he enjoys the thrill, the "challenge," of a day at the races. Before venturing out, he spends the morning studying the racing form, using a multitude of different-colored marking pens to note significant facts and figures about the various horses and jockeys. When he arrives at the track, he buys two or three of the available "tip sheets" and the day's racing program.

Mark never takes more than a $300 "investment" with him to the track. When he wins, he chalks victory up to a hard day's work and skillful interpretation of the facts. When he loses, he is not anxiety-ridden. He did the best he could and sometimes luck beats out reason. Besides, he was prepared to lose the $300 he brought with him. For Mark it is "play money" and is an insignificant loss that doesn't impact his financial lifestyle. A total loss, however, will keep Mark away from the track for weeks, maybe months. Mark, a typical Moneymax Entrepreneur, knows how to set limits on his risk tendencies, how to make risk work for him and not against him. His approach to risk is quite different from the Moneymax High Roller (discussed in Chapter 7) who risks money for excitement and adventure—for the thrill of it all.

The Moneymax Entrepreneurs are surprisingly fatalistic (average scores in the trait of self-determination), meaning that they do believe in good luck to some extent. Other Moneymax Profiles with similar levels of affluence have higher scores in self-determination and do not credit good luck as having an impact in their financial lives.

How could the Entrepreneurs possibly consider good luck as an integral part of success? They are exceedingly confident and motivated; they are the captains of their ships. The fatalism component may seem perplexing and quite out of character, but the answer is simple: they are convinced that luck is on their side. The Entrepreneurs' passion and confidence are so strong that they can't conceive of losing. Dedicated to the pursuit of their goals, they won't let anything get in their way. They can win; they deserve to win; they will win. The creation and actualization of the dream, or vision, is such a powerful and positive force that it assumes an infusion of good luck. In the back of their minds is the thought, "I know I'm right. I'm working damned hard. Surely the 'fates' will cooperate."

These fatalistic tendencies feed right into the risk-taking personality of the Entrepreneur. If the fates will cooperate, why not step out a little further? And then maybe a little further. Fortunately, Entrepreneurs are calculated risk-takers and for the most part their risk-taking tends to be a plus, not a minus.

HARD WORK—AND SMART WORK—PAY OFF

How is it possible for the highest income earners, the Moneymax Entrepreneurs, to be motivated more by a sense of work achievement than by the prospect of profits? The Entrepreneurs do not require money incentives to make them work harder. They work hard, provided there is an opportunity to achieve something. Financial rewards or profits are the concrete feedback which tells them how well they are doing. Yet, they still earn significantly high sums of money in the process.

It is the task at hand that rewards this high-achieving group. They are willing to take personal responsibility for solving problems and achieving goals. They are more concerned with achieving success than with avoiding failure. Successful Entrepreneurs cannot conceive of failure. Obstacles will not stop them. "I'm going to do it anyway" is their attitude. Courage is entirely consistent with the Entrepreneurs penchant for taking the complex—and making it simple.

Entrepreneurs are self-reliant, independent, and action-oriented. Courage and confidence counterbalance fear. Entrepreneurs realize that any business venture may meet with failure but usually formulate contingency plans to ensure success. They understand their value in the marketplace. They become bored, restless, and impatient with bureaucracy and routine chores. These traits often cause Entrepreneurs to leave structured businesses and corporations and strike out on their own.

Jennifer typifies the Entrepreneur locked inside a bureaucratic system. A college graduate with a liberal arts degree, she came from a small town, middle class background. After graduation, she worked for ten years in a publishing company and five years in a public relations firm. Both firms were small, creative environments. Hard work and long hours paid off for Jennifer. She found it easy to excel and rise through the company ranks. At age thirty-seven she landed a plum job —director of public relations with a Fortune 500 company in New York City.

After a year, the glamour began to fade. While she was praised for routine projects and assignments, Jennifer wanted to create new concepts and plans. Working sixty hours a week, she turned out proposal after proposal. While many of her ideas and plans were innovative and exciting, they rarely survived the corporate system and were approved. The usual response from senior management, handed down to her through her boss, was: "Nice but not for us; well executed but out of line with the company image; good job but let's do this the way we did it last year." Jennifer's file cabinet was overflowing with proposals that were going nowhere.

In addition, it was clear to Jennifer that she was going nowhere in the company. Of the five hundred corporate employees, not one woman held the title of vice president, the next level up from her job. For a while she tried to convince herself that it didn't matter. She was making $55,000 a year; she enjoyed the travel; she liked having a prestigious job.

However, Jennifer was convinced that her ideas were good, her plans were solid. With optimism and energy, she plunged in again. For another year, she worked long weekdays and weekends. Finally, one of her proposals, with a $5 million budget, was approved. Her elation was quickly dowsed upon hearing that her boss claimed credit for the project, acknowledging that she had been a fine "support" person.

Jennifer was at an impasse. Most of her plans never saw the light of day. When they did, she remained in her boss's shadow. Maybe she needed to polish her skills at corporate gamesmanship, but she didn't want to win at the corporate game. For two years she had poured enormous energy into her work but only felt overworked and frustrated. It was during this time that Jennifer participated in a seminar that featured the Moneymax Profile and learned that her profile was that of an Entrepreneur.

Jennifer wasn't particularly surprised. She had always been a hard-working, achievement-oriented person and, like most Entrepreneurs,

Jennifer had a difficult time adjusting to slow-moving bureaucratic systems and rules. When she had a good idea, she wanted to formulate a plan and put it into action. As we discussed her Entrepreneur personality traits, she admitted that starting up her own company was a venture that excited and energized her. The Moneymax Profile had confirmed that Jennifer did indeed exemplify the Entrepreneur—independent, self-reliant, confident, visionary, and willing to take the risks necessary to reach desired goals. She had been all of those things in the Fortune 500 company but those assets had not been fully appreciated or rewarded.

As Jennifer began to formulate a plan to leave the company and start her own business, she sought out the advice of family and friends. The feedback she received was mixed. Her father, recently retired, had worked as an auditor for a state government for thirty years. Never particularly satisfied or happy with his work, he nonetheless was proud that he had been able to provide financial security for his wife and family. He had survived the bureaucratic system, had put two kids through college, and now had a comfortable pension. He was delighted that Jennifer had a good job and was making more money than he had ever dreamed of. He cautioned her to reassess her situation and not to make a rash decision.

Jennifer's mother was more encouraging. She had taught Jennifer to be independent and always pushed the adage, "Nothing ventured, nothing gained." Jennifer's brother didn't have much to say except: "I understand your frustration. Your problems aren't all that different from mine. I'm frustrated too, but I earn less than half your salary. If I made as much money as you, I could learn to live with your problems. Don't take everything so seriously. You're doing just fine; hang in there."

Greg, Jennifer's husband, was an engineer who worked for a large firm and earned $60,000 a year. His advice was filled with confusing signals: Go ahead and step out on your own, but remember that you aren't getting any younger and it might be hard for you to get back into the corporate world; we can certainly live comfortably on my salary, but no more European vacations for a while; I wish I could leave the engineering firm and start anew, but two of us can't be taking that kind of risk.

Whether or not to leave her job was not an easy decision for Jennifer. But she had to admit that she was beginning to loathe her every day at work. As she put it: "I asked myself a hundred times why I stayed in a job that was making me so miserable. I worked long hours, had no social life, and was totally stressed out. Obviously, the money had something to do with it. I was earning a good salary and didn't want to give it up. So I said to myself, 'You just gave up a year of your life for $55,000; how many more miserable years are you willing to endure for that kind of money?' Then I asked myself the bigger questions: 'Was I confident that I could start up a company and make it successful? And what if I failed?' Once I started to concentrate on what I wanted and what I could do, instead of what I was giving up, the decision was easier."

Jennifer decided to leave her corporate job and begin her own company, a research and writing firm that specialized in business communications—annual reports, newsletters, speeches, staff publications. Before handing in her resignation, she formulated a detailed business plan and looked at all the costs that would be involved. Although she investigated the possibility of renting an office, the costs were too high. Instead, she decided to convert a second bedroom in her home into an office—that would give her a tax advantage and keep her overhead down. She figured that she had six months' living expenses saved, enough to support her as she launched her business.

For the initial months she would have to do everything—court the clients, do the projects, handle all money negotiations and accounting. As soon as the business was on its feet financially and she had built up a solid client following, she could afford to hire independent contractors to help with the work. Eventually, she reasoned, she would be able to have full-time help and rent an office.

Jennifer knew she was gambling on her talent, business savvy, and dedication. That didn't worry her. The Entrepreneur is self-assured and willing to accept responsibility. But, as Jennifer said when talking about her Entrepreneur profile: "I know that I have to watch how much I risk when it comes to money. I would love to have a beautiful office to go to every day and I'm tempted to hire a few people so I can concentrate on getting more business, but right now I think I'll have to work very hard and do practically everything. However, as soon as the business really starts to show a good profit, I won't hesitate to expand. Right now, I know I can get clients and do excellent work, but I don't want to get ahead of myself by incurring too many money problems. I would hate to be running an excellent company that was overextended and in serious debt."

At the end of a year Jennifer was able to hire independent contractors to help her on the company's projects and a part-time assistant to schedule and track her various jobs. At the end of two years she was able to rent a small office and hire a full-time secretary/bookkeeper.

As her profits began to accumulate, she knew it was time that she give some attention to investing her money. Referred by a friend to an accountant with some financial planning expertise, Jennifer made an appointment. Since she had no retirement plan, Jennifer chose to put $5,000 a year into a Keogh plan, which would help build a nest egg for the future and help decrease her taxes. In addition, with $10,000 she purchased common stock of two companies that had consistently high earnings over the past eighteen months. She liked the stock market and was willing to take risk because the more her investments paid off, the faster she could keep expanding her business. However, if she gambled too much, she would jeopardize her future business plans.

As Jennifer entered her third year of business, she was more convinced than ever that her decision to become an entrepreneur had been a wise one. She had created for herself all the elements formerly missing from her corporate job and those elements were the same that satisfied her entrepreneurial spirit: independence, control, innovation, personal and emotional and financial satisfaction.

Not all Entrepreneurs choose to trade one career in for another. There are some who choose to remain at their salaried jobs but also work independently outside of those jobs. Alan was one of those two-career workers. A computer programmer, he had worked for county government for fifteen years. His job was sometimes bogged down in red tape, but he was the manager of a small special unit and was usually immune from the hundreds of rules and regulations that plague government workers.

Alan had, on several occasions, considered leaving his job and going into business for himself. If he were single, the choice would have been fairly simple, but he was married and had five children. The financial responsibility for his family weighed heavily on him. He was ready to take some risks, but he had to make plans and execute them over a period of time. Before marrying, he had not been particularly security conscious but his head of household role forced him to make some compromises.

To vent his creativity, Alan wrote a book on computer programming. Even though he had never made a living at writing, he was confident that he had found a unique way to teach the art of writing computer programs. It took him a full year to find a book agent and sell the book to a small publisher. The book sold only 1,000 copies; certainly not enough to reimburse him for the time he had invested in it. However, he felt encouraged and used his earnings to buy a computer system to facilitate the writing of his next book. The second book was bought by a major textbook publisher and sold much better than the first book.

Juggling a full-time job, family obligations, and a writing career had not been easy. Alan's work week often exceeded seventy hours. Despite the lack of free time, he was motivated, content, and confident.

His books have led to several invitations to speak at college campuses and he is actively pursuing invitations before major computer seminars and conferences. In addition, he has taken on a few consultant jobs with small companies. Eventually, Alan hopes that the books and the consulting will enable him to leave his government job and still provide a comfortable living for his family.

His "grand plan," as he called it, is to eventually get several companies to put him on retainer as an independent consultant so that he can count on a certain amount of fixed income a year. When that income and his book income add up to his government salary, Alan plans to strike out on his own.

Alan's wife got very nervous when she heard him expound upon his future business plans. As is true with many Entrepreneurs, their spouses tend to experience anxiety when Entrepreneurs talk of leaving the security of permanent jobs and moving out into independent ventures. The tension over money security can be particularly troublesome when children are involved.

To ease his wife's concerns, as well as his own, Alan sought out the services of a financial professional who could map out a strategy to provide college educations for each of his five children. Together they looked at the issues involved: the ages of the children and how long it would be before each was of college age; how much money Alan would need to accumulate to put the children through school; how long it would take him to accumulate the college fund; how much money he could afford to invest; how often he would invest. At first, the plan seemed somewhat awesome to Alan, but the financial professional charted the plan into easily understood segments.

When looking at the amounts of money he would need to save, Alan felt confident that his job salary plus his outside income could handle the savings commitment and would not put too much of a strain on the family budget. After considering a number of investment options, Alan chose to accumulate the money in an interest-bearing account initially and planned to move the money into an appropriate investment vehicle at some point in the future.

Once Alan and his wife made a decision about providing for the education of their children, both of them felt more comfortable when discussing Alan's plan for someday leaving his job and working for himself. The stress of family financial responsibility was alleviated and Alan was better able to concentrate on writing a new book and expanding his consultant services.

CONTENT OR NOT CONTENT?

Are the highest wage earners content with their money? On the contentment scale, the Entrepreneurs have moderate, or average, contentment. As a matter of fact, some Entrepreneurs will probably never be content with their money.

The Entrepreneurs use money as an achievement benchmark, a way of keeping score with themselves and their peers. Their high standards of excellence and competition have a significant impact upon money attitudes. It's not that they perceive themselves as financial failures or unable to accumulate a vast amount of money. Quite the contrary, they are very proud of the way they handle their money.

But their financial personalities continually drive them to perform to their highest potential. Since they believe they can succeed, they are always moving forward. When one goal is reached, they move on to another. The Entrepreneurs can't stop themselves from pursuing the excitement of creating something from nothing. Some build better mousetraps while others create better services. Some climb the mountain to benefit others, as well as themselves. And yet another group will climb the mountain "just because it's there."

Basically, the end goal is never in sight. No matter how much cash and material possessions accumulate, money contentment remains linked to achievement contentment.

Frank was an inventor. At age fifty-five he had wound his way through a myriad of jobs—restaurant manager, appliance salesman, and construction worker. Since he was a kid, Frank had been obsessed with gadgets and toys and labeled himself a "master tinkerer."

For ten years Frank had been marketing and selling his inventions. He had crafted everything from water pistols and dolls to toy soldiers, board games, and kitchen utensils. While none of his inventions had attracted nationwide fame and popularity, Frank made a sizable profit.

He and his wife Marion lived in a comfortable home, had a late model car, and every year went on a two-week vacation. Royalties from three of his most successful products combined with family savings and profits from several good investments gave Frank and Marion sufficient money to live on.

When Marion and Frank argued, they generally argued about two things: Frank's all-consuming commitment to his work and Frank's reluctance to pay more attention to the money he earned. Marion complained that she was tired of spending so much time alone and resented the fact that she often had to turn down dinner and other social invitations. What bothered Marion even more was the couple's future financial picture.

Frank was somewhat blasé about money—he earned enough of it and didn't have the time to devote to managing it. His occasional investments in the stock market had been successful and a small apartment building the couple once owned, then sold, also reaped them a nice profit. They had a money market account, some life insurance, and Frank just couldn't be bothered with thinking about money when he was earning enough and planned to work for many more years.

Frank, like most Entrepreneurs, preferred to concentrate on work more than money. As long as income is sufficient and work is satisfying, Entrepreneurs are optimistic that money will always be plentiful and never a problem. This is not to say that they are not involved in money management. They certainly are, but it should be pointed out that they are the least involved of the three affluent Moneymax groups. Money is important but is only a measure of success. The same kind of equation holds true for money contentment. Entrepreneurs can only be as content as they believe themselves to be successful. Until they reach the top of the mountain, total contentment with money will remain elusive.

The Entrepreneurs like to zero in on their dreams, their visions, and the achievements that are still to come. In Frank's case, he had a board game that he believed was better than Monopoly and a building-block puzzle that was far superior to Rubik's Cube. He was convinced that it was only a matter of time before he could get a major company to mass produce and promote his games nationwide. On the shelves in his workshop were scores of successful games and toys which served as a reminder that his days of glory were imminent. According to Frank, "I didn't come from a rich family. Everything I have, I earned. You don't need a college degree to be successful—it takes a lot of hard work and mostly, you don't give up. I don't want to slow down. My work and my fun are one and the same thing."

While Frank didn't worry about the future, Marion did. If Frank should ever become seriously ill or disabled, what would they do? Or, if he died, what kind of financial position would she be in? Just how long would their money last? Marion wanted to consider possible investment options and make a long-range plan for financial security. Frank said she was needlessly worried and he couldn't spare the time to shop around for a financial whiz.

For years Marion had been sounding the same alarm and had gotten nowhere. Finally she decided to take some action on her own. After discussing the issue with several friends, she learned that Frank's best friend, a man who Frank liked and respected, had used the same financial adviser for more than ten years. She invited the friend to dinner one evening and skillfully turned the conversation around to finances and financial planning. Frank's friend was quite candid when talking about his investments and some of the strategies he had adopted. While Frank seemed impressed, he again remarked that he didn't have the time to be too concerned about money since he was so busy earning it. The friend then suggested that Frank and Marion call his adviser, whom he highly recommended and trusted.

Without too much maneuvering and behind-the-scenes tactics, Marion had used a third party to try to make Frank reconsider her financial concerns. Eventually, the couple did meet with the adviser and ended up with a diversified portfolio of investments that relieved Marion's anxiety about money. The investments they chose included current income vehicles, and some that provided tax shelter. With her money problems solved, Marion resolved to try to get Frank to leave his work more often and to take more vacations and develop some hobbies—a goal that is probably impossible for her to accomplish.

MIXING BUSINESS AND A PERSONAL LIFE

Entrepreneurs devote considerable time and effort to their work and, in some cases, spouses and friends are relegated to the sidelines. If forced to choose between a career and a relationship, the Entrepreneur may choose, like Alex, to forgo a relationship in order to single-mindedly pursue the business vision. A personal relationship can be particularly difficult if both parties are Entrepreneurs.

Alex was supposed to become a professional photographer. No one in his family, including Alex, had ever exactly stated that; it was assumed. Alex's father, Walter, was a noted photographer and the recipient of numerous awards and honors. The oldest of three children, Alex was snapping pictures at a very early age. His father made sure that Alex had the best camera, the best lenses, the best teacher.

Walter taught Alex the tricks of his trade, and as Alex grew older, his father often took him on weekend assignments. They spent some evenings developing the film and reviewing the quality of the prints. By age fifteen Alex was good; he was very good. He enjoyed photography, was the staff photographer for the high school yearbook, and had won a few local photography contests. While Walter seemed proud of his son, he always found something wrong with Alex's pictures. Alex should have used a different lens, a slightly different angle or composition. None of Alex's pictures seemed worthy of unqualified praise. Alex often wondered what his father really thought of him. Photography was their only common interest, and except for that subject, they had little to say to each other.

Graduation from high school forced Alex to think seriously about a career. Photography, the obvious choice, had a certain amount of appeal. He had some contacts for jobs—acquaintances met over the years when his father dragged him along on assignments. He was a recognized talent and he did enjoy the work. But he had too many misgivings. What if he never measured up to his father? Even if he did, his father would never acknowledge it. If he was able to ignore his father's indifference, people would still say, "Of course Alex is good. Look who he had as a father." And if he did gain more notoriety than Walter, his father would probably resent him. Somehow, much as he liked photography, Alex didn't think he could cope with being in the same profession as his father. He didn't want to be compared with Walter and he didn't want to be indebted to him either.

Six months after graduation, Alex got a job in a small advertising agency, owned by a friend of his father's. He worked in the traffic department with no title except "grunt runner." Nonetheless, he was a diligent worker and thrived on the daily dose of excitement and trauma. After a year, he was promoted; after two years he was promoted again. Then he moved to a larger agency, then to an even larger agency.

Finally, at age thirty-five, Alex was making his mark in the advertising world. An account executive with one of the nation's top firms in New York City, he was making $150,000 a year and had his mind locked in on the job of president. He knew he could get it. Nobody put in more hours than he did. Considered demanding and tough to work for, he was still respected and envied. His photography experience gave him an edge in graphic design and he was exceptionally good at courting clients and making presentations. His talents bridged both spheres of advertising, the accounting side and the creative side. The fact that he was good-looking and personable only added to the image that he carefully crafted.

The image was very appealing to the women who pursued Alex. He had little time for a social life, but he dated a number of women and when he couldn't be generous with his time, he was generous with gifts—flowers and jewelry in particular. When he was thirty-seven, he married Joan, an attractive secretary who worked in his firm. Because of company policy, which prohibited spouses from working in the same company, Joan quit her job. She was quite content to remain at home and be Alex's wife. Two years later she and Alex had a son.

While Joan was not oblivious to Alex's ambition, she didn't realize what a peripheral role she would play in his life. He worked late almost every night and spent most weekends in the office. When they did socialize, the conversation always revolved around Alex's work at the agency. Joan was bored and angry and insecure. She resented his work and began to nag him about the way he was ignoring her.

Alex couldn't stand her chronic complaining and demands for attention. He was doing the best he could for both of them and for their son. Joan had once worked in the same office; she should understand his commitment and the kind of pressure he was under. She had dated him a year before they were married and knew the kind of life he led. Why did she expect things to change now? Alex asked her for a divorce and Joan reluctantly agreed.

With one failed marriage, Alex figured that marital bliss was not yet in the cards for him. Eight months later he met Susan, a business consultant with a firm that had national and international branch offices. Not only was she attractive, but she had her own life, her own set of ambitions, and didn't make unreasonable demands on him. They spent many hours discussing business deals and how they were advancing in their careers. If Alex had to work late at the office and had to cancel a date, Susan was rarely agitated or angry because she often had the same time constraints. The relationship was great for Alex; he was involved with a lovely, dynamic woman who somehow seemed to fit well into his frantic life. Three months later they decided to live together.

Their first big argument came after dinner at a restaurant with Alex's boss, Tom, and his wife Marsha. Since it was the first time Susan had met Alex's boss, she was particularly charming and vivacious. Tom and Marsha were intrigued by the kind of work she did and asked Susan quite a few questions about her job and her company. The conversation never stopped, and at the end of the evening all agreed that they should get together again soon for dinner and the theater.

As soon as Alex and Susan got into their car, Alex erupted. How dare she embarrass him in front of his boss? Didn't she realize that Tom was one of his prime supporters in the agency and would have a lot to say about Alex's future? How could she have been so stupid? Susan was bewildered and could only ask what she had said or done that had sent Alex on a rampage. He angrily retorted: she monopolized the conversation; she talked on and on about herself; she sounded arrogant and pushy; she laughed too much and too loudly. Susan defended herself: everybody had a good time, she spoke about herself in answer to questions—and anyway, why shouldn't she talk about herself? She didn't monopolize the conversation. What was Alex's problem? Perhaps, one evening out of the limelight was more than he could handle? Maybe Alex was so used to center stage that he was unwilling to share it, even with her? The next day at work, Tom raved about Susan—how wonderful, how intelligent, how lucky Tom was. Tom apologized to Susan but the next crisis came quickly.

Susan got a promotion and her new position required a lot of travel, frequently abroad. For the next three months, she was out of town on the average of twice a month. Mostly, she flew to the company's offices in Paris and Tokyo. The job was exciting and Susan was immersed in new challenges. Alex was unsettled. Susan was hardly ever at home; he had no companion and no dinner. When she was home, all she wanted to talk about was her damn job. Finally, he gave her an ultimatum. Give up the travel and return to work in the home office or risk losing him.

Why did these two Entrepreneurs attract and repel each other? Susan and Alex, both strong-willed and independent, were attracted to each other because their energies and personalities ignited one another. They seemed to have it all. Susan said she couldn't believe they had so much in common. Alex remarked to his friends that he had finally met the perfect woman—he loved to look at her and he also loved to talk to her. In addition, Susan shared many of the same attitudes and ambitions about work as he did. She certainly was unlike Joan, who had nothing in her life except him. While Alex once believed he wanted a woman who was content to be a wife and mother, he found that Joan's dependency on him was suffocating.

However, the very qualities which attracted Alex to Susan were also causing him great stress once the couple began to live together and tried to work out a life together. According to Alex, Susan was too independent and her priorities often put her work before him. Alex was frustrated and angry, yet he didn't express his feelings because he was afraid of losing her. Instead, he sulked, complained a lot, and drowned himself in his work.

The distance between them became increasingly difficult for them to overcome. They were dancing to different tunes and neither one of them was quite sure how to change the rhythm. Alex and Susan were very much in love with each other yet couldn't deal with the critical issues that would allow their relationship to survive and grow. Alex had never felt out of control before and he didn't like the feeling. He remembered how he felt when his ex-wife nagged him to spend more time with her and he was not going to act like his ex-wife and grovel for attention. Susan felt she was doing her best to accommodate Alex but she wouldn't give up her job for him since she would never expect him to do that for her.

The time they spent together was either wonderful or traumatic or distant. Finally, Alex was unable to cope with the situation any longer. The stress was affecting his work and his confidence in himself. When Susan refused to give up her new position and return to the home office, he announced that the relationship was over, he was moving out, and he did not want to talk about possible reconciliation. His mind was made up; he was leaving so he could feel good about himself again. Obviously, Alex and Susan had some issues other than their work schedules to deal with, but they never reached a stage where either was willing to openly discuss their problems and make compromises.

Alex personifies another of the traits of the typical Entrepreneur—the desire for a certain degree of power and prestige with money. He lived in an affluent section of New York, dined at the best restaurants, and knew how to impress women. He was generous with gifts to women and didn't hesitate to invite a female companion on a last-minute trip to the Bahamas or Puerto Rico. While he did earn a sizable salary, he spent much of it and rode his credit cards to the limit. However, while Alex paid all of his bills on time, he was not very good at accumulating money.

He was driven to become president of his advertising firm because he wanted the power and the control that came with being in first position. Like his father, who was recognized and admired, Alex too wanted to gain recognition—but he wanted to carve it out in his own way. Recognition, money, power, and achievement are all tied together for the Entrepreneurs, and Alex was no exception. The fact that he had captured some major accounts for his agency put Alex in a very strategic position for advancement. The president's job was definitely within reach and he would settle for nothing less.

Alex was interested in discovering his money personality primarily because he was concerned about how his lavish lifestyle was impacting his financial future. When I first met him, Alex assured me that for most of his life he had been a pretty diligent saver. However, since moving to New York, he explained, he seemed to have fallen victim to the glamour and glitter of the city. He felt that competing with his peers necessitated keeping up with them in terms of material possessions and it was essential that there be no question in any one's mind that he was successful. Most people, he continued, judge your success by what they see—where and how you live, what you have, how you dress. Overall, he was uncomfortable with his spending habits, but he was more concerned that people might not understand how accomplished he was.

When Alex reviewed his scores on the Entrepreneur profile, he gained some insight into his behavior. First of all, Entrepreneurs are rational with money and are, by nature, savers more than spenders. Since Alex was an Entrepreneur, it is easy to see why he was unnerved by his spending. Recognizing that he also had a certain power need, it made sense to him that he was using money, and the spending, to assure himself of the power he desired. His power motive and his risk-taking tendencies, however, were causing him to live on a financial precipice. He really wasn't in control of his money. Even though Entrepreneurs don't need as much control as other financially successful Moneymax groups, they do like, and need, to be involved in money management.

Until he really analyzed his money personality, Alex blamed his spending on a need to keep up with his peers and on the women he dated—the kind of women he dated, he said, didn't like home-cooked meals or anything farther back than tenth row center seats at the theater. Once he honestly reviewed his behavior and attitudes, Alex was ready and willing to make some changes in his money life. What Alex really wanted to do was buy a house in the Hamptons but he lacked the capital to make the purchase. Recognizing that he needed a new money strategy, he decided to seek out investment advice.

Entrepreneurs, like Alex, are very good at juggling many aspects of their lives and coming out on top in most areas. This skill tends to make them think that they can keep adding more and more tasks and still manage to do everything well. Sometimes the time constraints, however, require a reordering of priorities. Once Alex felt that it was all right to let someone else enter his financial picture—he didn't have to be perfect in everything—he began to make financial progress.

After carefully selecting a financial planner, Alex embarked upon a new financial strategy. His initial portfolio of investments included limited partnerships in both a video production company and an office building complex—the second being more conservative than the first. Also, since he was eager to quickly acquire enough money for a down payment on a house, he invested in some high risk stocks that he hoped would turn some big profits in a short time. For more safety and liquidity, he allocated some of his money to conservative growth stocks that had had a good track record for at least ten years and put some money into a certificate of deposit.

The conflict between Alex's work and his relationships with women was not as easy to resolve. After the relationship with Susan ended, Alex made a commitment to himself to remain single until he was president of his company and all of his career goals were reached. As he put it: "I know the rules at work and how to design a winning game plan. In relationships, I lose all insight and rational thinking. At work, I can call all the shots and there's something concrete to deal with. When you're in a relationship, you're dealing with two people who have different beliefs and feelings. I tried it two times with two totally different women and it still failed. At least my career makes me happy. While I'm single, I can conduct my life on my terms without feeling guilty about hurting anyone's feelings because I am not living up to their expectations. At this stage of my life, I prefer it that way. I negotiate enough at work, and I don't want to have to do it in my personal life too."

POWER AND PRESTIGE

Are you motivated by the prestige and status that your money brings you? Or, are you uninterested in receiving public recognition with your money? Entrepreneurs rank fourth highest of the nine profiles in the desire for power and prestige. They do want their financial success and achievements to bring them status in their communities, and often with the public at large. This desire for prestige and power with money is more pronounced in the Entrepreneur profile than in the other profiles with similar levels of affluence.

The desire for power and prestige is a reflection of the narcissistic culture that the Entrepreneurs live in. The average age of the Entrepreneurs is forty-five. This generation of Entrepreneurs has become accustomed to affluence—more than any other preceding generation. Postwar affluence has given them a sense of entitlement. Part of the "Me Generation," they subscribe to a new lifestyle, a new set of values and expectations. With unassailable optimism, they expect to be stimulated, challenged, and rewarded. The Entrepreneurs find no dignity in being poor. They have worked very hard to achieve success and feel no guilt in surpassing the financial status of their parents.

Money, and what it buys, is a constant reminder to the Entrepreneurs that they have made it; that they are respected and recognized for what they have accomplished. It signifies their personal merit— their creativity and intelligence, their vision and fortitude, their ambition and courage. They deserve to have "the best" whether the best is a car, a bottle of wine, or a box of imported chocolates. And they want to pass on their competitive advantage to their children by sending them to the finest schools and buying them the latest computers and educational toys.

Money differs from other forms of social power in that it can be precisely measured. In addition, money is influential with a greater number of people and over a wider range of circumstances than any other social power. Money, by itself, has no power, but we respond to it as if it did.

The maître d' of a small, but very elite, restaurant in Los Angeles was recently interviewed about how he decides which tables to give to his customers. The restaurant, which caters to the rich and famous, has five tables which are acknowledged as the most visible and prestigious. When recognizable celebrities, or regular patrons, arrive, there is no doubt as to where they will be positioned. But what about the lesser-known people, perhaps out-of-towners, who may not be instantly recognized but nonetheless are prominent, influential figures?

How does the maître d' know who is important and thus save himself the embarrassment of placing a VIP at an inappropriate table?

The maître d' explains: "It's quite simple. I look at what they are wearing. The cut of the man's suit, the design of a woman's dress. It's particularly easy with women because they have so many accessories. I can spot a Gucci handbag and a Rolex watch a mile away. I can tell fake jewelry from real gems. For ten years I've been watching people go in and out of this restaurant. I don't need to see the car they arrive in to be able to tell where I should seat them. I'm getting so good that I can just about judge the women by their brand of perfume. No, it doesn't take a genius to figure out who's who—just a practiced eye. I've made very few mistakes."

Entrepreneurs are proud of their money and their possessions because they are proud of themselves. It's all right to prefer mahogany over Formica, cashmere over corduroy, a Mercedes over a Volkswagen. While some may be bargain hunters and shop the sales for appliances, furniture, and clothing, they do believe in rewarding themselves with the best products and services available. Because the Entrepreneurs place such a premium on time, it follows that they are likely to buy computers, microwave ovens, car phones, and gourmet frozen foods.

Some Entrepreneurs may flaunt their possessions, but they are just as likely to be against conspicuous display. Creature comforts, albeit nice creature comforts, don't have to be flaunted in order to be enjoyed. Entrepreneurs are amply rewarded by the power and prestige which their money confers upon them: they stand out from their peers and are recognized; they enjoy a good measure of self-esteem; they take great pleasure and satisfaction from their work.

EVOLUTION OF THE ENTREPRENEUR

The very word entrepreneur conjures up images of success, wealth, status, independence, and notoriety. According to Professor Karl H. Vesper of the University of Washington's School of Business Administration, "There's been a radical rise of entrepreneurial spirit. There's a latent lust for it in all of us—it's the American way." The word hasn't always evoked such reverence. Forty years ago entrepreneurs were considered egotistical, self-promoters, followers of pipe dreams. Believed to be impetuous, greedy, and bold, they created their own business opportunities not because they were rugged individualists, but because they didn't have what it takes to make it in the business mainstream. Those who were truly talented and hard-working had secure, salaried positions in respectable companies. In 1950, only 19.5 percent of employed Americans were self-employed. By 1960 the number had dropped to 13 percent; by the early 1970s less than 6.5 percent were self-employed. In 1969 a study by the Institute for the Future predicted the demise of self-employment by 1985.

Today that trend has taken a revolutionary turn. In 1985 more than 670,000 new businesses were formed—up by more than 25 percent from 533,000 in 1985. The number of new-start businesses has been staggering, especially in light of the fact that 50 percent of all new businesses fail within five years and eight out of ten don't survive to the tenth year. In addition, the previous statistics do not take into account the "subterranean economy," a term coined by Peter M. Gutmann, professor of economics and finance at the City University of New York's Baruch College. The subterranean economy, according to Professor Gutmann, consists of underground, "off-the-books" cash and barter business activities that could amount to as much as $420 billion a year.

More than 200 colleges and universities across the United States offer courses in entrepreneurship. In 1985, President Ronald Reagan, in a speech urging support for his new tax reform plan, called the eighties the "age of the entrepreneur." He said: "We have lived through the age of big industry and the age of the giant corporation, but I believe that this is the age of the entrepreneur, the age of the individual. That's where American prosperity is coming from now, and that's where it's going to come from in the future."

Corporate America, afraid of losing its talented and valued employees to the new entrepreneurial wave, has been making adjustments in its structure. According to one vice president of management development, "The challenge is to create islands within the organization where the creative spirit can flourish." Companies are altering promotion structures, increasing salaries, and putting a greater emphasis on flexibility, autonomy, and personal growth. "Intrapreneuring," stimulating entrepreneurial innovation within a corporation, is a term invented by Gifford Pinchot III, who wrote a book on the subject. One of the most popular buzzwords of the eighties, intrapreneuring and intrapreneurs made Pinchot an overnight entrepreneur. A former blacksmith and dairy farmer, he quickly parlayed the success of his book into a profitable consulting business and lecture tour. In the true spirit of the entrepreneur, Pinchot assessed his achievements: "There are some people who think intrapreneuring is the flavor of the month. If so, give me a few years off, and I'll come back with something else. Or, I can always go back to blacksmithing."

H. Ross Perot is an excellent example of a would-be intrapreneur, who, when thwarted, became an entrepreneur. Once a salesman for IBM, he always reached his monthly sales quotas early and was on the lookout for more work. When he got the idea to create a company division to service computer software, he took it to IBM executives. They weren't interested; they wanted to continue concentrating on hardware. Perot eventually left IBM and with $1,000 started his own company, Electronic Data Systems (EDS), in Dallas. Today, he is one of the richest men in the United States, worth over $2.5 billion.

"New-style entrepreneurs" or "lifestyle entrepreneurs" are terms designed to reflect the attitudes of the entrepreneurs who work to live instead of living to work. Unlike the archetypical entrepreneur who is on a fast track to create new products and services and to conquer unmapped territories, lifestyle entrepreneurs have a more humanistic approach to business. Their businesses tend to be smaller, conservatively financed, and easily controlled. Family, friends, and leisure time are as important, or more important, than the business. Sometimes the lifestyle entrepreneurs create their own products and services; sometimes they sell and market the services of others. Given the opportunity to "go big," they may refuse if expansion alters their original goals or interferes with their lifestyle. This prioritization of values does not imply that they are not totally dedicated to their businesses. Many have become very successful—and on their own terms.

The faces and success stories of entrepreneurs fill the pages of newspapers and magazines and flash across the screen on the evening news. Their names have become familiar—Steven Jobs, H. Ross Perot, Frederick Smith, Donald Trump, Mary Kay Ash, George Lucas, Liz Claiborne, Ted Turner, Lee Iacocca, and many more. Not so visible are the countless others who have ventured out to create their business and personal lives according to their own talents, convictions, and ideals. They make, sell, and market everything from egg rolls and kitty litter to computers and exercise equipment. They run take-out restaurants, housecleaning services, cheerleading clinics, business seminars, telephone installation companies, gourmet catering services, and childcare centers. They put together mail-order catalogues, electronic data bases, and traveling health clubs. Famous or not famous, each has carved out a distinct entrepreneurial niche.

MONEY MANAGEMENT STYLE

1. Although one might think that Entrepreneurs have so much drive and ability that they can make the best investment decisions on their own, the opposite is sometimes true. Entrepreneurs have a tremendous ability to build successful businesses but can fall short when trying to make their own investment decisions. Because they are so consumed with their work, they cannot be an expert in all things. They will find overall superior investment results by using competent investment advisers. With assistance they can make well-informed decisions, rather than expeditious ones. Sometimes they find time constraints forcing them into impulsive decisions, or no decisions at all, neither of which is comfortable for Entrepreneurs.

2. Entrepreneurs are the number-one investors in common stock, both individual and mutual funds, but prefer direct ownership of individual shares.

3. They are not very satisfied with fixed-dollar investments like T-bills, T-notes, and CDs; nor are they interested in investments that provide tax-exempt income like municipal bonds.

4. They also have not been particularly satisfied with the investment performance of insurance products. They are the greatest investors of all nine groups in whole life insurance (60.5 percent), but of all their investment vehicles, they like whole life the least. Their dissatisfaction with whole life policies may stem from its performance before 1980. Historically, whole life insurance had not provided good returns in comparison with other investment opportunities. However, a major

shift in the past few years in the insurance industry has fostered much better returns, which is having a positive impact on investors who were previously disenchanted. The tax-sheltered growth that is part of the cash accumulation in whole life has been very attractive to many investors, especially in light of the Tax Reform Act of 1986 and the current returns whole life is paying.

5. They are most satisfied with limited partnerships, along with the Money Masters, and are second to the Money Masters in highest use of this investment. Limited partnerships are attractive to the Entrepreneurs because the investment provides limited liability while they take the risk necessary to reap higher returns. Also, there are broader investment opportunities available in limited partnership form, thereby expanding the options to diversify—which is highly attractive to the Entrepreneurs who are opportunistic investors. Their satisfaction level might increase if they expanded their use of limited partnerships, but the investments should be carefully selected in order to maximize the new opportunities and find the best quality available.

6. Even though the Entrepreneurs are the number-one users of futures contracts and commodities, the High Rollers—the highest risk-takers—are more satisfied than the Entrepreneurs with these investments.

7. The Entrepreneurs invest in coins and stamps more than any of the other Moneymax groups and share the highest level of satisfaction with this investment, along with the High Rollers.

THE ENTREPRENEURS— FINANCIAL STATEMENT

The Moneymax Entrepreneur encompasses the traditional entrepreneur, the new-age lifestyle entrepreneur, the corporate intrapreneur, and others who don't fit into those categories. Regardless of their individual situations, they share common financial personality traits. They have an unrelenting drive to excel and are confident of reaching their goal or vision. They make their money through hard work and taking higher than average risks. They are proud of their achievements and believe that luck will always be on their side. Convinced that their own individual efforts are inexorably linked to their success, they enjoy the power and prestige that they have earned. They are predominately male, the highest income earners, and are moderately content with the money that success has brought them. Individual efforts and total commitment, more than college degrees, have unlocked the doors of business opportunity.

6

Hunters

One's own self is well hidden from one's own self: of all mines of treasure, one's own is the last to be dug up.

—Nietzsche

GUIDELINES
Hunters

. . . Find it easier to make financial decisions if they can rely on someone else's advice.

. . . Experience feelings of self-doubt and inadequacy in dealing with their money management.

. . . Spend their money impulsively, according to how they are feeling at the time.

. . . Lack pride in the way they have handled their money.

. . . Find that they spend as much as they make, and save very little.

. . . Are motivated to buy status symbols as personal rewards for their hard work.

. . . Would like more money in order to make them feel more powerful.

The following comments were made by three participants in a six-week seminar, "Making Sense of Your Money Mind," for people who, through use of the Moneymax Profile, were able to learn more about their money attitudes and how to change their money styles:

"Finance is not a second nature of mine. I wish I felt better about money than I do. I don't trust my financial decisions. I wish I did. When I was answering the questions on the Moneymax Profile, I almost lied on some of the answers. But then I answered truthfully. Guess I was a little nervous. Money always makes me nervous. I always thought I'd be married and money wouldn't be much of a problem. Don't get me wrong; I love working and I always plan to work. But I'm thirty-eight, divorced, and still very single. Guess I should start thinking about taking care of myself, and that's why I'm here."

(Margaret, a paralegal and a Hunter)

"I'm curious about what my money style is. My job doesn't pay what I think I deserve in a salary. I have even thought about starting my own business—maybe that's my ego talking. I know I've got what it takes to be successful and I want to get there before I'm an old man. I don't understand why I haven't done better so I'm here to find out how to get on the right money track."

(Joe, a personnel manager and a Hunter)

"I saw the brochure and loved the title of this seminar. I want to learn more about my money so I can have some knowledge in case it's ever necessary for me to take care of myself by myself. My husband doesn't care if I work or not; financially we're doing okay. Actually, Andrew, my husband, doesn't think I need to have a career but he says that I should know a little more about money management."

(Donna, a housewife and a Hunter)

Comments like "guess I should" and "in case it's ever necessary" are characteristic of the excuses Hunters use to prevent themselves from financial *action*.

Of all nine Moneymax groups, the Hunters have the highest percentage of women—76 percent. They are very well educated and they top the list of Moneymax Profiles in the number of college graduates (tied for first place with the Achievers). They also have the highest percentage of professional/managerial positions as well as the highest number of clerical workers. Surprisingly, their income level is average for all the Moneymax groups (fifth of nine) and their assets are even lower (sixth of nine). Indeed, they are the youngest in age, but they also have the least number of dependent children. Their average age is forty, with 30 percent of them under thirty years of age. Hunters tend to be divorced and single.

One dominant trait of the Hunters is "emotional spending." They spend their money when they are depressed and frustrated and it makes them feel better. Spending their money is a way of rewarding themselves. For what? Having to work so hard, being so alone. Not having the help and support they think they deserve. They spend their money rather than save or invest it, and therefore have a difficult time becoming financially independent. They are impulsive buyers, not practical planners. Because many Hunters secretly want to be financially rescued, they need to counteract their self-doubt and anxiety. Their emotional spending certainly erodes their self-confidence. In addition, the Hunters have low feelings of pride in the way they handle their financial affairs. They have educated themselves, are career-oriented, have acquired professional and managerial professions—yet they don't have the income or assets to validate their accomplishments. Today, more than ever, they are judging their accomplishments and personal merit by how much money they earn. Yet they are not doing enough to get their hard-earned money to work for them, like investing it properly in order to maximize their returns.

It appears very important that the Hunters have the services and material possessions of their desired social status. They probably can't afford to live in the neighborhoods they desire and the same is true of the clothes they like to wear and the cars they drive. Because they feel like underprivileged members of their class, they go out and buy products reflecting their desired social status. They want to feel valuable and worthwhile by today's economic standards.

The Hunters generally reflect today's younger generation, particularly those who have been educating themselves and pushing themselves into more professional careers while they strive for greater financial success. Yet they sabotage their ambitions by using money as a mechanism to reduce stress and anxiety. They spend it instead of using it more wisely. This short-term gratification, however, is a poor substitute for a more thoughtful and analytical approach, which would ultimately lead to and foster greater wealth accumulation. Spending never reduces their stress. In fact, their money management style only adds to their stress in the long term.

The Hunters are not composed solely of younger people. They are also characterized by older men and women who have always exemplified a "live for today" consumption style. Some Hunters become aware of their style too late to make an impact on the money they can accumulate. Many others, however, gain the insight and motivation to change their style and increase both their incomes and assets.

There is, however, much encouraging news for the Hunters. They are definitely well educated, career-oriented, ambitious, hard-working, and upwardly mobile. If the Hunters improved their self-regulatory system, they could take care of their personal, social, and financial needs and at the same time accumulate assets. For the Hunters, money reflects self-esteem by projecting an image of prosperity and success— the success to which they aspire but can't quite actualize because they sabotage themselves along the way. Society has not delivered according to their expectations, but the Hunters aren't quite sure how to make society pay up.

MISGUIDED AMBITION

The saying, "As a woman thinketh in her heart so is she," embraces the whole of the female Hunter personality. Unfortunately, the Hunters are blinded to their true abilities because they grew up believing they could only make the kill if their scout found the prey and they executed the winning shot. Female Hunters move out fast and ambitiously train themselves (get an education) to hunt the prey (money), but take along a scout (usually a man) because they don't totally trust their skills and are afraid of failure. In other words, they need help; they are not able to master the hunt alone. They really don't believe they have money skills so the hunt for money is never predictable and always frightening. They don't reap the rewards of their hard work.

Margaret complains, "I don't give myself credit for what I know and I don't have confidence in what I know. Well, I guess I'm trainable." Whenever Margaret has to make a financial decision, she immediately panics. So do many Hunters. Not only do they lack confidence in their financial decision-making skills, but of all the personalities, the Hunters are, by far, the emotional spenders, using money to work out their emotions. And the emotional spending can lead to overspending.

They may shop at Bloomingdale's even though their budgets may dictate J. C. Penney's. They can live in neighborhoods they can't afford, or be the first to get the latest model car, or VCR, or gourmet appliance. Spending makes the Hunters feel better—even if they get depressed later. Money is a mood elevator. That's what they think while they are spending. However, after the immediate short-term high, reality sets in and the powerful feelings of the moment are over. Emotions guide their decisions and cloud their ability to be practical money managers. Money emotionality only reinforces their self-doubt.

When I met Margaret, she was a paralegal and was thinking about going to night school to get an MBA. Five years earlier, Margaret had received $30,000 as a result of an insurance settlement from an automobile accident. She told me: "The settlement was my lottery ticket to the future. I almost used it as a down payment on a condominium. I've always wanted to be a property owner. At first, I didn't even think the realtor took me seriously. For a whole week, I hardly got any sleep. Was I ready to take on such a big financial commitment? What if I lost my job and couldn't meet the monthly payments? I got scared and backed out of the deal at the last minute."

Instead, Margaret bought a new car for $15,000, spent $8,000 on a vacation to Europe, and "frittered away" the rest of the money on clothes, household items, and other material goods. In addition, Margaret had a problem with her credit cards. She said, "I was making pretty good money and I ran my credit cards up to the hilt. Finally, I realized they weren't made of money. I'm still paying off some of them and some of my cards have been taken away."

Had Margaret sought some professional help at that time, she might own the condominium today. Instead she had nothing to show for her $30,000 windfall gain. As a home owner, she would have been accumulating equity, learning about appreciation, saving taxes, and feeling proud of her financial accomplishments. But Margaret robbed herself of those opportunities and spent the money on a car she didn't need and a vacation that could have been postponed. Margaret's inability to manage her money typifies what Hunters do to themselves. They are their own worst enemies when it comes to financial wellbeing and future prosperity.

Margaret was extremely bright, insightful, and articulate. She vowed that she would never again squander away such a large sum of money. She repeatedly said that she needed to set goals for herself; she needed to "get focused." As she put it: "I'm really good on tenacity but I've never been very good on focus. But you see, I'm almost afraid to get that focused because that's almost like signing a death warrant that I'll be alone."

Alone was a very ominous word for Margaret. In her mid-twenties she married a teacher but the marriage only lasted fifteen months. She stated, "I don't want to anticipate a future without a husband. I've come a long way in coming to grips with that Pollyanna syndrome that someone's going to come along and take care of me but it takes a lot of time and effort. I'm still working on it. Does it happen to a lot of women?"

Yes, it does happen to a lot of women. When they face this issue and make a commitment to take care of themselves, they often become depressed. Margaret's depression and inner turmoil convinced her that a choice had to be made between career advancement and the pursuit of a relationship. As she put it, "I get angry with myself for spending so much time in school, betting on my own education instead of investing it in a relationship—a relationship which I don't have. I mean, I'm giving away opportunities to meet that special person. I lose opportunities every day because I choose to spend my time improving myself instead of being out in the bar scene, the health spa scene, or the party scene."

Margaret was driven to achieve, but she kept getting in her own way. She resisted the fact that she was a bright and competent, achievement-oriented person. With or without a man, she would never be fully satisfied unless she fulfilled her own goals and dreams. Margaret had difficulty developing a healthy self-concept and never would if she looked for it in the familiar framework of male relationships. She had to muster up the strength and courage to pursue career and financial freedom. If she didn't she would remain fused to her parents' identity, particularly her mother, who lived life solely through her husband and children. Instead of being "lost in isolation," as she claimed, Margaret needed to rely on the fact that she was moving toward self-fulfillment. For many women, this reckoning with financial management and self-sufficiency is one of the last, most significant milestones to achieve. It is a symbol of reaching financial adulthood.

It is not uncommon for people to wind up with similar money styles as their parents even when they are consciously motivated to be different. When I asked Margaret to explain why she was driven to achieve financially, she responded: "I was just generally angry. I wanted to get out of my surroundings. My parents were divorced when I was about six. My father died when I was nineteen. I lived at home until I was twenty-five. My mother is a high school graduate who married young and had three kids. She never taught me anything about money. She was an assembly worker so we never starved; we had clean clothes and food and a roof over our heads. But my mother has always lived hand to mouth. I don't want to live like that. She's still fairly self-reliant but she has rheumatoid arthritis and there will come a day when she can't take care of herself. And I do not want to take care of her. I have to be in a position where I can afford to hire someone to take care of her."

Margaret got her education despite her parents: "I got my undergraduate degree and my paralegal certificate at night school. I'm the only one in my family who has a college education. I started working at seventeen for an attorney. It was a turning point. I started to get an appreciation for education and saw a standard of living that was foreign to me, yet very attractive. It clicked. Since I had a strong work ethic—to get ahead—education became important to me. I remember my mom saying, 'You're working too hard going to school.' During finals she'd tell me to throw in the towel—I was working too hard. She never gave me an 'atta boy'—almost never. In certain ways my education has been a wedge between me and my family. In certain ways I've lost them. They left me. Because I think I remind them of a lot of things that they aren't and never will be."

Women like Margaret have a much more difficult time with the quest for financial independence. Men are raised from an early age to think about providing financially for themselves and their families. They know they have to make a switch from a dependency on Mother to identifying with Father, the provider role—the person out there in the world making money. Many women, on the other hand, stay attached to their mothers. They aren't encouraged to make that switch to Father. They don't have to come to grips with their financial dependency until much later, usually in adulthood. Some Hunters never do.

The feeling of dependency is really a mask, a fog or detour, for a lot of women. Hunters sabotage themselves by confusing their need for attachment as women with financial dependency needs. They fool themselves into believing they are truly dependent—not necessarily so. Female Hunters are achievement-oriented and want the symbols and measures of success that men have always had. The female Hunters differ from the female Entrepreneurs because the female Entrepreneurs have been able to break away from old connections and traditions. They take risks with their lives, their investments, perhaps even starting businesses of their own. The female Entrepreneurs don't saddle themselves with the old myth of dependency. Margaret, as well as many other Hunters, is still struggling with the problem.

Another trait which impacts the Hunters' personality is self-determination. Hunters are average scorers on self-determination. The highest scorers on self-determination are the Money Masters (tied with the Achievers), who firmly believe that success comes from personal effort. The Money Masters clearly attribute their financial success to their skills and persistent, diligent efforts. On the other hand, for the Hunters, financial success or lack of success is a toss-up—they can attribute their money status to themselves or to fate.

Margaret needed to believe that responsibility for her life was within herself; that her financial successes were a result of her talent and hard, smart work—not good luck. Otherwise, she would always be placing the source of power and responsibility for both her successes and failures outside of herself. Any future dreams of success would be hazy since she couldn't always predict or control outside forces but could deal with internal ones. If Margaret thought she had the ability to make money, she would be more likely to make it instead of wondering whether or not this was her lucky year.

Margaret's secret ambition was to become a lawyer. She had abandoned the idea because of "time commitment, energy required, and lack of financial resources"—which sounded reasonable—yet she was considering going back to school for an MBA. Those were not the real reasons that kept her from going to law school. It was a lack of self-confidence; she had high expectations for failure. The same feelings driving her lack of self-confidence in managing her money were driving her reluctance to go to law school. This was how Margaret reasoned: "The law firm I work for is very uppity and recruits only from the top 10 percent of law schools in the United States. I work with some pretty brilliant people. I might not get into the top 10 percent. I'm a good student but I might not be the crème de la crème. I mean, I would have to take classes at night and plod along just like I always have. And besides, I'm not quite sure I fit into that world. If I get an MBA, there are more options open to me; it's more flexible; there are more fallback positions."

The question of "worthiness" was important to Margaret as it is to many Hunters. They question whether they can ever really have financial independence. If they don't believe they deserve money and status, then they never get them. Or the Hunters give money away or lose it whenever it becomes too plentiful. If their sense of themselves, often unconscious, is one of deprivation, struggle, and unworthiness, then their beliefs and actions serve that end—a kind of financial self-fulfilling prophecy.

Margaret needed to develop her own career goals and begin an investment education program. She needed goals that would stretch her abilities and not allow her to fall into mediocrity. Sabotaging thoughts such as "I'm not sure I'm good enough" and "Can I really do it on my own?" needed to be replaced with specific action steps that would reinforce more positive beliefs and feelings about her ability to succeed.

Money is a significant symbol of personal achievement. It reflects how people feel about themselves. For the Hunter, it is a source of frustration and drive at the same time. The Hunters are motivated to succeed, have certainly equipped themselves with education and careers. But they are too often missing the internal building blocks to support and encourage their desires for financial success.

BEYOND THE SPENDING LIMITS

Joe, the personnel manager for a large printing company, said he came to the Moneymax seminar because he wanted to "get on the right money track." While that was true, it wasn't entirely accurate. His parents, part owners of the company where Joe was employed, strongly urged that he seek advice for what they called his "money problem."

At age twenty-seven Joe had been in the family business for five years. His mother, Alice, had inherited a 50 percent share of the company after Joe's grandfather died. The other half of the business was owned by Alice's brother, Stanley. Even though Joe had gone to college, his parents wanted him to learn the business from the bottom up and started him out in an entry-level position. After five years he had moved up to personnel manager but still wasn't a part of the management team. His cousin, Roger, Stanley's son, was also employed in the firm. Three years older than Joe, Roger was two notches above Joe on the company ladder and headed for a top spot. Joe hated competing with his cousin and thought his parents belittled him by not advancing him further in the company.

Joe's money problem was one dimensional; he spent every dollar he earned. While he lived at home and had no household expenses, Joe lived well outside the boundaries of his income. He drove a Porsche Turbo, dined in the finest restaurants, and was impeccably dressed. Not only generous to himself, Joe was financially magnanimous with friends. He was always the first to reach for the dinner check, the first to pay for theater and football tickets. And he never forgot his parents or friends—on their birthdays, anniversaries, and holidays. When asked if it bothered him that he had nothing saved, had no investments for the future, Joe replied: "Look, I know I spend a lot of money. But that's what money is for—to enjoy life. I expect to have a lot of money in my lifetime and I'm not about to act like a pauper. There's plenty of time ahead to plan for the future. Too many people lose out on life because they are so hung up on money. I'm never going to fall into that trap."

Joe's parents were anxious and upset about his cavalier lifestyle. Over the past three years they had lent him money on three occasions. The largest sum, $20,000, was supposedly for a down payment on a house but instead went toward buying his Porsche. After Joe's parents learned what he had done with the money, they gave him an ultimatum—either seek help to change his irrational spending habits or move out of the house and assume total financial responsibility. Joe opted to see a professional and was referred to me.

Joe was as perplexed about his parents' money style as they were by his. He said, "It really annoys me. The way my parents spend money. Or, I should say, how they don't spend money. We still live in the same house that I grew up in. Some of the furniture we have is twenty years old, even though my mother had it reupholstered and it's in pretty good shape. My father drives a compact car and my mother clips coupons as if we were poor. It drives me crazy when I see her going through the newspaper with a pair of scissors in her hand. Our newspaper has a special food section every Thursday, and every Thursday night while she watches the news she clips coupons. I don't understand that kind of mentality. My family isn't going to make the Forbes 400 list but they have enough money to live a lot better than they do. If you met them at a party, you'd think they owned the neighborhood grocery store."

Despite his ambivalent feelings about his personal finances, Joe did fairly well at work. Except for the trouble over his expense account, his parents didn't complain very much. He took his job seriously, hardly took a sick day, and worked overtime when it was necessary. Still Joe felt that he could never quite measure up to Roger, and for most of his life he had been compared with his cousin. Now that they were working in the same company, Joe resented the fact that he might never outdistance Roger. Joe was never quite as savvy or sophisticated. Joe worked hard but not as hard as Roger. Joe was a college graduate but Roger had an MBA. Even though Joe's parents owned half of the company, Roger's father, Stanley, was really the boss and ran the day-to-day operations. Joe's mother, once very active in the business, rarely went into the office. Even though Joe's father had a top position, he reported to his brother-in-law. Stanley was an admired and respected boss, was active in the community, and served as president of the local chamber of commerce.

Joe went to college because he knew he was expected to work in the family business. He said, "I almost scrapped college and applied for a job on a local newspaper. I'm a good writer. But I figured that was a sure way to get myself disinherited. I'm an only child and I've always been told that one day I would run my grandfather's business. So now I have my college degree, I got educated, and they tell me I don't know anything about money. I should have a better title by now and more money; I've been with the company for five years. But the place is entrenched in the nineteenth century, very resistant to change. I've come up with some good ideas about how to get more business, more clients. Most of my plans have been axed because they are either too unusual or too costly. My family doesn't understand that you have to spend money in order to make money."

Joe went on to say that maybe he would go back to school and get an MBA: "My parents would pay for that. If I'm staying in the company, I'm sure as hell not going to end up working for Roger."

Joe was reluctant to accept his Hunter profile. He was not comfortable with his scores and wanted to know what he could do to change them *now*. He believed himself to be a Money Master. Joe would never have had the external trappings of his current lifestyle if he had not had a father who was a Money Master and a mother who was an Achiever. His parents had always overindulged him, and Joe didn't have a realistic view of what he could accomplish at this point in his career and at his age. The only thing he knew was that he wanted the "right" car, classic clothes, money to compete socially—he wanted to exude financial success, a motive which drove him as it drives other Hunters.

Joe never felt like he had total control over his life and the situation was getting worse. He felt that his fate was in the hands of his parents and uncle, and he never saw that he had a clear choice—to stay and show them he could cut it or to leave and find another job. The latter was not a viable option for Joe since he was not ready to be that independent. He clearly wanted his family's monetary support and felt he needed it to be "somebody."

Joe certainly never understood nor put into practical use any rational money management systems. Especially in his personal life, he made too many impulsive financial decisions. A lot of his decisions, he said, came from his gut: "It depends on how I feel at the time. If I want something, I feel I deserve it. I've made mistakes sometimes, yeah. But that's how I am."

Joe's greatest barriers to his financial success were his poor self-expression and self-regulation. Unlike Margaret, who was willing to be more systematic about getting there, i.e., through education, Joe wanted his family to give him the "setup." Both Margaret's and Joe's self-image and self-esteem were dependent on external factors. For Margaret, it was the love of a man; for Joe it was the "right status at work" and the "right pay." He needed the self-respect of his family and friends to feel good about himself.

Joe could not afford himself. He was continually depending upon his family to fund his lifestyle, and most of his purchases were a reaction to his frustration. Joe was trying to make himself feel worthy through tangible symbols of perceived wealth. His parents never really had the social class or style he wanted them to have, not like his uncle and his uncle's family. Roger, his cousin, always seemed to be a few steps ahead of him. Roger knew exactly what he wanted and where he was going. Joe didn't have a clue and wasn't particularly interested in finding out. It was too overwhelming; he'd rather not think about it. As quickly as Joe made money, he spent it—short-term pleasure but no long-term accumulations of capital. He was continually dependent upon his parents (his scout) to supplement his expensive lifestyle.

Joe needed to make changes in his personal life: 1) Move out of his parents' home; 2) Create a spending, savings, and investment plan to ensure independent financial responsibility; 3) Eliminate any future loans from his parents; 4) Monitor his newly created financial plan on a consistent basis; 5) Determine one-year, three-year, and five-year career goals.

Joe was asked to track his spending for six weeks—down to the most minute purchase or expenditure. At the end of that time, he categorized and totaled his expenses and we were then able to prioritize how he really wanted to spend his money. Through a negotiation process, Joe eliminated many expenses that were unimportant and we were then able to redirect that money to a savings and investment plan. Six months later he had saved several thousand dollars and purchased a few investment-grade rare coins. Owning rare coins appealed to Joe's desire to stand out from the crowd and acquire a touch of status and prestige, like other Hunters. As it turned out, the coins were a solid investment choice for Joe. In addition to coins, Hunters also like to invest in rare stamps.

Joe, like most Hunters, couldn't reconcile his current income with his perceived social class. Being the underprivileged members of a social class, for the Hunters, creates a significant degree of discontentment, feelings of failure, high anxiety, lack of trust in others, and frustration which is acted out in emotional spending on nonappreciable items. The spending is a mood elevator which will often crash when financial reality strikes.

Male Hunters typically don't have to struggle with money dependency issues since they have been taught to provide for themselves. However, some, like Joe, can find it difficult to break away from financial caretaking. The thought of being responsible for himself depressed Joe as it did Margaret. Neither wanted to come to grips with reality.

Hunter men can have more resistance to changing their profile than Hunter women. They have more of a sense of identity tied into their money. If a man cannot adequately provide for himself and his family, his sense of identity, as well as his sense of power, is undermined. If male Hunters feel socially inferior, they need more props like Joe's Porsche to mask inadequate financial prowess. They are more reluctant to analyze their sabotaging money traits, and understandably so because of the emotional significance of the issue.

Given the same kind of behavior, female Hunters are more easily excused than male Hunters in our society. Women, so the story goes, don't understand money, don't want to understand money, and just like to spend and enjoy it. Men, however, are expected to be more knowledgeable, more rational, and better able to identify and correct any misjudgments in money management. Thus, Joe would be judged more harshly than Margaret. However, if society continually excuses the female Hunter, she may never improve.

THE STRUGGLE FOR FINANCIAL INDEPENDENCE

Donna married Andrew when she was thirty-seven; he was forty-eight. It was her first marriage, his second. Donna was working as a marketing manager for a department store when she met Andrew. He was an executive for a large manufacturing company. One year after they were married she was fired from her job, and it was a devastating experience. However, Donna said that Andrew was wonderful during her "time of need." He suggested that she not look for another job right away. She had been working too hard and deserved a break. She should relax, accompany him on a few out-of-town business trips, and go back to work only when she was ready. According to Donna, Andrew said, "Honey, it's all right with me if you never go back to work. You don't need to. Why don't you just enjoy yourself for a while?"

Four years after Donna lost her job, she still wasn't working. And she and Andrew were fighting, mostly about money. Donna said: "I don't consider myself a spendthrift. When I stopped working, I finally had some time to fix up our house so I did some remodeling, especially the kitchen, living and dining rooms. Andrew was very angry when he saw the bills. He said the costs were much too high and that I didn't need to get the best of everything. We entertain a lot and the house really looks wonderful now. After the remodeling, he started to complain that I spent too much money on clothes, yet he loves it when somebody compliments me on how nice I look. Women's clothes, quality stuff, cost more than men's. Andrew doesn't understand that. He dresses pretty well but it's easier for men—all they need are a few good suits. I rarely buy anything at full price. I always shop the department store sales. I'll admit that I love to go shopping, but most women do. It fills up my time. When my husband suggested that I go on a budget, I blew up. I hate that word because it makes me feel poor. And we are not poor. This generous man I married has turned into a tightwad.

"I pay all the bills but he reviews them. I hate to fight about money. My parents always fought about money and they didn't have much to fight over. Even though my mother worked, she didn't make very much and always had to ask my dad for money. He used to keep their spare cash in a metal box in their dresser in the bedroom. Every time my mother needed money, she had to put a slip of paper in the box. She had to write down how much she spent and what it was for. Sometimes, even when she was really mad at him about something other than money, she would make up with him just because she wanted to buy something and had to ask his permission. I knew even then that I would never buckle under to any man for money."

After her four-year hiatus, Donna decided to go back to work. She admitted, "I was scared, nervous—and over forty. I decided to look for work again because I was getting bored. I was tired of ladies luncheons and volunteer work. I did travel with Andrew and that was nice for a while but he spent most of his time in meetings and the trips got shorter and more hectic. I decided that it was time that I got some mileage out of my college degree—after all, it took me ten years to pay off my college loans."

For six months Donna went on job interviews—mostly in her job area—marketing. She did get some job offers, but none of the positions seemed right. Either the position and salary weren't good enough or she didn't really like the people. Finally she decided to go back to school and get a master's degree because it would "make a difference in the salary I can command and I can afford to go full time, so it won't take me that long to finish the program."

Nine months into the master's program, she was doing well. Her grades were good and she was studying "just like the good old college days." Her marriage, however, wasn't doing as well. She never went on business trips with Andrew because she was always studying. He claimed that he had been abandoned. She was still spending too much money, he said, and she had her priorities mixed up. Donna defended herself: "When I get this degree, it will be easier to get a good job and a good salary. For most of our marriage, our lives have revolved around Andrew—his job, his friends. He says there is nothing wrong with being a housewife; that I went to college, worked for fifteen years, and have nothing to be ashamed of. When he first called me a house-wife, I broke down and cried. Is that really what I am?

"The bottom line," said Donna, "is that I will not break up my marriage. I love him very much and I think I can make him under-stand how important this is to me. But if I have to make a choice, it will always be Andrew. My marriage is more important to me than my career. I can always do some part-time work—maybe some con-sulting. That would keep me busy but give me more free time. It took me a long time to find somebody like Andrew and I'm not going to lose him."

Women have traditionally been motivated to establish and maintain relationships as their primary need and drive. This need for affiliation has generally exceeded both their needs for achievement and for a sense of power. Female currency in a marital relationship has usually been love and emotional support while male currency has been money for the financial support of the family.

Now that women are moving into the work force in great numbers, we are seeing a shift in the priority of their needs. The drive for achievement and power is becoming as important as the need for affili-ation. However, women such as Donna are still motivated more by the need for affiliation. For many women, giving love and receiving love are more essential to a sense of themselves than achievement and power. Because of this, their money management skills and the pursuit of financial independence are secondary. Even though the Hunters are ambitious and have a desire for power with money (higher than the power motive for most Moneymax groups), those needs can still be subservient to personal relationships. These priorities may very well change in the future as women acquire different motives—i.e., a career instead of a family.

ENTREPRENEURS IN HUNTERS' CLOTHING?

When the financial traits of the Hunters are compared overall with the financial traits of the more affluent groups, the Hunters come closest to mirroring the Entrepreneurs. The two groups are closely aligned in self-determination and somewhat aligned in work ethic and power. The greatest disparity shows up in the traits of emotionality, anxiety, risk-taking, and pride.

First, a look at the similar traits. The Hunters work hard but seem to struggle a lot; the Entrepreneurs work hard and with a lot less struggle. The Entrepreneurs clearly define their goals and systematically go after them with great diligence and every available resource. The Hunters, on the other hand, have a difficult time defining their goals. Usually they get too caught up in the process and the potential rewards and don't concentrate enough on a systematic plan to get the desired results. For example, Margaret's process was education, as it is for many Hunters. She believed that more schooling, more degrees, eventually would have to lead to financial success. She put an enormous amount of effort into getting an undergraduate degree, then went back to school to get certified as a paralegal. Now she is thinking about getting an MBA. Margaret really wants to be a lawyer and has worked in that field since she was seventeen. Had she been able to define her real goal earlier, Margaret would be practicing law today. But she continually engages in the process, i.e., education, instead of pursuing a specific result. She has invested much time and energy in a goal that still eludes her. Hunters do many of the "right" things but too often they get lost along the road to success. Entrepreneurs first look down to the end of the road, find out exactly at what point they want to be, and then begin the process of planning how to get there.

Surprisingly, both the Entrepreneurs and the Hunters have average scores in self-determination, meaning that both groups believe that financial destiny is partly attributed to luck. This is not debilitating for Entrepreneurs, who are so certain of success, so action-oriented, that they push forward, confident that luck will lend an assisting hand. When Hunters score a win, they don't give themselves personal credit but feel lucky; when Hunters lose, they feel they just had back luck on their side. In short, Entrepreneurs expect good luck because they deserve it, while the Hunters use luck as an excuse to reward or punish themselves.

Both groups desire a certain degree of power and prestige with their money. The Entrepreneurs get their power through achievement and feel powerful because of their accomplishments. They have personal power. The Hunters want power but they aren't quite sure that they have a right to be powerful or that they can exercise power. Being powerful means commitment, responsibility, willingness to act. The Hunters equate money with power but since they fear money, they also fear power. For the Hunters the equation between money and power results in a paralyzing action. When they get money, they spend it.

Emotionality with money is one of the four main differences between Entrepreneurs and Hunters. For Entrepreneurs emotional spending is a nonexistent problem. They are practical and rational with their money. The Hunters are the opposite and try to buy self-esteem and confirm their sense of worth through the purchase of material goods. Their possessions give them a sense of controlling their lives. The material goods wrap around them like a big security blanket. Shopping brings on a sense of excitement and instant gratification that temporarily counteracts feelings of depression and powerlessness. For the Hunters "purchasing power" has a literal translation. When they have money, they are afraid that the "good fortune" money symbolizes will vanish if they hang on to it for too long; so they spend it. This behavior is counter phobic, meaning that Hunters do the exact thing that they are afraid of. They fear that they will be financially out of control and dependent, and they spend their money, which only reinforces that fear. Hunters have a low tolerance for stress. Their personal problems make them anxious and to relieve the anxiety they spend money. But the spending only causes more anxiety.

Anxiety is the second big difference between Hunters and Entrepreneurs. When making financial decisions, Entrepreneurs are confident and trust their financial abilities. The Hunters experience great self-doubt. As Margaret so aptly put it, "Money makes me nervous." And when Margaret got nervous, she went shopping.

Winston Churchill once said that only when you risk more than you can afford to lose do you know what the game is all about. The Entrepreneurs would applaud that statement, but nonetheless their risk-taking is usually very calculated. For them risk-taking works, and it complements their action-oriented philosophy and pushes them faster and further toward their goals. The Hunters, however, are risk aversive. They haven't learned how to analyze the risk-reward ratio. Since they don't know how to make their money work for them instead of against them, the Hunters overall are very conservative risk-takers. A loss of money may mean a loss of identity. Finally, the Hunters have low pride with how they have handled their money while the Entrepreneurs have high pride.

The Entrepreneurs have a clear vision of what will bring them financial and personal satisfaction and they move through the jungle with ease and confidence. The Hunters know they want more than they have, but their vision is obscured by the thick of the jungle. Oftentimes the Hunters adopt an avoidance approach. Margaret was avoiding the dependency of her mother and Joe the lifestyle of his parents. Both followed a strategy of avoidance, focusing on what they didn't want (dependency for Margaret; lack of prestige for Joe) rather than on what they did want (financial independence and security for Margaret and power and prestige for Joe). Margaret worried about being on poverty row and Joe worried about living a life of boring mediocrity in an old Volkswagen. While Hunters react to life, Entrepreneurs act upon it. Entrepreneurs plan for the future; their primary financial goal is growth. The Hunters live for today; their primary goal is current income.

Hunters can become affluent. They can become self-sufficient and increase their incomes as well as their assets. Demographically, they outshine the Entrepreneurs in education and occupation and have considerably fewer dependent children. They need to become aware of what is sabotaging their success and adopt new financial strategies.

MONEY ACTION PLAN FOR THE HUNTERS

Hunters have the qualifications necessary to play in the money game, but they need to know how to play the game better and they need to believe that they are capable of playing the game alone. They need to become more realistic about who they are, what they want, and what they can realistically do with their money. They need to maximize their personal assets in order to maximize their financial assets. I have worked with many Hunters, and once they are armed with the knowledge and skills necessary to succeed, they become quite capable of drawing their own road map to financial independence. Their hunt becomes exhilarating and challenging. They move ahead financially (more income, more assets) and emotionally (less anxiety, more pride, more contentment). They learn how to set their own price tag for self-esteem and realize that the best investment they have is themselves. The money action plan for the Hunters:

1. *Set definitive goals and put them into a realistic time frame.* Hunters do not need to bootleg the visions and passions of others. They have enough ambition of their own. Set the goals, set them high, and don't plan for *how* to get them until you have a clear picture of what they are. Capitalize on your own skills, abilities, and desires.

2. *Create a spending plan.* One of the most important ingredients of a successful money management strategy is to know where your dollars are being spent. Track your spending for six weeks so that you can determine which items are appropriate, or inappropriate, to spend money on. Tracking your expenditures will help you to control expenses and resist impulse buying.

3. *Understand how the financial and economic system works.* Educate yourself by enrolling in financial seminars, adult school, or college classes. There is a great abundance of financial books, magazines, and newspapers available. The investment world need not be a mysterious realm.

4. *Step out of the comfort zone.* You won't feel comfortable about

money until you begin working with it—not only earning it, but saving it and investing it. Work on disarming your risk-aversive tendencies but only take calculated, reasonable risks.

5. *Fail optimistically.* Financial reverses are a part of the money game. With proper planning, your gains will more than offset your losses and the knowledge gleaned from failure will add to your money management expertise.

6. *Seek the advice of a financial expert.* A reputable professional will assist you in establishing long-term financial goals. Hunters need to stop living in the economic present and plan for the future. The only way to accumulate wealth is through investing.

7. *Take responsibility for your financial well-being.* Hunters don't need scouts. They have a multitude of options and don't need to dilute their ambitions. Having economic clout does not mean a loss of healthy, rewarding relationships.

MONEY MANAGEMENT STYLE

1. Even though they are risk aversive as a group, the Hunters who do own individual common stocks and mutual funds are pretty satisfied with them. A monthly investment program in growth mutual funds can be set up so money is automatically withdrawn from a bank account and invested. This approach allows options, is disciplined, and forces the Hunter to make systematic investments. Thus, in the future they have a much greater assurance of building some capital for themselves. They can be as involved or uninvolved as they want. The key is finding a financial adviser who can direct their money to the appropriate funds at the appropriate times and make changes when necessary. Many Hunters who don't own individual common stocks appear to be successfully investing through this concept.

2. Dissatisfied with money market funds, Hunters view the funds as a parking space for dollars, and Hunters don't park their dollars—they tend to spend them.

3. Hunters like investing in investment-grade coins and stamps probably because of the status and prestige appeal and aesthetic qualities.

4. The Hunters strongly favor "current income" as their number-one financial goal. Since spending is a problem, they would profit from prioritized spending plans and need the discipline to follow the plans. Otherwise, they may never accumulate sufficient assets.

5. Since they have an interest in commercial property, the limited partnership form of investment in high quality commercial properties has been a worthwhile consideration even though Hunters generally have not expressed as much satisfaction with this investment vehicle as they have with others. There are many of these available through reputable syndicators who have good records of making money for their investors. According to financial professionals, the limited partnership form of ownership provides an investor with limited exposure to risk as well as more opportunity for gain because these public programs typically have a few—to many—properties in a partnership. The investor's risk is limited to the amount invested ($2,000 or more) and many of the partnerships provide cash flow during the operating stage as well as an equity position on sale, for even greater returns. The properties are professionally managed as well. All these factors make them a viable investment for an individual who has difficulty gaining control over money management.

6. A financial education program is recommended for this group even though there may be some initial resistance since Hunters generally are not future planners, but geared more to immediate gratification and to living for today.

7. They are satisfied with their IRAs and Keoghs, which are a start toward future financial planning—not their strong suit.

8. Although Hunters are motivated by a desire for power with their money, they do not express satisfaction or a preference for commodities/options and futures contracts, unlike some of the other profiles— such as the High Rollers and the Producers—with similar power motives.

THE HUNTERS—FINANCIAL STATEMENT

"I want it now" is indicative of the Hunters' money attitudes and behaviors. This Moneymax Profile has the highest percentage of women of all nine Moneymax groups; it is the youngest group with 30 percent under the age of thirty. Collectively they are also the least married and the most divorced. In addition, they have the fewest number of dependent children under twenty-two years of age. The Hunters are professional and managerial workers and have the greatest number of people with higher levels of education (tied with the Achievers). However, their income level is average and they are one of the lowest Moneymax groups in accumulation of assets. They certainly don't have the assets they should, relative to their income level and education. Of all nine groups, the Hunters scored the highest in the trait of emotionality. They also are the highest believers in spending and enjoying their money—rather than saving it. They use their feelings to guide their financial decisions, which translates into emotional spending. The number-one financial goal for the Hunters is current income. The Hunters need greater involvement with their money, significantly lower emotionality, lower anxiety, and more confidence in making financial decisions.

7

———————————————

High Rollers

During the first period of a man's life the greatest danger is: not to take the risk. When once the risk has really been taken, then the greatest danger is to risk too much. By not risking at first one turns aside and serves trivialities; in the second case, by risking too much, one turns aside to the fantastic, and perhaps to presumption.

—Kierkegaard

GUIDELINES
High Rollers

. . . Enjoy the thrill associated with taking risks with their money.

. . . Are discontent and frustrated with their current financial situation.

. . . Let their emotions guide their financial decisions.

. . . Are not very proud of the way they have handled their money.

. . . Experience anxiety in dealing with their money management.

. . . Desire that their money bring them feelings of power and prestige.

. . . Get greater enjoyment in spending rather than saving their money.

Money is a psychological thrill for the Moneymax High Rollers. They have a strong desire to command attention, get recognition, and influence others with their money. This need for power and prestige often causes the High Rollers to set impossibly high goals for themselves—goals they attempt to reach by taking inordinately high risks.

Of all nine Moneymax groups, the High Rollers are the highest risk-takers. They seek sensation-filled lives and would rather spend money than save it. While some High Rollers earn large salaries and have considerable assets, on the average they are one of the lowest groups in income and assets (seventh and eighth respectively). They tend to be young, single, or divorced.

The High Rollers enjoy living on the edge of the unknown and would rather be financially insecure than bored. Some step over the edge into the world of gambling, for the essence of that world is risk; others don't even remotely resemble the stereotyped Las Vegas gambler. High Rollers are usually creative, extroverted, competitive, and energetic. They work hard and they play hard. Regardless of occupation and lifestyle, the common thread that pulls them all together is risk.

Risk is inherently a valuable commodity. Without it, Columbus wouldn't have set sail for the New World, the Wright Brothers would never have flown at Kitty Hawk, the astronauts would never have landed on the moon. The history of the United States reflects the accomplishments of an impressive array of risk-takers who dared to invent, to innovate, and to push the boundaries of the country from east to west. Risk requires courage and action. It demands that you trade in the realm of certainty for the fear of the unknown. The rewards for successful risk-takers are plentiful. They enjoy personal as well as financial success. They believe in their own abilities to control their lives and can turn unrewarding lives into productive lives, or already productive lives into even more productive lives.

WALKING THE FINANCIAL TIGHTROPE

The Moneymax High Rollers understand that to reach a goal they must push themselves beyond their limits and that risk is part of the process. However, there is a difference between goal-oriented risk-taking and risk-taking for the sake of sensation. Goal-oriented risk-taking requires perception, evaluation, confidence, and assuming responsibility for action. It also requires a focus on the goal so that the energies expended are directed toward the desired results. Sensation-seeking with money is not conducive for wealth accumulation as is goal-oriented risk-taking. Instead, risking for the experience of sensation, like trading stocks for the thrill of the transaction instead of the profit, creates short-term pleasure rather than long-term gain.

The Moneymax High Rollers want to experience thrill and excitement in financial transactions and money management. They have a great propensity and tolerance for risk but too often their attitudes and behaviors do not advance them toward realizing their financial dreams and goals. They can be compared with the inveterate political campaigner who works very hard and is continually excited by the campaign—meeting new people, extensive travel and speeches—yet never wins the election. His thoughts, feelings, and behaviors are never directed toward winning, just running and campaigning. The High Rollers are financial campaigners.

We live in a society of "fast lane economics" and the High Rollers are right at home. They pride themselves on being money savvy but do not like admitting their discontent with their present status—financial and personal. They continually struggle with what they know would make more sense—a practical way of handling their money—yet they are emotionally torn by the desire to gratify their sensation needs. Translated into financial terms, that means that the High Rollers go for the long shot instead of taking small, boring, and laborious steps. They can't resist the temptation of the fabulous deal in lieu of a more sensible step-by-step money approach.

Some Moneymax High Rollers are financially solvent and can afford to indulge their desires for sensation and risk-taking while others can only express a vicarious longing for the "good life." Many of those in the latter category might very well be in a more affluent position someday if they can set specific financial goals and commit themselves to a long-range strategy for achieving the goals.

The High Rollers are too enamored with the financial journey. They set the journey up to be filled with risk, excitement, and big payoffs. They enjoy meandering down the road and like any distractions that happen by. The thrill is in the journey, not in the destination. In some cases High Rollers are disappointed and uncomfortable if they meet with financial success because they achieved a goal in spite of themselves.

Security is not a necessary goal for High Rollers. In fact, it can be their nemesis. Only 18 percent of the High Rollers choose "safety" as their number-one financial goal versus 46 percent who chose "current income." Only 22 percent put "growth or appreciation" on top of the list of financial objectives. If life becomes secure, some High Rollers feel compelled to search for new sources of excitement and novel experience. Boredom—a state that is dull and tedious—is unacceptable to the High Rollers. When they are bored, they can indulge in risky financial investments, new business creations and adventures.

Choosing and investing in emerging growth companies is viewed much more enthusiastically by the High Rollers than by most of the other Moneymax groups. If a High Roller and a Hunter both invest in the same emerging growth stock, which is considered more risky than many investments, the High Roller contemplates the choice with more excitement than anxiety while the low risk-taking Hunter experiences a great deal of nervousness and little excitement. This tendency to desire and assume risk varies significantly from person to person and influences a wide range of areas, from personal to financial. Knowing whether you are a "high" risk-taker like the High Rollers or a "low" risk-taker like the Safety Players (to be discussed in the next chapter) is very important. It is crucial to managing your money and planning your investment strategies as well as choosing a career and even a potential spouse or business partner.

Most Americans, per the results of the nationwide Moneymax survey, do not seek risk with their money. That is because most people cherish certainty and security and fear the possibility of losing money. The horror of losing money is a very powerful emotion and stops many people from taking very many, if any, risks with money. Some people can accept a loss on a good risk better than they can accept letting a good risk get by them without acting on it. Others are much more conservative and take very little risk yet get angry at themselves when a very safe investment suffers a loss.

Obviously, investors willing to define and confront the negative emotion of fear when investing stand to outperform others as long as they truly understand their tolerance for risk. As one Wall Street analyst says, "Lots of people will tell you that they are risk-takers or risk-averse, but they really don't know."

The downfall for the High Rollers is that big gains are most often matched by equally large losses. The same kind of counter phobic financial behavior the Hunters experience in emotional spending, the High Rollers experience in gambling and unwise investment choices and schemes. They fear they will lose and act out that fear, thus creating a self-fulfilling prophecy—loss. The High Rollers are not expecting to win—not really. They have no specific strategy, no game plan to win like the Entrepreneurs. The High Roller approach is more trial-and-error, fantasizing about the deal of the cards, the thrill of the horse race, the whims of the marketplace. They do not systematically hedge their bets but go for the long shot, hoping for a magical windfall gain.

For the High Rollers, money is magic. Here one day, gone the next. They don't face reality and make a rational commitment to make the essential moves and significant changes necessary in their money systems and styles to assure more success. They resemble the Hunters in this respect—stuck in a self-sabotaging money style. The unrealized financial potential of the High Rollers and the Hunters is never really put to the test because both groups don't take an earnest look at themselves and what they've been doing to distract themselves from getting ahead. It's easier to deny, distort, and ignore those feelings.

The High Rollers experience less pride than the Hunters in the way they handle money. While the Hunters score the highest in the trait of emotionality—that feelings guide financial decisions—the High Rollers are right behind them in second place. Both groups use money to act out how they are feeling at the moment. In addition, both groups are back to back in low contentment with money; the Hunters are just slightly less content than the High Rollers.

Someone once said that an opportunity is born every second and we have the choice to seize it or ignore it. The High Rollers often ignore the opportunity because their minds are shooting around so quickly that they miss it. They lose sight of what is important in getting the job done. The old adage, "Don't be in such a hurry to make a living that you don't make money," applies to the High Rollers. Their sensation-seeking and emotional money style prevents them from achieving the financial success they desire.

Of all nine Moneymax groups, only two groups are comfortable with taking risk—first the High Rollers, second the Entrepreneurs. The Entrepreneurs are the number-one income earners; the High Rollers finish seventh of nine in income. Obviously, the Entrepreneurs have learned how to manage and capitalize on risk. For the High Rollers, risk can be a disaster.

High Rollers, like the Entrepreneurs, tend to take a chance if there is an opportunity that might pay big dividends. While the Entrepreneur's sights are always set on the gain and the "financial win," the High Roller gets distracted by the thrill of the ride—seesawing from high achievement to near disaster. The High Rollers are usually overly optimistic about their ability to win even when they are aware that the odds are against them. Little time is wasted in regret over mistakes. The Entrepreneurs are much more analytical in assessing the odds and if they make mistakes, they use them as learning tools for future opportunities.

Many a High Roller enjoys the thrill of a stock transaction even more than the payoff. Since the Entrepreneurs are motivated more by ultimate performance, they set up goals and standards by which to judge the success of their stocks. The stocks become an investment game in which Entrepreneurs gather and hone skills and confidence for future transactions. For the High Roller, the investment game may be more like a roller coaster ride with no specific goal in mind or standards to judge any level of success. Rather, the thrill and exhilaration of the ride is what's most prized. Often they don't have a particular goal or strategy and even if they do, they tend to lose sight of their destination. Generally, the Entrepreneurs will walk away from the craps table when they are losing whereas the High Rollers might hang in there until there are no more stakes for the roll.

While the Entrepreneurs use their tolerance for risk to their advantage, as one of their assets in getting the job done, the High Rollers may use it to their detriment by making it their all. They get lost in the thrill of the journey, taking every path and side road just so they don't miss anything of value along the way. Unfortunately, the High Rollers don't see that the value lies down the road if they'd just continue walking at a reasonable pace and straight ahead.

Risk-taking can be described as betting. Whether you are buying a house or car, starting your own business, or playing the stock market —you are still betting. In most circumstances, you either bet on yourself or on fate. When you play the roulette wheel or jump on a "hot" stock market tip, you have no direct opportunity to affect the outcome. You are at the mercy of the odds combined with the skills of others to determine the likelihood of your win.

High Rollers prefer to keep themselves out of the financial equation. They would rather risk the odds by betting on fate and chance than by betting on themselves. Sometimes they spend large amounts of time and energy trying to predict the outcome of high risk investments or games of chance. Yet these same people may not feel comfortable betting on themselves whether they are playing in a tennis tournament, starting their own business, or competing for a job promotion. They avoid situations where their skill is challenged or their abilities become an integral part of the financial picture. David was such a High Roller.

STEPPING OVER THE EDGE

David never seemed to be able to please his parents. From his earliest memories through adulthood, the love of his parents was conditional. It depended on what he did right or wrong. His father was a very successful corporate executive in the clothing industry who had difficulty coping with a high stress job.

David's mother suffered from a variety of physical ailments, and a recovery from one usually signaled the onset of another. As soon as David was old enough, he became partly responsible for taking care of his younger sister. He walked her home from school, helped her with her homework, and made sure she got to bed on time. In addition, David had a daily list of chores that included helping out with the cleaning and cooking.

When David was twelve, he started to rebel by hanging out at the local park with a group of older classmates. His gang didn't commit any serious offenses, but they were a neighborhood nuisance. They drove bikes across manicured lawns, made crank phone calls, stole cigarettes from their parents. Once David and two friends got caught shoplifting in a drugstore but the owners didn't press charges and the boys got away with only a stern warning not to do it again.

David got a charge out of getting away with pranks. He sneaked out of the house to go on dates, drove cars without a license, made a little spending money by playing penny rummy and nickel craps. He wore his hair long and dressed in T-shirts and jeans when most students were wearing madras shirts and khaki pants. He liked being different. David had learned at an early age that he got a lot more attention for doing something bad, instead of doing something good. Despite his unruly appearance and cocky attitude, David was a good student and usually reaped As and Bs in his classes—grades that somewhat perplexed his teachers.

David gained admission to a nearby state university. His father wanted him to major in business or engineering—good solid professions with well-paying jobs. Instead, David majored in liberal arts. He loved being away from home, particularly away from his father's critical eye. For the first time he felt free and alive. Campus life was fun, exciting, full of new people and experiences. David, however, had a difficult time with his classes because earning good grades in college was much harder than in high school. He couldn't seem to concentrate and quickly became listless and bored. His grades were below average and he worried that perhaps he really wasn't good enough to be in college. Maybe the competition was too tough.

He sought escape and distraction by organizing a weekly poker game in his dormitory. While some of the guys played well, David was the best. Like many High Rollers, David was a strong competitor and gambling at cards gave him a psychological thrill. He won more often than he lost and the extra money was a welcome supplement to the meager financial assistance from his parents. The weekly poker games became nightly poker games as David recruited more students to play. By the end of the second semester, he had enough cash to buy a secondhand car and a new stereo system. He felt good about himself. He was earning a living before he even graduated from college.

The stakes in the poker games got higher and higher and David got richer. He was hooked. He was making money at something he really liked and he had become an expert. Because the games often lasted until the middle of the night, David frequently skipped his morning classes, and his grades plummeted. When his parents refused to give him any more money for tuition and housing, David dropped out of school. Somehow, he'd find a way to make a living without a college education. He found his way by gambling.

Until David was forty-six years old, he gambled for a living. Gambling was a refuge where no one could call him a failure because no one knew for sure when he would be lucky or not. His track record certainly spoke for itself. He bragged that he usually had a six-figure income and he won cars, real estate, and other high ticket items when opponents couldn't meet their debts in cash. At thirty-two David had enough saved to start lending out money at a 20 percent rate of return for second mortgages. He had found another way to make a lot of money. For David, it all seemed so effortless, and he was flying high. He began to spend some of his money on mens' favorite toys—a nice power boat, a place at the beach, a Rolls Royce. He took his dates on plush vacation trips and spared no expenses.

High Rollers like the power base that they feel is gained through money. Material possessions, recognition and status, and the exciting lifestyle gleaned from money provide them with a sense of self-worth that can otherwise be absent. For David, the benefits were particularly intoxicating because he had the money to buy whatever he desired.

David drifted from one card game to another, traveling internationally for bigger stakes and more excitement. Everything was going fine and yet it wasn't. Something was missing. He decided that he needed an important relationship in his life. He became involved with one beautiful, flashy woman after another, and the relationships bolstered his self-image. Soon the chase became boring and he felt no better; in fact, he felt even more frustrated. He had gone through a lot of money, taken time off from playing poker, and had nothing to show for it.

His overall dissatisfaction with his life led him to seek professional advice. When working with David, I tried to make him aware of how he had always been afraid to really risk putting himself on the line. He was willing to take many risks but none that involved his own self-esteem, typical of High Rollers, who can insulate themselves from their feelings through high stimulation with their money. Focusing on a goal, making a commitment, and applying himself were too close to what his parents seemed to want but never really encouraged or reinforced with their actions. David was not in touch with the fact that he wanted security and a feeling of success for himself. At least by playing poker, he was making money. He had chosen an offbeat, risky way to make a living, but gambling was a safety zone for him. Even though he had chosen an activity which many friends thought unworthy of his talents, he had proven to himself that he was capable of doing something. He was making money, not getting into too much trouble, and enjoyed poker and the kind of people it attracted.

It was difficult for David to risk his self-esteem because if he did fail, it would confirm what he felt from his family all along—that he was a loser and not worthy of respect. When High Rollers, like David, set themselves up for failure time after time, what they are really doing is playing out the you-will-be-a-failure theme prevalent in their unconscious or conscious mind. It is a rebellious act—a way of getting even and the way they have always gotten attention.

David tried his hand at several full-time jobs before he found his niche as a commercial real estate broker. Today he orchestrates deals all around the world.

David still takes greater risks than most people would be willing to take with money. He still lends money for second mortgages but says he has only been burned once and his risks are now "covered." David has, however, diversified his investment portfolio and now owns several apartment buildings, which he anticipates will appreciate substantially over the years. In addition, he gave up his singles' apartment at the beach and bought a small home in a suburb of Los Angeles. This is in contrast to his previous "income only" High Roller investment style, which had no provisions for his future or his financial independence. After many years of living without security, David has adopted a more conservative philosophy in his life as well as his investments.

POWER, GAMBLING, SENSATION-SEEKING LIFESTYLES

High Rollers want more than profit and creature comforts with money. They want power. Of all nine Moneymax groups, the High Rollers rank first in the desire to have their money bring them power and prestige. The High Rollers are not content only to be rich. They want to be rich and famous; it's a lot better to be rich and famous as opposed to rich and anonymous. Money is an instant passport to prestige, a ticket to the top of the heap. Money allows them to stand out from the crowd; it makes them feel respected, powerful, and influential.

American society glorifies and envies the rich. If you've been successful at making money, then obviously you have been doing something right. Money brings instant power and recognition. It enables the High Rollers to leave behind any feelings of worthlessness and move into the arena of self-respect. Money becomes an indicator of achievement and social value and shines like a bright medal on the lapels of those who have it. For the High Rollers, money provides a quick trip up the ladder of success, which is preferable to climbing up the ladder rung by rung. As a barometer of personal adequacy, money gives High Rollers a legitimate claim to status and public recognition.

Today, flaunting one's money, in the form of conspicuous consumption, is acceptable as long as you observe some decorum of good taste. Power dressing, power cars, power possessions—whether they are full-length sable coats or designer sunglasses—are a means by which most people quickly size up net worth and personal worth. The High Rollers are keenly aware of the rules of the status contest. Being dynamic competitors, they surround themselves with the material goods that become natural extensions of themselves. Prestige possessions are not purchased for intrinsic value and quality but for the success and affluence they represent. Even if High Rollers lack a solid financial base, they need to surround themselves with the accoutrements of the good life—concrete reminders that they are valuable.

High Rollers can be generous but too often their generosity can also be a ploy for power. The person who buys the tickets to the football game usually controls the arrangements for the day—what time the group will leave, how they will get to the stadium, where they will sit, if they will have dinner afterward. When High Rollers extend dinner invitations, they usually choose the restaurant, recommend items from the menu, choose the wine, pace the conversation, and decide when the evening should come to an end. They like being in command, making the necessary decisions.

Wanting and exercising power can be a positive personal asset. Power has, unfortunately, acquired many shades of meaning, most of them negative. The precise dictionary definition of the word is "the ability or capacity to act or perform effectively." Nonetheless, most of us equate the desire for power with a desire for dominance and thus believe power to be egocentric, vile, and evil. If you are powerful, I must be powerless. If you win, then I must lose. Phrases like "power hungry," "power driven," and "power crazy" reinforce our negative attitudes.

Those people who have power, in a constructive sense, have the ability to seek out opportunities, influence people, and get the best out of life. They get good jobs and good promotions. In a world of constant negotiation, they act upon life rather than waiting to see what will be dealt out to them. They take risks and assume responsibility and control over their lives. They make good managers and good leaders whether involved in business, government, sports, or social clubs and organizations. The rewards for those who successfully use power as a source of personal strength are obvious: self-esteem, praise from their peers, financial gain.

The High Rollers have not properly channeled their need and desire for power. They believe that the power they extract from money can cure, or at best alleviate, personal problems that are unrelated to and unresponsive to money. They use money instead of themselves as a power base. Money, like other forms of social power, whets the appetite for more. Each new gain in power is reassuring for the High Rollers, but the security it brings is temporary.

Someone once said that there are three ways to get money: "You're either born into it, you earn it, or you marry it." Some High Rollers have a fourth avenue; they gamble for money. Public gambling is very attractive to people who want power because they have a chance to excel in front of others by being big risk-takers and big winners.

A 1976 report of the federal Commission on the Review of the National Policy Toward Gambling revealed that 80 percent of Americans approve of gambling and two thirds have participated in some form of gambling. The United States offers many outlets for would-be gamblers—lotteries, bingo, casino games, horse racing, dog racing, sporting events, billiards, neighborhood card games. Generally, most Americans indulge in gambling to an extent that does not harm their family lives and work habits or push them into debt or bankruptcy. However, compulsive gambling can lead to personal as well as financial ruin.

To date, not much research has been done on the personalities, backgrounds, and motivations of compulsive gamblers. Estimates on the number of compulsive gamblers in the United States range from 1 to 9 million. Television and movie portrayals of gamblers tend to show them as either downtrodden, alcoholic deviants or sophisticated, attractive ladies' men like Nicky Arnstein (Omar Sharif) in *Funny Girl,* who wore ruffled shirts and tuxedos. Both portrayals are inaccurate, but it is difficult to typecast a gambler. A study of 400 gamblers treated at the Johns Hopkins University Compulsive Gambling Counseling Center provides some very interesting, sometimes surprising, information. According to the center's findings, gamblers often come from a middle to upper middle class background. They are articulate and intelligent with IQs that range from 120 upward. Most first learned about gambling from a member of the family, and most, when in their late teens or early twenties, had a "big win" that made a lasting impression on them.

Other treatment center studies and surveys describe gamblers as confident, independent, energetic, aggressive, and adventurous. As one expert says, "These people are not strung out. They're not sitting on curbs. They're bright, they're producers. The characteristics that go into making a pathological gambler frequently include those you look for in 'good people.' "

In their book on compulsive gambling, *When Luck Runs Out,* Dr. Robert Custer and Harry Milt draw a composite picture of the gambler: "He is a friendly, sociable fellow, cheerful and enthusiastic, generous and full of good will. He is clever, energetic, hardworking, and he generally does successfully whatever he undertakes. In social, organizational and business situations, he is confident, assertive, persuasive; he moves spontaneously and naturally into the role of leadership. Restless, hyperactive and easily bored, he is in constant need of stimulation, excitement, change. Bland, predictable situations with an assured outcome don't interest him. He thrives on challenge, adventure, risk. The key to his personality is competitiveness. He needs to control, to win, to be better than everybody else, to be Number One."

Most studies show that from 80 to 90 percent of compulsive gamblers are men. Male gamblers tend to prefer games which require some level of skill like sports betting or card playing, while female gamblers are drawn to lotteries, bingo, and slot machines. Regardless of the game, gamblers are all seeking a sense of power, mastery, control, and recognition that "the action" provides. They thrive on the sheer excitement of gambling and the thrill that comes from winning. The excitement generated from gambling eradicates the problems of the outside world—stress on the job, family arguments, house and car payments.

Gamblers scoff at the fact that 90 percent of all gambling ends in a loss. They are a part of the winning 10 percent. Immune to the odds, they have an almost limitless capacity for self-delusion, believing that the next wager will result in a windfall gain. When they are ahead, on a roll, they rarely quit. When they lose, they feel betrayed and anxious. The only way to overcome the anxiety of losing is to return to the game and get even, get ahead. Walter Matthau, an actor who has played his share of roles as a gambler and con man, describes the motivation of the compulsive gambler as follows: "Pain is what he's searching for—the emotion of pain. It's much greater than the emotion of pleasure. Bigger, larger, stronger. Therefore, more interesting."

When the losses reach overwhelming proportions and debts mount up, compulsive gamblers get desperate, insecure, angry, and hostile. They empty joint savings accounts, pawn or sell jewelry, cash in insurance policies, borrow money from family and friends. When necessary, they embezzle money from their companies, fully intending to pay it back as soon as their gambling debts are paid and their luck returns. Gambling for them can be an addiction as destructive as alcohol or drugs.

Of all the Moneymax groups, the High Rollers will most likely contain the majority of compulsive gamblers and others who enjoy gambling. That in no way means that all High Rollers are gamblers or compulsive gamblers. As mentioned earlier, all High Rollers take risks with their money. That is not to say they risk at gambling casinos and racetracks.

Sensation seeking with money can be, for some High Rollers, one aspect of a lifestyle of high sensation. Those who like to speed on the freeways and listen to loud music may also like to ride the river rapids and ski the most challenging slopes. They may choose high risk jobs, have a variety of sexual partners, be the last to leave a party. They may jump from one thing to another—changing careers, investments, spouses (of all Moneymax groups they are eighth of nine in married, second of nine in divorce).

For all the High Rollers who are flamboyant and daring, there are an equal number who live fairly conventional lives—work full time, raise a family and put children through college, spend a vacation visiting relatives rather than taking a trip to Hawaii. Whatever the chosen lifestyle, High Rollers generally take chances with money. Be it high risk investments or high risk gambling, High Rollers want a big return on their money in a short period of time.

Even though many High Rollers claim they have no need for security, their behavior is often quite paradoxical. Many do have secure jobs, earn respectable salaries, and seem exemplary of conservative Middle America. Their outward appearances seem to make them unlikely candidates for speculative, high risk ventures or investments. Yet lurking beneath the mask of deceptive exteriors is a High Roller mentality. Such was the case of Georgia, a junior high school English teacher who lived far beyond her means.

When I first met Georgia, she was recovering from financial losses on two "economic ventures." More appropriately termed "adventures," one involved a spiritual pyramid scheme and the other was an investment in a building product invented by her brother.

The "spiritually oriented" pyramid was based on the premise that one doesn't have to work hard to make money; that if you can change your prosperity consciousness, then "the universe will provide." Structured around an airplane motif, each participant was first a passenger, then a crew member, and finally a pilot.

To qualify as a passenger, Georgia had to contribute $1,500 and bring in a friend who would also contribute $1,500. As more and more people joined, Georgia would move up to crew. When she became a pilot, she would receive $20,000. The participants met twice a week to discuss their strategies for getting more passengers to come on board. Georgia could start out as a passenger on as many planes as she wished—provided she contributed $1,500 for each flight. No money was ever exchanged at the meetings. When Georgia became pilot, she would be contacted by other participants who would each deliver a specified sum to her.

At Georgia's first meeting there were seventy-five people. At the second meeting, three days later, the attendance had grown to almost two hundred. She was ecstatic. She said, "It was such a fun way to make money. You couldn't believe the energy level of those people.

And they weren't nobodies. There were lots of doctors, dentists, other very professional people."

Georgia never got her $20,000. Before she reached pilot level, the police raided one of the meetings. Georgia was out $1,500.

Six months before she became involved in the spiritual pyramid, Georgia gave $5,000, her entire savings, to her brother, who had invented a new construction material that he assured her would revolutionize the building industry and make him a millionaire within a year. But he needed some start-up money and asked all of his friends and relatives to invest. Georgia was a supportive sibling and a willing investor.

Together they estimated how much money Georgia would make on her $5,000 investment. She too would become wealthy, and within a short time frame. She withdrew the money from her savings account and happily handed it over. Within a few years she would be fabulously rich and she envisioned all the things she could buy and the trips she could take.

Within five months the dream was shattered. Georgia had never asked if her brother had a business plan, how he planned to get the necessary capital to support the business through its early years, whether her brother had a business manager lined up, none of the questions she should have asked. Georgia learned too late that while her brother may have been a creative inventor, he was a poor businessman. While he had been able to raise $25,000, he quickly paid off some of his debts and took his family on a vacation to celebrate. Confident that he was going to line up some more investors, he spent the bulk of the money he had raised. He wasn't able to interest any companies in his product; there were no more investors on the horizon; he declared bankruptcy. Georgia got none of her money back.

Georgia's teacher's salary was hardly sufficient to cover her investment losses. In addition, she was heavily in debt, due to excessive spending habits, particularly summer vacations spent in Europe. She thought nothing of taking off on a trip and charging the vacations to American Express, although she knew she couldn't cover the bills when she returned.

Georgia despised her job as a teacher, despised being in a bureaucracy which she said was paralyzing and depressing. To compensate for her less than rewarding job, she found out what real life was like by traveling. "The only salvation in being a teacher," she claimed, "is the three months off each year. If I didn't have that I would go mad." Beneath Georgia's acquiescence to her boring and unfulfilling job was a High Roller desire for adventure and stimulation—desires that were satisfied by travel, spending sprees, and high risk investments.

In her late thirties, Georgia had been a teacher for more than fifteen years. She lived in an apartment and had a host of monthly payments, including obligations on furniture, a car, and fourteen credit cards. Usually she was able to get friends to bail her out when payments of the bills were long overdue. The only reason she had the money to invest with her brother and in the spiritual pyramid was due to a lucky break in the stock market. Since her profits didn't even begin to cover her debts, she decided to reinvest them and take the chance on multiplying her money. If all had worked out, she could have paid all of her bills and had a lot of money to spare.

The two losses had come at a very bad time. Georgia had run out of people to rescue her and she was very worried. She said, "I know this is going to sound really stupid, but sometimes I think I might end up like a bag lady, one of those sad creatures you see in reports about the homeless. I know I shouldn't feel like that; I still have a job and all. But I'm afraid of ending up alone and poor."

Georgia knew she didn't belong in the school system. Out of frustration and boredom, she became involved in a variety of outside activities; she joined health clubs and meditation groups, worked for several volunteer organizations, and took language classes in French and Spanish. She was always juggling a lot of projects but was skating around the most important issue—that she was very dissatisfied and wanted to make changes in her life. Mostly she wanted to switch careers but was hesitant to give up her secure job. "Single, in debt, and pushing forty," she said, "is not exactly an ideal combination to be taking big risks."

It is interesting to note that while Georgia was willing to take risks with her money, she stopped short when it came to risking a change of career. This is not atypical for High Rollers because they find it a lot easier to risk when it doesn't involve a personal commitment. Risking and losing on an investment or a game of chance was a lot more endurable for Georgia than risking possible failure in a new career.

Georgia did not perceive herself as a risk-taker. She was quite taken back to learn that her Moneymax Profile was that of a High Roller. She said, "I've taken some chances with my money and sure I've lost out but I've never lost that much, not like the kind of money that real gamblers lose."

Georgia constructed a new financial and career game plan as a result of counseling sessions geared to her Moneymax Profile. She realized that hard work and discipline, over a long period of time, would be necessary to alter her money behavior, but she felt that the potential end result was worth the price.

One of Georgia's liabilities was her impulsive decision-making with money—as it is with other High Rollers—and she worked on transforming her emotional spending into a structured savings program so she could ultimately start to build financial security.

After reducing her debt to a manageable level through personal sacrifice, which including paying off eleven of her fourteen credit cards, Georgia was ready to make investments. She began by opening a money market account, and every month forced herself to deposit at least $500. Discipline doesn't come easy to the High Rollers, and changing her spending behavior did cause Georgia some anxiety. However, she was able to sustain her financial commitments because she was altering the dead-end course she had been on.

Georgia is rebuilding her financial life very slowly and now understands that her high tolerance for risk, if properly handled, could become an asset. She currently has a systematic monthly investment plan in conservative growth mutual funds. This kind of slow and diligent process is usually not attractive, nor tolerable, for the High Rollers, who prefer faster and more exciting action but this is a strategy that will work for them.

Within the next few years, Georgia wants to start looking for a home so she can start to build equity, and her forced savings plan will provide her with the cash for the down payment. She hopes eventually to make a career change and saving her money will enable her to do that with more financial security and peace of mind, both of which she has learned to value.

IN PARTNERSHIP: TWO HIGH ROLLERS

Flo grew up in a small town outside of Eugene, Oregon. Her father, a quiet and unassuming man, worked for the city government, made a modest income, and always stressed the importance of frugality and saving money for his retirement. Flo's mother was a housewife, had never worked, and took great pride in her family and her home.

When asked how her mother was with money, Flo replied: "She never had enough. You see, my father had a college education and she didn't. Mother always felt that he always put her down because he was more educated. Whenever they had a fight about money, she told him that he was the one with the college education, and if it was so valuable, then why wasn't he making more money. My uncle, who was a plumber, made more money than Dad. My mother always reminded him of that when she was mad. Mother wasn't exactly a spendthrift, but she always bought the things that her friends had, even if she really couldn't afford them. She grew up in a big family—was the youngest of nine. I guess her family was pretty poor. She always talked about how she never got anything new; she always got secondhand things like her sister's clothes and her brother's bike. When I was growing up, she was the one who paid the bills but my father made up the budget. She always complained about his numbers, especially for food and household things. She tried to get him to go shopping with her so he could see what things really cost but he would never go with her."

When Flo graduated from college, she moved to Los Angeles to take a job in the accounting department of a large hotel chain. It was an outstanding job and she wanted to move to Los Angeles because her sister and brother-in-law lived there. Flo worked her way through the company ranks and eventually was promoted to controller. During her early years with the company, Flo lived with her sister, paid minimum rent, and saved most of her money. She earned a good salary and bought a duplex in an upwardly mobile, trendy area, which she rented out. Flo was quite proud of her real estate investment and continued living with her sister until she met John, her future husband.

John was a real estate broker so they had a lot in common, and Flo was grateful for all the advice John gladly shared with her. He was handsome, dynamic, and quite different from the intellectuals she usually dated. While he was rich on paper and thin on cash, they went out frequently even if only to a movie and an inexpensive restaurant. Flo was captivated by John's take-charge style; he was a real decision-maker and a man who had great ambition and drive. He talked as much about the future as the present and was confident that life offered vast rewards for those who had the courage to go out and get them. John was attracted to Flo because she wasn't a man hunter, the dependent and desperate type. She had her own career, was a shrewd businesswoman, yet had a female vulnerability and sweetness that were very appealing. And she didn't try to change his strong-willed ways; she didn't try to "rein him in," as he put it. They were married less than six months after they met.

Soon after they were married, John located a large tract of land on the outskirts of Ventura County, perfect for a small shopping center. He convinced Flo to sell her rental duplex and relinquish a second trust deed she had acquired several years before. He also persuaded her sister and brother-in-law to invest and was even able to squeeze a small sum of money from her father. Flo's boss at work contributed $150,000 and became a general partner. John developed a very professional prospectus and attracted several other investors. He quit his job and at the same time bought a new house for Flo on the west side of Los Angeles. While he continued to work on the shopping center complex, John zeroed in on another prospective windfall, a piece of land suitable for an office complex. He asked Flo for what was left of her meager savings and set out to get more capital. John was feeling great; he was his own boss and the future looked very bright indeed.

Almost one year after the shopping center deal began, it came to an abrupt end due to difficulties with a utilities company lease agreement for part of the land—something John said would never be a problem. All of the investors were in an uproar, particularly Flo's family and her boss. John and Flo lost their new home and had to declare bankruptcy.

John's calamitous business dealings placed an enormous strain on Flo's personal and professional life. Her parents were furious and her boss barely spoke to her. Until she met John, she had been a good money manager; she made a living from her knowledge of sound financial practices. Now she had a bad credit rating, no assets, and no money except for her salary. Her marriage was in serious trouble and she recognized that she and her husband needed professional help. While John refused to seek marriage counseling, he did agree to try financial counseling.

At our first meeting, he said, "Well, I guess I had to come close to losing everything before I woke up. First my money, now my wife." He was concerned about "his" money even though the money he lost did not belong to him. He felt little, if no, remorse. In the second meeting, John spent fifteen minutes trying to negotiate a lower fee and asked that he not pay anything up front but be billed for all meetings. John canceled the third meeting and never returned. Flo continued to work on solving her financial problems even after she divorced John.

John was a grand manipulator, a man who was not only self-destructive but also took his destruction out on others. He was a High Roller who never intended to test his own merits but used others for his own self-aggrandizement. Flo was also a High Roller even though she had had a good financial start. The hole in her armor was her vulnerability to John and what he represented. She risked everything for him—her career, her family, and her self-respect.

John obviously did not want to change his money style. For him the pain was only momentary and it was a lot easier once again to go down the path of least resistance rather than to take a hard and honest look at himself. For John it made much more sense to cash in on what others had accomplished with their money.

Flo, on the other hand, has a good chance of becoming financially successful and secure. She may have lost for the last time. She was attracted to John's High Roller style because she too was a High Roller. Flo's style was a lot less obvious than John's but she did want to feel powerful and important, even though much of her need was played out vicariously through John's escapades. Her desire for an exciting life stopped her from seeing personal and financial reality. Her perceptual skills were contaminated by her need to believe in John and all of the promises he made.

REFRAMING POINTS FOR HIGH ROLLERS

As a group, High Rollers have many positive, admirable characteristics. They have keen perceptual skills and move with ease from philosophizing about an idea to taking action. They have the ability to approach a problem from many angles and come up with creative interpretations and solutions. High Rollers can function effectively in unstructured work environments. They seek out the novel and uncertain and are willing to take risks to succeed. However, their poor money management skills tend to counteract their inherent creative and ambitious nature. The following guidelines can serve as a beginning for change for this Moneymax Profile:

1. *Reevaluate your risk-taking.* If you are risking, have a thorough understanding of all the ground rules. Some ventures can be won; some cannot. Learn to know the difference; calculate your risks and act accordingly.

2. *Set your priorities.* Monetary success requires definitive goals and a plan to achieve them. Establish high standards of excellence and continually evaluate your progress against your standards.

3. *Choose moderation over extreme.* Moderate goals are preferable to long shots.

4. *Know your limits.* Be realistic about your current financial status and don't risk more than you can afford to lose.

5. *Get control over your money.* Assuming full responsibility and control over your money will replace anxiety with confidence.

6. *Remove emotions from your money.* Risking out of rebellion, fear, hurt, or anger contaminates goal-oriented risk-taking.

7. *Reevaluate your drive for power.* Use power for your own benefit and not to impress others.

8. *Take time to grow.* Patience may be a hard pill to swallow but diligence combined with talent and goal-oriented risk-taking will pay off.

MONEY MANAGEMENT STYLE

1. The High Rollers are tied with the Hunters for the highest satisfaction with the results of owning commercial property, perhaps because of their strong motive for power and prestige with their money. However, successful investing requires a rational instead of an emotional approach such as knowing how to evaluate a property as to its price and profit potential versus an emotional approach, which is often the High Rollers' style and downfall.

2. Interestingly, they perceive commodities/options and futures contracts as highest in risk of all investment vehicles and are the most satisfied with these investments. Obviously, because High Rollers derive a great deal of their satisfaction from the emotional charge they receive from their money, this seems logical. In contrast, the financial tools that least interest the High Rollers are savings accounts and whole life insurance (lackluster vehicles).

3. The High Rollers are satisfied investors in money market accounts. They and the Money Masters are the most satisfied of all nine groups with this financial vehicle.

4. Even though the High Rollers are the most satisfied of all groups with money market accounts, they are even more satisfied with commodities/options and futures contracts.

5. They express a significant preference for use of commodities/options over futures contracts.

6. When they invest in common stock, the High Rollers have a tendency to choose direct ownership versus mutual funds. With individual common stocks, there is more of a personal challenge involved in selecting stocks as opposed to the mutual fund concept, which has professional management.

7. The High Rollers have the lowest satisfaction of all Moneymax groups with all insurance vehicles.

8. It is advisable that High Rollers seek professional guidance when making investment decisions. Such an adviser should have the ability to counsel this risk-seeking money personality type. The adviser should have not only a broad base of investment knowledge but also a fundamental understanding of the motivations, shortcomings, and potential for maximizing financial success that are possible for the High Rollers. High Rollers should consult with someone who can educate

them about various investments and who can determine the percentage of the portfolio that should be allocated to the different levels of growth, safety, income, and tax advantage.

HIGH ROLLERS—FINANCIAL STATEMENT

Of all nine Moneymax groups, the High Rollers are the highest risk-takers and the group that wants the most power with money. The need for "money power" tends to make them take extreme risks or set impossibly high goals because the desire for prestige and status is greater than the desire for financial achievement. Whether they are making an investment or waging a bet, the High Rollers do not clearly size up the probability of success or, conversely, the probability of failure. The High Rollers experience a great deal of anxiety when managing money, making financial decisions, and thinking about decisions already made. They have low pride and contentment with their financial accomplishments. Like the Hunters, they are highly emotional with money.

In income the High Rollers rank seventh of the nine Moneymax groups; in assets they rank eighth of nine. A lack of goals, game plans, and focused persistance are their financial downfall. Once corrected, their ambition, drive, and penchant for risk will likely result in an escalation of both income and assets. They have a definite predilection for becoming Entrepreneurs. The High Rollers rank "current income" as their number-one investment priority—before appreciation, safety, and tax advantage. They tend to be young, single, and divorced.

8

<hr />

Safety Players

Security is mostly a superstition. It does not exist in nature, nor do the children of men as a whole experience it. Avoiding danger is no safer in the long run than outright exposure. Life is either a daring adventure or nothing.

—Helen Keller

Human felicity is produced not so much by great pieces of good fortune that seldom happen by as by little advantages that occur every day.

—Ben Franklin

GUIDELINES

Safety Players

. . . Believe that their financial fate is often cast by forces outside of their own control.

. . . Have a tendency to be more passive with their money than to actively take charge of their money management.

. . . Don't often feel in control of their financial security but don't particularly worry about it.

. . . Have a tendency to make financial decisions without a lot of analysis.

. . . Are skeptical of whether financial success can be attributed to hard work.

. . . Have a high level of doubt that people can be trusted when their money is concerned.

. . . Tend to disbelieve that people will be financially generous with others less fortunate.

Do you believe that being in the right place at the right time is the main reason you landed a good job, or a promotion, or an increase in salary? Or do you believe those accomplishments were earned by your ability and experience? When your investment nose-dived, did you chalk it up to bad luck or to a poor decision? In other words, do you believe you are mainly responsible for your financial success or failure, or do you attribute financial outcomes to fatalistic, external forces?

Your answers indicate whether you are self-determined and feel primarily responsible for life's events; or whether you are fatalistic and perceive yourself more as a money victim, subject to outside forces which are beyond your control.

If you believe that money comes and goes as a result of luck or fate, that it is under the control of powerful others, or that money gains and losses are unpredictable because of the great complexity of the financial structure, then you believe that your money life is governed and shaped by the world around you. You are fatalistic, externally controlled. If, however, you believe that who you are and the actions you take directly influence the outcome of financial decisions, then you accept responsibility for financial losses and are proud of financial gains. You are therefore self-determined or internally controlled.

People are not totally internally or externally controlled with their money. Belief in self-determination is a continuum, and everyone falls somewhere along that continuum. It should be emphasized that the money behavior of an individual in any given situation is a result of many converging factors and self-determination tendencies may vary accordingly. However, the Moneymax continuum with self-determination at one end and fatalism at the polar opposite definitely characterizes Moneymax Profiles as having one tendency or the other.

Self-determined Moneymax Profiles like the Money Masters and the Achievers believe that financial rewards come through skills, brains, and perseverance. Any monetary mishap or failure means that more effort must be put forth. Outside influences are considered but play only a minor role. These profiles believe that they can put their own plan for financial success into effect; they have complete confidence in their own abilities to move ahead, and they will assume all responsibility for doing what has to be done to succeed. If they fail, they will fail because they did not put enough time and effort into the plan, and not because they did not have the right skills, or because fate stepped in at the last moment and brought everything crashing down.

The Moneymax Profiles who take a more fatalistic position, like the Safety Players, tend to see both monetary success and failure as a matter of luck, a gamble that worked, or a gift bestowed by the money gods. As fatalistic money believers, they steer toward structured, bureaucratic work environments and tend not to enter the entrepreneurial arena. Safety Players would like someone else to assume responsibility for their money actions and the consequences of those actions.

A Safety Player investor who lost money might protest, "My stockbroker led me astray." A self-determined profile like the Money Master would say: "My stockbroker's got to give me more facts before I decide to buy again. I should have spent more time evaluating that investment."

When Safety Players do acquire profits, they often attribute their financial success to reasons such as, "I was just lucky that the market was doing well," "that broker certainly chose the right stock," "the competition wasn't that hot." And when they fail, Safety Players don't look to themselves for the answer but feel that the fates intervened at the wrong time, that they trusted the wrong person, that the decks were stacked against them.

The Safety Players are average income earners and accumulators of assets. They are comprised of many two-income families and many have dependent children in the home. They are predominantly married and are older rather than younger—46 percent are over fifty years old and 13 percent are under thirty. As many live in the city as in the country, as many live on the West Coast as on the East Coast, as many have college degrees as have only high school diplomas.

Savings accounts are, by far, the most preferred strategy for Safety Players—no worries, no effort. Of all the Moneymax groups, the

Safety Players have the highest use of savings accounts; 89 percent of them have had or currently have savings accounts. However, of all the Moneymax groups the Safety Players are the *least* satisfied with savings accounts. After savings accounts, they use whole life insurance, residential/rental properties, and government bonds.

Since their expectations are low for financial growth and asset accumulation, Safety Players are reluctant to investigate other financial vehicles. For example, they show little interest in corporate bonds (80 percent of this group have never owned or want to own corporate bonds). The Safety Players probably perceive this investment as beyond their understanding and expertise because it relates to an unfamiliar set of financial circumstances. If they were to spend time in understanding this investment, either through their own individual efforts or those of a financial adviser, more of the Safety Players would learn, as some already have, that high quality corporate bonds can be better investments than savings accounts—the return is greater and there can be ample safety. Since the Safety Players' highest financial objective is current income, corporate bonds or bond funds, properly selected, as well as other investment opportunities, like tax-free municipal bonds or government securities funds, would likely meet their desire for current income. Those Safety Players who have put their money in corporate bonds or bond funds have been satisfied with their investments.

Safety Players take the easy way out by placing their money in the bank, recognize and admit that savings accounts are a source of dissatisfaction, yet are reluctant to change their habits and money management style. While they do want to become better money managers, they feel incapable of affecting desired financial results. They have intelligence and formal education but lack confidence and motivation.

The Safety Players share many similar demographic characteristics with the Money Masters. Both have basically the same educational background, are roughly the same age, and have a similar percentage of professional/managerial careers. However, there is a vast difference in net worth or accumulated assets—the Money Masters have a third more in net assets than the Safety Players.

The reasons for this significant difference lie in their financial personalities. The Safety Players and the Money Masters are at opposite ends of the spectrum when it comes to attributing the reasons for financial success, the control exercised over money management, trust in the financial honesty of others, and the degree that hard work contributes to financial success in life.

The Money Masters know how to make a dollar stretch for maximum benefit, usually make wise financial decisions, and are in control of their purse strings, aware of what comes in and what goes out. The Safety Players are more passive and allow outside events and people to take charge of their destiny. Safety Players enter the money game by betting that they will be either the beneficiaries or victims of luck and fate. They would rather rely on the advice of others instead of digging in to challenge themselves, improve their performance, and assure their success. They want to go on the money ride but would rather sit in the passenger seat than drive.

The Money Masters, who have the highest scores in self-determination, are also the greatest accumulators of assets and the most content with their money. Whereas, the Safety Players, who have the lowest scores in self-determination, are fifth of the nine profiles in assets and are not content with their money status. The Money Masters also have the highest trust that people are basically honest in dealing with money, while the Safety Players are skeptical that people can always be trusted with financial transactions.

The Safety Players do not assume control of their money, would rather be passive, yet at the same time, don't trust that others will be honest in financial dealings. Thus, they find themselves in a very uncomfortable predicament: they are reluctant to assume responsibility to improve their financial status and they don't trust the advice and expertise of others who might be of valuable assistance.

It may be easier to believe that you are in control of your money when you are financially successful, but the Safety Players are far from financially destitute. They are middle income earners with average asset accumulation. When compared with the other Moneymax Profiles, it is very evident that the Safety Players could have even more assets and be more prosperous and content if they would alter their orientation about money.

In my practice I have counseled Safety Players by suggesting that they adhere to the following game plan:

First, outline your financial objectives for the short, intermediate, and long term. For instance, during the next twelve months, what are your needs and desires and how much money will it take to meet those goals (a new car, appliance, vacation, home)? The same type of thinking should then be applied to three-to-five-year goals and then for the next six to fifteen years or longer—college for the kids, retirement, a vacation home, and so forth.

Second, write down your assets and liabilities, and make a list (from canceled checks if necessary) of everything you spent money on during the previous one-year period. Preparing this list may be one of the hardest tasks you have ever faced since most people don't really know what they spend money on, and frankly don't want to know.

Step three is to seek out several different advisers: accountants, brokers, or financial planners who have the proper credentials and a good reputation (be sure to check references). After you have decided which of these people you want to work with and a plan has been prepared, give yourself a chance by adopting some of the recommendations. Watch the results and the quality of service over time and build slowly and cautiously. Remember that a Safety Player money personality feels much greater peace of mind when eased into financial and investment planning instead of being overwhelmed initially.

This approach is geared to help Safety Players really change their behavior from a lack of involvement and a fatalistic approach, to an action-oriented, take-charge strategy. Without this kind of plan, the Safety Players will likely repeat their past mistakes.

The Safety Players need to develop a good internal barometer and perceptual system so they can better detect and read the internal and external forces that impact their money management style. They need to realize that some things are under their control and others are not, and the first step toward financial well-being is to learn which is which. Their financial plight in life is not predestined. Financial struggles and unfulfilled aspirations need not be a continuing part of life.

The Safety Players need a new belief system about financial success —that luck is when opportunity meets preparation. No doubt the equation is tricky. Some people earnestly believe that success comes from being in the right place at the right time. I prefer to believe that it takes skill, persistence, and initiative to be in the right place at the right time. Oftentimes, successful investors will hit upon what they call a lucky stock choice. But if they examine their previous behavior, what they often find is that their experience gave them the knowledge and confidence to go with that choice at that time instead of passing it up or deliberating until the opportunity was gone.

The Safety Players play it safe because they are unsure of the outcome, the probability of success. When they are challenged, they invest less effort, time, and personal resources than do other more affluent Moneymax groups. Whereas the Entrepreneurs would adopt a strategy to maximize the number of favorable monetary outcomes, the Safety Players would likely rely on hunches or stick with a plan used previously in a similar situation. The Entrepreneurs want to assure themselves as much as possible that they will win. Even though the Entrepreneurs are not conservative planners and do take risks, they try to control fate. The Safety Players are creatures of money habits. They rely on what seemed to work the last time or what felt most secure. By remaining in the comfort zone, they don't stretch themselves and don't push forward.

Safety Players rarely sit down and say, "I'm afraid of financial responsibility." Admitting that truth is painful and suggests that one should examine the fear and take action to correct it. Most Safety Players like to think that they do take advantage of opportunities as they are offered—even if they don't. Take those Safety Players, for example, who are offered, but refuse, promotions from one department in a company to another department. They rationalize and justify the reluctance to make a move by saying: "Well, I know everyone over here. We work well together and get along. There's a good morale. The extra money isn't that much and won't be worth much if the new job doesn't work out. I don't want to leave here." Those statements may all be true but may not be the genuine reason for turning down a job promotion.

If someone can establish a solid job performance and good relationships in one position, why can't they be established in a new position? The Safety Players don't think the situation through for themselves because it might reveal some personal feelings that they would prefer to avoid. Because the Safety Players attribute success or failure to forces outside of themselves—not their knowledge, nor their skills, nor their energies—they are just as likely to anticipate failure as success. Low expectations for success have a great influence on the likelihood of hard work culminating in financial success.

Fatalism certainly impacts their belief in the work ethic. Safety

Players can become very disillusioned and lose incentive and drive when they are unsure of whether all their efforts will pay off. They can become cynical rather than trusting, indifferent rather than ambitious, and cautious about change rather than ready and willing to risk. They say they are somewhat proud of the way they handle their money but not very content. They say they don't feel very emotional about their money nor extremely anxious or worried about it, but that may be a rationalization.

Safety Players have learned to deny their discomfort with their financial status. They try to deny reality—pretend it's different—and make excuses for not taking control of their financial destinies. They hold onto their self-esteem by undercutting their ambition and the role of money in their lives: "I don't care about having money; it causes too much trouble anyway. Look what it's done to Uncle Sam or Aunt Rose or the Tompkins next door."

Safety Players assume a role of indifference and nonchalance. It is difficult for them to take risks and attempt to change when the game is to pretend that they simply don't care. So intent on maintaining the status quo, the pretense that everything is okay, the Safety Players don't prepare or motivate themselves to step out and take a look at how they feel or what they really want. So what that a Camaro is in the garage instead of a Lincoln? Moving into a new home in a better neighborhood would be nice but it's not that necessary. Compared with others, they aren't doing badly; they're not interested in planning, doing, risking.

The "I'm doing just fine" pretense serves the purpose of saving face regarding money or lack of ambition. Safety Players value the facade because it protects their self-esteem and plugs up the holes in their armor. They typically don't try to win the money contest but either pretend to try or make some excuse about why they weren't able to do their best. Thus, they can rationalize failure to themselves and save face with others if the reason for not winning is because they didn't put their "all" into it.

They do not allow themselves to go after what really matters to them. They deny their desires, rationalize them away. Somehow they manage to sidestep opportunities—lack of time, sickness, family emergency, some reasonable excuse. They are good at pretending that the reason they are not really involved with money is because they choose not to be involved.

Success is intellectually and emotionally a foreign game to them. Acknowledging their skills and intelligence and allowing others to watch them stumble, climb, and risk is too threatening. To be evaluated by someone else's standards puts the Safety Players in too vulnerable a position, so rather than risk failure and rejection, they back off. Whatever they do with money usually lacks active participation, which results in money and greater wealth being "out of their control." Sometimes the frustration of not having control leads to impulsive financial decision-making. Safety Players will jump into an investment and then jump out just as quickly, leaving a cloud of dust for someone else to cope with.

They can be provocative, both personally and financially. A Safety Player will tell you that he wants to invest in a time-share ski condominium, that she wants to splurge and go to a four-star restaurant, that he will take a hotel room with a full-ocean rather than a partial-ocean view, that she prefers the orchestra seats in the theater to the balcony, that he can be counted on in the next group outing to the seashore. When the time comes for them to show up or pay up, the Safety Players are often missing.

They want to believe that they are participants and more importantly that others see them as participants. They go through the whole rehearsal of getting ready for the theater, the restaurant, the vacation, but back out at the last minute. Maybe they didn't want to spend any money at all; maybe they would have gone if the seats had been balcony instead of orchestra; maybe they weren't interested in the particular activity. Nonetheless, they didn't want to acknowledge the truth and risk not belonging to or alienating the group. A Safety Player will agree to play golf on Saturday morning with the guys from the office, then phone in and cancel late Friday night. On Monday morning, he will congratulate the winner and in the spirit of camaraderie say, "You might not have won if I had been there to give you some real competition. I feel bad that I had to cancel. But wait until the next time."

Safety Players want to be viewed as active participants, as part of the team. Unfortunately, they often promise what they cannot deliver. They can disappoint and anger others when they don't follow through on a commitment or own up to the truth or say yes when they really mean no. When confronted and pinned down to account for their contradictory behavior, they have a fistful of excuses and a "who me?" attitude.

Some Safety Players are easy to recognize because they play it safe in every area from investments to careers to personal relationships. Others are much more difficult to identify. A Safety Player may buy a new car every few years and purchase a top-of-the-line washing machine but may balk at staying at any hotel above budget prices or shopping anywhere but a discount store. A Safety Player husband may wholeheartedly promise his wife a European vacation if they should ever have an extra $10,000. The truth is that if the $10,000 ever appeared, he would probably head straight to the bank, perhaps holding back a small sum for a week's vacation at a nearby resort.

A Safety Player who is a compulsive saver and budgeter may generously volunteer his time and services to friends—fixing appliances, painting a house, paving a driveway—yet accept not a dime in compensation. Again, the money pretense appears: this is who I want you to think I am even if I'm not. Not all Safety Players will send out the same signals or clues but there is an overall pattern to their behavior.

Many Safety Players spend entire lives acting out money roles that are very close to the money styles they desire but won't go out and build. They don't see the difference between their pretend money style and self and their real money style and self. The defense systems, shored up and rationalized over many years, are quite sturdy and invincible to bolts of reality.

Safety Players are typically resistant to change. They disavow the fact that they are truly the center of their financial system because they have a lot invested in disbelieving. Initially, they tend to reject the suggestion that they create a better money self with more positive attitudes and behaviors. They feel uncomfortable with financial responsibility, thinking it may somehow leave them overwhelmed, vulnerable, and poor.

But their acquiescence produces anger and frustration that become trapped within themselves even though they try to detach them. If financial problems, disappointments, unresolved ambitions are detached or put out of focus, then the Safety Players have no reason to be anxious or bothered. Then the way they have conducted their financial lives is justified according to the way they believe the money system works.

Despite their superb powers of rationalization, Safety Players have a deep, unresolved feeling that they deserve better, but they don't trust that feeling and put it to the test. They'd rather not know than be disappointed. It's easier to stick to their basic philosophy: "Life is a struggle. I must be careful with my money. Most people don't get what they want no matter how hard they try. Even if I made more money, it might not make me happier and I'd just have to pay more taxes. I should be satisfied with what I've got."

Safety Players are motivated more by avoiding failure than by achieving greater financial success. The way for them to avoid the evils of money is to protect themselves and minimize loss. They are also afraid of the unknown. They understand their present financial situation and even if they have misgivings about money management, it's better to be safe than sorry.

Safety Players need to risk placing themselves inside their money ambitions. By remaining detached, they have created an unrealistic "secure and safe" financial environment which leads to stagnation and frustration. So while they opt for security and safety, they do so at the expense of variety, stimulation, and creativity.

They carry around a lot of "what ifs?" and unrealized potential. Despite all this, the Safety Players rank fourth in income and fifth in assets among all Moneymax groups. They could substantially increase their net worth if they would change their current money patterns, consider new investment opportunities, and assume more control and responsibility for their finances.

ENTERING ALIEN TERRITORY

A Safety Player is unlikely to welcome the prospect of being in business with an Entrepreneur but such was the case with Fred, who at age forty-six had been co-owner of an independent car repair shop for nineteen years. The death of his partner, Karl, meant that Karl's half of the business was passed to Peter, Karl's only son. Fred and Peter had known each other for years but Peter had never worked at the repair shop and it was quite a shock when Fred learned that Peter intended to quit his job and become Fred's full-time partner.

Fred had been working since he was twelve years old. His father was an alcoholic and, unable to hold down a full-time job, had moved through a number of part-time positions. Everyone in Fred's family worked; his mother was a cashier at a grocery store and his two younger brothers, like Fred, started at a young age to mow lawns, paint houses, and do other neighborhood jobs to bring in money. Fred had to turn in a portion of his weekly earnings to his father, who usually complained that it wasn't enough or that Fred was withholding too much for himself.

When he was older, Fred got a part-time job bagging groceries at the market where his mother worked. The owner of the market was a car buff who tinkered with repairs on his own car on weekends. Fred, always in need of money, helped the owner on weekends and by the time he graduated from high school he was skilled enough to get a job as a mechanic at a local auto repair shop.

For ten years Fred worked for several different repair shops until he met with a business offer he couldn't refuse. One of his coworkers, Karl, wanted to open his own repair shop and needed a partner. The deal was very appealing to Fred since Karl would put up most of the money needed for start-up and Fred could pay him back, with interest, out of his earnings. They would be equal partners, sharing in all profits and all decisions. Fred was somewhat hesitant to accept since, like most Safety Players, he felt more comfortable with a secure, permanent job and never thought much about being in business for himself. However, the offer was too good to pass up. He didn't have to invest much money and if the business failed, he could still get another job.

The repair shop was located on a heavily trafficked boulevard in Los Angeles and since the city's lifestyle is built around the automobile, the new business got off to a good start. Both Fred and Karl worked in the shop five days a week and closed on weekends. They serviced both foreign and domestic cars and after five years had built up a loyal clientele. From time to time they hired a few extra mechanics but for the most part they worked with a small crew.

Even though the business could have doubled or tripled in size, they chose not to expand. Each wanted to spend time with his family— Fred had married and was the father of one son. They were able to service a fair number of cars a day if the work was mostly tune-ups and minor repair jobs. When a larger job was involved, Fred simply told the customer that they were a small outfit, did excellent work at reasonable prices, but the cars would have to remain in the shop for three or four days. The thought of expanding was an option Fred never seriously considered. Safety Players are not about to take too many chances, especially when it comes to money. To expand the business would have required some risk, a certain amount of planning, and a lot of personal involvement. Unless the outcome is certain, Safety Players prefer not to rock the boat. As long as Fred's business was providing him with an adequate living, he wasn't about to leave his comfort zone and step into alien territory.

Fred's wife Sarah worked a full-time job but came in twice a week to do the bookkeeping and his son came in during summer vacations to clean up and learn the business. Sarah complained that Fred could afford to hire someone to do the books but he refused, saying that it was an unnecessary expense. His son also complained about spending his summer vacation in the shop since he really wasn't interested in making a career out of his father's business. But Fred insisted that everyone in the family had to put some work and effort into the business.

Fred was certainly a better provider than his father had been. He was proud of his shop; it brought in enough money to support his family even if they couldn't take fancy vacation trips or buy some of the things that his wife wanted. He owned a small two-bedroom house, had two cars, and a savings account that he added to every week.

He was, however, concerned about money for his retirement. Neither he nor his wife would ever benefit from pension plans and Fred was particularly concerned about what would happen if anyone in the family became seriously ill. As long as his wife worked, they were all covered by a medical plan even though the plan was not very comprehensive.

As he got older Fred became so worried about retirement that he decided to take some of his money out of the savings account and try a few investments. By the time he was forty-six he had accumulated a fairly sizable nest egg due mostly to the fact that he was a very diligent saver.

At first he tried investing in a few blue chip stocks but he always seemed to buy when the market was up and didn't hold the stocks long enough to make a decent profit. (Safety Players, as a rule, avoid investing in the stock market.) He selected his investments after hearing how several good friends had made some money in the stock market. They must have known what they were doing since they had turned a profit and Fred didn't have the time to become a financial whiz. He was too busy working. He never sought investment advice from a professional (clearly a mistake for the Safety Player) and rarely read the business pages of the newspaper. His first foray into personal investing resulted in a loss of $3,000.

After his first loss, Fred returned to putting all his money into his savings account to try and recoup what he had lost. Then he read a magazine article about tax-free municipal bonds, which appeared very safe, according to the magazine. However, he still wasn't able to evaluate market risk and he got trapped again. As the market for bonds turned downward, he waited too long, and before he knew what was happening, the underlying value of his bond portfolio depreciated significantly. He sold at a loss—this time for $2,500. Again, he had relied on his own limited financial expertise and again he had lost money.

Fred was frustrated and angry at himself but still too distrustful and stubborn to trust anyone else's advice about his money. However, he knew that taxes and inflation were eating away at what was left in his savings account. He did receive flyers in the mail and calls from investment counseling services and brokerage houses. But he didn't believe that the financial professionals were giving him good advice; they were just trying to make a commission. All in all, it was easier to keep his money in the bank where he knew it was safe.

Fred had succumbed to one of his strongest money personality traits —lack of trust. Of all the Moneymax groups, the Safety Players have the lowest belief that people can be trusted when talking about or dealing with money. Even though his forays into the investment world were not successful, Fred's lack of trust prevented him from listening to professional financial advice.

Two years after his second loss, Fred was feeling better about his financial state as he was trying harder than ever to rebuild his savings account. Then his partner died. It was a terrible shock since Karl was only fifty-six, ten years older than Fred, and seemed to be in good health. They had never discussed what would happen to the business if either of them died or wanted to sell out. They had an ongoing joke about how they would work right up to retirement, sell the business for a "fortune" if neither of their sons wanted to take over, and go on a long vacation trip around the world.

Three months after Karl's death, his son Peter asked Fred to spend a Saturday with him so they could discuss the future of the business. Fred assumed that he would continue to run the business alone, that Peter would be a silent partner but share equally in all the profits. But Peter presented Fred with a business plan to expand the shop. Peter said he had been studying the books and that the shop could make considerably more money. He wanted to buy a small vacant lot next to the shop so they could expand and service more cars and hire a few more employees. Peter also proposed that they move into body and paint work in addition to servicing cars. He had already been to several banks about securing loans and thought Fred would be impressed with how much work he had done.

Fred was so overwhelmed that he only muttered that he would think over Peter's proposal and call him in a few weeks. For several nights Fred hardly slept as he pondered his options although none of them seemed right. He could sell out to Peter but he wasn't sure how much to ask and even if he did sell out, he was too young to retire and he didn't want to go out and look for a new job. He could try to talk Peter out of the expansion idea, hoping that his long friendship with Karl would count for something. Or he could go along with Peter's plan and take the chance of losing everything he had worked for all of his life. Fred did not want to expand the business, did not want to put his own money into it, nor did he want to take out a bank loan. All he could think of was bankruptcy. He had a copy of Peter's business proposal but it didn't make much sense to him. Fred was angry and unnerved and wondered how something like this had ever happened to him.

If Fred had not been forced into such a position, he probably never would have sought financial advice. Peter, realizing what a dilemma he had created for Fred, made an appointment for both of them with an accountant who used the Moneymax Profile. Once they realized how far apart their money and business attitudes were—with Peter profiling as an Entrepreneur and Fred as a Safety Player—they decided to see if they could make some compromises and still stay in business together.

The issues they had to discuss revolved around the differences in their money personalities: Safety Players are not very involved with money while Entrepreneurs are highly involved; Safety Players are not willing to take risks but Entrepreneurs are quite comfortable with risk; Safety Players have low expectations for success while Entrepreneurs are self-assured and expect to win; Safety Players manage to sidestep opportunities but Entrepreneurs seek out and create opportunities; Safety Players are more concerned with avoiding failure than achieving success while Entrepreneurs don't worry about failure and are confident of success.

Eventually they did expand the business, not to the extent that Peter proposed but enough to make the shop more profitable. In the process Fred had to learn considerably more about money and business. At first, he was constantly agitated and nervous about every decision. They did take out a small bank loan but one that Fred said he could learn to live with. As he became more confident, and as the business continued to do well, Fred became more comfortable with his financial picture and began to realize that his business was his own best investment.

After talking with bank loan officers and the accountant, he wasn't so perplexed by financial issues and finally sought out some professional advice on what to do with the money in his personal savings account. Remember that Fred, like most Safety Players, was reluctant to take some additional risk with his money in order to stay ahead of inflation and taxes, but he decided to ease himself into the process. Fred agreed that a diversified group of investments geared to monthly income but also with some growth aspects would be suitable for him. After carefully studying the options presented to him, he withdrew some of his savings and invested it in growth and income mutual funds.

Fred is still having a little difficulty dealing with his new financial life, but he has given up thoughts of bankruptcy. As his income and assets continue to grow, he will become more aware of how he can continue to enhance his Moneymax Profile and make the most of opportunities that are available to him.

FEAR OF FAILURE AND LOSS

America is labeled the land of great opportunity where the promise of competition, success, and affluence are embodied in the national philosophy. Because we are the most success-oriented nation in the world, it follows that we can also be viewed as a nation of winners and losers. Success suggests achievement, recognition, pride, honor, self-worth, and money. Failure suggests loss, nonperformance, insolvency, weakness, disgrace, humiliation, self-doubt. Many of us believe that the best thing about success is the absence of failure.

While much has been written about success, it still eludes exact definition, and the path to success lacks a blueprint to follow. Failure, about which little has been written, is less ambiguous. Business and personal conversations are likely to be more focused when talking about failure than about success. Reasons for failure are more identifiable: He didn't try hard enough. She couldn't stand the pressure. He doesn't know how to play the game. She didn't have the right connections. He didn't follow through with the plan. She is all talk, but never gets results. He didn't have enough money to get started. She was way out of her league. He can't get along with people. She just can't zero in on the problem.

Everyone has experienced a number of failures in life. Fortunately, in this greatest of all democracies, everyone is given some share of failure. It crosses boundaries of age, sex, race, job status, money status. We fail in school, in careers, in personal relationships. And usually there is a way to measure the degree of failure for ourselves and others to see—report cards, job performance evaluations, marriage certificates and divorce decrees, financial statements. No one likes the feelings that accompany failure—depression, anger, terror, fear, guilt, betrayal, vengeance.

Unfortunately, some of us have never learned that there can be a positive, constructive side to failure. Painful as it may be, it teaches us much about who we are, what we need to change, and what pitfalls to avoid when we next move forward. Failure allows us to better evaluate options presented to us and gain mastery over many parts of our lives. It can build stronger backbones and survival skills. Once you truly believe you are a survivor, it becomes easier to step out and risk a little more the next time. The bottom line is that unless you are willing to risk failure, it is not likely that you will achieve very much.

Failing in a job or personal relationship can be devastating, but both have built-in avenues of escape—namely, other people to share in the failure. The boss was a jerk, the boyfriend was a loser, the company was poorly managed or in financial difficulty. If that's not enough, there is another lineup of candidates waiting to share blame—your parents, your upbringing, your bad luck, your education, even "the system" that is omnipotent and unjust. However, if you alone are managing your money and if you fail to do a top-notch job, there are fewer scapegoats around. Lurking inside is the persistent, nagging thought that you are doing something wrong. Safety Players can become quite astute at ignoring the fact that they need to take a second look at their financial situation. Money equals hard-earned security and to risk losing that security is a hard corner to turn.

George, a Safety Player, was fifty-eight and had retired from a management position with a state government agency, after having worked there for thirty-two years. He was having a tough time adjusting to retirement—depressed, anxious about money, frequent stomach ailments, weight loss. It was a marked contrast to the healthy and jovial image George usually conveyed. He wasn't sorry that he left his job; thirty-two years with the government had been quite enough.

His wife, Joyce, and children, Jason and Lisa, had numerous suggestions about what he should do with his free time but George vetoed practically everything, especially any suggestion that involved his money. George's father had lived to be eighty-five, his mother to be ninety-one. If longevity ran in the family, George expected to be around for another twenty-five years and he refused to be a financial burden to anyone. He could take care of himself as long as he had enough money.

George grew up in a family with six children and learned to be independent at a very early age. The house was run by a very strict set of rules, especially his father's rules about work and money. George swore he would never run his own household the same way, but in fact he did replicate his father's military style of discipline.

Both of George's children had to work their way through college, though George did contribute as much as he thought he could afford. When his children were very young, he bought U.S. savings bonds for them. In addition, an insurance salesman convinced George that both of his kids needed life insurance policies. When each child was ready to enter college, George cashed in the life insurance policies—each one amounted to a little over $2,000.

Joyce was bewildered by her husband's money style. Throughout their married years, he had kept a careful watch over their money. She paid the bills and shopped for major purchases but he controlled the budget and made all the deposits and withdrawals from their savings accounts. George only agreed to spend money on necessities, never on any luxury items, yet he indulged himself by spending money on rare books, which he claimed were a good investment.

While Joyce always had a hard time getting money from George for clothes and home furnishings, George was generous when it came to picking up the dinner tab when they ate out with friends, buying his secretary a gift at Christmas, and buying presents for his three grandchildren. About midway through their marriage, Joyce started to work part time as a secretary and bookkeeper so that she could have spending money of her own.

George was very secretive about his money and Joyce wasn't sure how much money they really had. According to her best estimate, they had at least $100,000, but George always refused to give her an exact accounting. She knew most of their money was in savings accounts and CDs but had a strong suspicion that George had a sizable sum stashed away in a safe deposit box. For years she had tried to get him to make a will and set up trust funds for their grandchildren, but the subject only stirred up his anger and resulted in an accusation that she was after his money. Finally she ceased asking for financial information because it only caused an argument. Besides, they were making ends meet on his monthly retirement income of $1,400 plus the extra money she brought in from her part-time job. They had paid off the mortgage on their home and owned both of their cars.

A loving and devoted grandfather, George spent much of his time with his three grandchildren. Aside from that, he worked on crossword puzzles, read books and watched television, did small repair jobs around the house, and worked in the garden. He went bowling and played cards with friends but stopped going on the annual two-week vacation to Lake Tahoe that he and Joyce for many years had taken with their neighbors. Now that he was retired, he also stopped spending money on his rare book collection.

George's anxiety about money grew worse over the next few years. He was nearing age sixty-five, when the medical insurance he received from the state government would end and be replaced by Medicare. He knew that Medicare insurance didn't cover catastrophic illness or long-term health care in nursing homes. George was terrified that if he or Joyce should become ill, they would lose all of their money and perhaps place additional financial burdens on their children. While his wife assured him that they could buy additional insurance coverage from a commercial insurance company, George was not at all convinced. He didn't trust insurance companies any more than he trusted banks. Like many Safety Players, George had spent a lifetime being somewhat indifferent toward his financial affairs. Until his retirement, he had coped fairly well by denying his discomfort with money and money issues. Since leaving his job, however, he had had to take a hard look to determine whether his money would, or would not, be sufficient to provide for his living expenses as well as cover any health problems that could occur.

The financial strain reached a crisis point when George suggested to Joyce that they sell their home and move into a small apartment. He said that they didn't need a house any longer since the children were grown up and it would be much easier for her to take care of an apartment instead of a three-bedroom home. George's motive for selling the house was not to make life easier for Joyce; he wanted to sell the house so that he could put the money in the bank. Joyce was adamant in her refusal to sell the house. This time, she and both of the children had a long, earnest discussion with George about money. They asked George to seek some financial advice and work out a plan to help alleviate all the stress he was experiencing.

In talking to me about how he felt about money and security, George told me: "I've always been reluctant to touch my money once I had it in the bank. For years, I've been scared of the future. I just lived day to day and kept socking money away. When Joyce and I were first married, I used to pay the bills but I hated to balance the checkbook and watch the balance decrease. So I asked her to pay the bills and I took care of our savings plan. I want to be sure that we can live all right for the rest of our lives without our kids having to bail us out. I should feel good about all the money I've saved but instead it's eating away at me—like I still don't have enough."

A person like George would probably not be able to tolerate his wife's going for professional financial help without his consent and prior knowledge, although many a spouse married to a Safety Player like George might be tempted to do so. In some cases, it could cause significant discord in their marriage.

The best way to deal with this personality is to slowly desensitize his fear and his distrust of involving others in money management—and "others" might even include the spouse. Safety Player spouses should tactfully try to initiate money conversations—expressing their fears and frustrations, in general, about the way the household expenses and other financial matters are handled or not handled. If the spouse does nothing assertive and takes the path of least resistance, nothing will ever change. The change, if it is to come successfully, will have to come in small, yet consecutive stages.

Eventually, George and Joyce met with a financial planner. The planner talked at length with them about the goals and objectives they wanted to obtain with their money. He recommended a diversified group of investments for them that would encompass liquidity, safety, income, and growth. George invested in municipal bonds that produced good tax-exempt yields and a corporate bond mutual fund with yields in excess of 10 percent. The mutual fund concept was both critical and ideal for George; he was getting a diversified and professionally managed investment. In addition, he purchased an interest in a real estate mortgage partnership which contained all first mortgages on multifamily dwellings. All the mortgages were insured by the federal government against loss of principal and interest; George had an equity position in the future value of the properties and the annualized return was around 12 percent. Finally, he invested in a low-risk equipment-leasing income fund designed to produce tax-sheltered income at 10.5 percent per year.

A diversified portfolio is usually important when considering investment strategies not only for the Safety Players but for the other eight Moneymax groups as well. All of the alternatives were unknown to George before he decided to reconstruct his Safety Player attitude and become more educated about his personal finances.

BUILDING FLEXIBLE, LIFETIME
MONEY PATTERNS

Regardless of age, Safety Players are capable of establishing new flexible, lifetime money patterns. That requires a better balance between work, leisure time, and financial matters. Devoting just one or two days a month to investigating new money options is a start toward assuming more financial responsibility. Subscribing to one of the many money magazines, attending free seminars given by banks and brokerage firms, occasionally reading the *Wall Street Journal,* talking to friends and relatives who have made wise investments, are all ways to begin learning more about money.

The formula for building confidence with money is self-acceptance and a willingness to change unsatisfactory money habits. If you want to build your confidence, you can't remain in a comfortable, safe position but have to pull yourself up by the boot straps, declare yourself, and take appropriate action. No matter what the outcome, you will learn that you can take risk, face the consequences, follow through, bounce back if necessary, and gain an increment of confidence.

You'll certainly feel better if the outcome is successful and positive, but feeling better is secondary to building confidence. Changing lifetime money habits and beliefs usually entails quite a bit of discomfort. Unless you devote yourself to a new money orientation, you will not become more financially successful. Because Safety Players have adequate income and assets, they tend to settle in with complacency and pull the mask over reality. But too often, they are not really content, secure, or in control.

For Safety Players, the step backward into money acquiescence dictates that they will become observers, reacting to a system they don't fully understand. Thus, they tend to reflect an unconscious outlook or attitude which says: "My life is essentially in the hands of others or a vast powerful force [or forces] out there and beyond my control. Therefore, I am the victim of the IRS, the politicians, my boss, my children's needs, my spouse's unreasonable demands." As a consequence, it makes little difference what the Safety Players want out of life. They have to learn to settle for whatever they can get, since they believe themselves to be relatively powerless.

One simple money truth is that every individual has more control over his or her money than he or she believes is possible. No matter how much of our lives is perceived to be unchangeable, under the control of someone or something else, there is always a part that is under our control and can be altered. Be it 40 percent, 20 percent, or 2 percent—it is almost always more than we think it is. You can increase that control. If you decide what it is that you want from your money and act on it, you will be infinitely more powerful and less of a victim. You will not sit by passively or accept second best. You will not just react, but learn to cause events—be actively responsible. Whatever is necessary for you to be and do your best, the one fatal mistake is to take no initiative.

Everyone wants greater success; everyone would like to have more money. We all have demands in our lives which consume our time, but most of us do find time for whatever is most important to us. How high are financial planning and your money management among your priorities? Decide how much involvement you want, how much time you are willing to spend in learning, assessing, and executing a new money management process.

Financial planning doesn't require substantial extra time and effort when looked at in the perspective of your total life. It can seem like hard work, not merely because of the self-discipline and determination that are needed, but because you may be entering alien territory and learning about financial matters that have seemed complex, mysterious, and designed only for financial experts. Good money management skills can become a habit if you continually exercise and develop them. Safety Players have to do some hard money thinking in order to determine what keeps them from using their intelligence, good sense, and talent to make money work better for them.

MONEY MANAGEMENT STYLE

1. Of all the Moneymax groups, the Safety Players most adamantly reject the stock market. Most have never had and are not interested in owning individual common stocks or mutual funds.

2. Their top three investments are various types of bonds. They probably perceive the favorite, government bonds, as safe but what

they haven't plugged into the equation is the inflation-adjusted rate of return. The following example was provided by a financial planner who worked with one of my Safety Player clients: If inflation is running at 4 percent and the return on a government bond is 7.5 percent, your inflation-adjusted return is 3.5 percent. You can't possibly earn enough to be financially independent by getting only 3.5 percent on your money. So, in fact, there is risk in putting your money in low net yield investments—risk that you will not have enough money to retire comfortably. Financial independence is not accomplished by investing all of your money in "perceived" safe vehicles, and even during times of low inflation, the potential for a negative rate of return is very likely. A negative rate of return results when the combination of your tax bracket plus the rate of inflation exceed the return you are receiving. The same is true with savings accounts, CDs, and money market accounts, because their after-tax, inflation-adjusted rate of return is insignificant, and could result in a negative rate of return even at times of low inflation. This just points out that Safety Players could benefit greatly from finding a trusted adviser who could direct them to low risk investments that produce greater potential returns than government bonds or savings accounts.

3. They do like IRAs and Keoghs and probably have them invested in bank instruments like CDs. My Safety Player clients indicate that although they are satisfied with their IRAs and Keoghs, the rate of return they receive is quite low compared with other viable alternatives. The rate is low because these Safety Players decide to put their IRAs and Keoghs in fixed-dollar investments, which also include guaranteed interest accounts as well as U.S. Government securities like Treasury notes and government bonds.

4. Even though Safety Players own insurance, they are the least satisfied of all the groups with insurance. Of all the insurance company vehicles, they are most satisfied with annuities. (Their number-one financial objective is current income and they are the third-oldest group of the nine profiles.)

5. Even though they perceive owning individual shares of common stock and owning commercial property as having the same risk, twice as many Safety Players—who don't own either—would like to own commercial property as would like to own common stock.

6. Safety Players score the lowest of all profiles in trust and are

difficult to steer toward a financial adviser. They could be helped im-
measurably if they could find an adviser they could trust, but working
with an adviser is a personal decision.

7. In general, Safety Players are discontented investors who don't
like most of the investments they have chosen.

SAFETY PLAYERS—FINANCIAL STATEMENT

Of all nine Moneymax Profiles, the Safety Players have the lowest
scores in the trait of self-determination—the extent to which they feel
in control of their own financial destiny. Thus, they are not very involved with money management nor do they reflect upon past financial decisions. They do not believe that people are basically honest
with money, are low risk-takers, and are not content with their financial status.

They share many demographic characteristics with the Money Masters but have significantly fewer assets. Overall, the Safety Players
rank fourth in income and fifth in assets when compared with all the
Moneymax groups. For the most part, they are married, older rather
than younger, and tend to be a part of two-income families. They
prefer to keep their money in savings accounts even though they are
very dissatisfied with the return on their money; 89 percent of them
have had or currently have savings accounts.

Despite their reluctance to assume direct responsibility for their
financial affairs, Safety Players do want greater prosperity. However,
they are not confident that they can take control of their money. If
Safety Players can become more assertive and more educated about
financial planning, they stand a very good chance of significantly increasing both their income and assets.

9

Achievers

Aim for the highest; never enter a bar-room; do not touch liquor, or if at all only at meals; never speculate; never endorse beyond your surplus cash fund; make the firm's interest yours; bread orders always to save owners; concentrate; put all your eggs in one basket, and watch that basket; expenditure always within revenue; lastly, be not impatient, for, as Emerson says, "no one can cheat you out of ultimate success but yourselves."

—Andrew Carnegie

GUIDELINES
Achievers

. . . Want and need to be integrally involved in their money management and investing.

. . . Prefer conservative, low-risk investments.

. . . Have difficulty delegating their money management to others.

. . . Are very proud of the way they have handled their money management.

. . . Are highly reflective and analytical in their financial decision-making.

. . . Are utilitarian, practical consumers.

. . . Have little interest in status and prestige with their money.

The Achievers earn the second-highest income (following the first-place Entrepreneurs) and are also second of all Moneymax groups in the accumulation of assets. Like the Safety Players, the Achievers have a low level of trust in others' honesty with money. In addition, both of these Moneymax Profiles have low scores in altruism, believing that financial responsibility is a personal matter to be handled individually. Both the Achievers and the Safety Players disagree with the statement that people are basically willing to help others in financial difficulty.

Because the Achievers and the Safety Players do not believe that other people are altruistic, it can follow that they themselves are not particularly altruistic. Perhaps Safety Players think that everyone must go it alone and look out for himself in a competitive, unfair world where it takes more than intelligence and hard work to succeed. The Achievers are convinced that people feel better about themselves when they are productive members of society, that people should have to work for the money they receive. Because the Achievers take tremendous pride in their own accomplishments, they believe that everyone has an opportunity to share in the American dream through diligent effort and perseverance. They may not be supporters of the welfare and unemployment systems which they may think undermine the American work ethic and the country's capitalistic foundation. Their value system does not imply that Achievers are necessarily selfish and contribute none of their money to nonprofit groups. They will donate to those groups that give them a sense of personal identification like educational and cultural institutions and organizations or to groups that foster their own beliefs like environmental and political groups.

Who are the Moneymax Achievers? For the most part, they are college graduates (tied for first place with the Hunters) and are married (most married of all groups) with two-income families. They are conservative with money, share traditional values, and have a strong belief in the work ethic. They do not take high risks with money, and are interested in protecting what they have earned. They are achievement-oriented and want to see the fruits of their own labor in everything they do. Achievers tend to be successful employees within businesses rather than entrepreneurs. However, they may be intrapreneurs, independent thinkers, and self-initiators who work for companies that provide security and structure. Because Achievers typically lack the comfort level with risk that it takes to start up their own enterprises, they carve out their financial journey in a more traditional way that balances their need for structure with their need for achievement. If their creativity is stymied in the work place, they find other outlets for their talents like hobbies or business and recreational organizations.

The Achievers score very high in self-determination and are assured that their hard work will pay off financially and their close scrutiny of money will ultimately reap the accumulated assets necessary to provide security for themselves and their families. Some Achievers tend to become hoarders but others spend money without guilt or anxiety. Because they have such high expectations and keep a watchful eye on goal attainment, the Achievers sometimes don't enjoy the process of becoming successful as much as they should. Nonetheless, they have a great sense of pride in what they have accomplished.

The Achievers score the highest in pride, the personal satisfaction resulting from the way they have handled their money. Confident of their financial skills, many of them had parents who were good role models and encouraged and nurtured ambition, self-reliance, and prudent money management. The Achievers have made financial blunders, but unlike the Safety Players, who become blocked by the threat of failure, the Achievers profit from mistakes and reign even tighter control over their money.

The difference in dealing with failure lies in the fact that the Achievers know that their skills and abilities will far outdistance a few mistakes, while the Safety Players, who don't have much confidence in themselves, see personal and monetary failure as a sign of what the future will bring.

Another distinction between the Safety Players and the Achievers is their desire for involvement with money—the Achievers score at top level of involvement while the Safety Players score at the bottom level. While the Achievers desire and need control over their money to have peace of mind, the Safety Players become frustrated when they have to make a financial decision and try to avoid managing and investing money.

Because the Achievers take charge of finances, they exert control and power over money, but the Safety Players allow money to control them and make them feel powerless. The Achievers don't ever want to find out how it feels to be out of control so they tenaciously hold on to every element in the money matrix, refusing to give fate a chance to play out its hand.

This strong desire and need for involvement and control is a positive characteristic as long as it does not generate anxiety. For example, the Achievers experience more anxiety in making financial decisions than the Money Masters, who have more trust that people are basically honest when making financial transactions. Interestingly, the Achievers are content, but not as content as the Money Masters with their money.

The interaction between trust and control for the Achievers exemplifies the proverbial case of the chicken and the egg: Since the Achievers tend to be distrustful of the way others handle their money, they need absolute control. Or, you might say that because the Achievers desire so much control over financial transactions and decisions, they won't trust anyone else to handle their money; they must be fully responsible and prefer unilateral decisions. Are the Achievers distrustful because they need control, or do they need control because they are distrustful? It's difficult to tell which trait came first but each significantly impacts the other. Thus, the Achievers find any negotiation process distasteful, a situation that affects both personal and business relationships.

THE NEED FOR ABSOLUTE CONTROL

Consider the case of Richard and Monica. Richard was an attorney who specialized in real estate. His yearly income had averaged $250,000 for the last few years, and he said he was proud of his financial accomplishments and generally content with his money. He was also extremely conservative with his money and lived in a lower middle class tract house and drove an old model car. He had over $500,000 in CDs in the bank and every year his income tax bill escalated. A very low risk-taker (Achievers are the lowest risk-takers), Richard didn't mind paying taxes as long as he could watch his bank account grow.

Richard grew up during the Depression, but his mother did a remarkable job of handling meager funds and even managed to save money. Richard admired his mother's thriftiness and his family's staunch work ethic. Richard probably would not have questioned his money personality except that his wife, Monica, was ready to walk away from the marriage because of his rigid money style.

Monica grew up in an impoverished family and never brought her friends home because she was ashamed of her family's house. She fantasized about being rich and believed that money should be spent and enjoyed. Here she was in an affluent position, wanted to enjoy the comforts that money could buy, yet had to ask Richard for permission to buy anything over a hundred dollars. She was particularly upset because she handled the money for the household budget; she was given the responsibility for their money but no power. Two totally different money styles, an Achiever and a Hunter, had merged in marriage.

People are influenced by the financial attitudes and behavior of their parents, and sometimes the imprint is so strong that it causes money-oriented problems in adulthood. These "money traps" can lead to poor investment decisions, extreme frugality or spending, interminable arguments with spouses. Correcting such problems can take considerable time, effort, and expense. But over the long run, the cure is usually worth the price.

Both Richard and Monica were attractive, bright, and sophisticated. In society's eye, they were the perfect couple. Yet, when I met them, Monica was frustrated and angry because of Richard's unreasonable rules about money. She had only a vague idea of where their assets were and how much they actually had. Richard retained extraordinary financial control. Throughout their eleven years of marriage, Richard held a tight grip on the purse strings, because Achievers like to have an exact accounting of where all their hard-earned dollars are being spent.

Richard preferred to pay taxes rather than have someone else, including Monica, try to reduce the tax bill through proper planning of their money. Richard's greatest pleasure seemed to be watching their bank account balance add up and get closer to his projected goal of $1 million. Only when he broke the million-dollar mark, he reasoned, would he truly be a success.

Richard had convinced himself that he had found the best way of dealing with his financial affairs—a way that would let him sleep at night. Richard knew the real cost of his inflexible and conservative style, that inflation was eating away at his profits, but he was willing to make the financial trade-off to gain peace of mind with his money.

Richard didn't need or ask for many creature comforts. Buying his wife a new car (a Toyota Corolla) was a monumental decision and one that he made under duress. As he continued to make more and more money, Richard still saved most of his earnings and begrudged anything that he was forced to spend. He didn't even want to buy the new dishwasher they desperately needed. As mentioned earlier, some Achievers can become hoardish with money and Richard certainly fit into that category.

Monica, on the other hand, loved to spend money. She liked pretty clothes, she liked to travel, and she wanted to buy a new house that would reflect their financial success. They had no children to provide for, Richard had a lucrative career that promised to get even better, and Monica was totally baffled by her husband's compulsive saving and extreme frugality.

According to Richard, Monica's need to spend money was very anxiety-provoking and emotionally intolerable. Even though he had built up a solid client base, he claimed that his income was unpredictable and it was important to have enough money to carry them through any lean years that might occur in the future.

Consequently, Richard felt more secure living in his lower middle class tract home, which was fully paid for, and refused to incur high mortgage payments on a new house. Of course, he also didn't want to take any money out of the bank for a down payment, and thus deplete his savings.

Richard and Monica clashed often over money. While opposites often attract, in this case money became the emotional football between two people with dissimilar lifestyles who were trying to keep together an otherwise happy marriage. Richard and Monica were so immersed in emotional turmoil that they couldn't understand the roots of their dilemma. They blamed all of their problems on money.

Knowing that Hunters are reluctant to take control of money and are prone to emotional spending and that the Achievers need total control of money to feel secure and confident, it is understandable how and why Richard and Monica were always in battle. Hunters like a money style that reflects status and prestige, while Achievers prefer a conservative style that denotes utilitarian, practical spending. Achievers are very reflective about money (number one of all Moneymax groups) and like to evaluate each and every money decision; Hunters would just as soon forget the past.

To comprehend Richard's and Monica's money profiles, it is important to consider their backgrounds, especially their childhoods. As was mentioned, Richard grew up during the Depression when money was very scarce, and his mother did a great job of managing the house and the money. She sewed clothes, baked bread, and always kept a clean and orderly house. Richard's father sold electrical equipment and often worked long hours and weekends. Richard remembered the many times his mother told him how much the family had been able to save because of her ability to "stretch dollars." That dogged saving allowed all of them to survive and feel safe and secure—a message that made a strong impression on Richard and a lesson he obviously never forgot. According to his wife, Richard was still living in the Depression.

Richard recalled the top buffet drawer where the money was kept until the family made a trip to the bank at the end of each month. He remembered how proud his mother was when she had money to deposit. His father's hard work and his mother's thriftiness were the money principles which made Richard an Achiever. His frugal childhood was clearly the internal rulebook that guided his financial behavior, even when he earned a six-figure income.

Monica, on the other hand, never felt a sense of security in her home. Her father worked sporadically and drank heavily, and her mother was submissive. Both she and her two brothers were emotionally abused children. Monica remembered how often she dreamed of being rescued from it all by a family that would want to adopt her. She recalled fantasies of living in a mansion with maids and servants doting on her.

Monica's money style signified a feeling of "reward yourself with money when you are blessed to have it." She wanted to use money to bring pleasure and joy into her life. For her, that meant living in a beautiful home and buying the pretty things she never had as a child. Monica was attracted to Richard because of his secure profession, personal strength, and apparent financial control over his life. Unfortunately, Monica wasn't reaping the emotional and financial rewards she had hoped for.

In deciphering what drew Richard to Monica, it became obvious that he had unconsciously married himself. Monica exemplified the person he wanted to be as a youngster, yet was never allowed to express and develop. Individuality was not fostered in his home. Richard still adopted his parents' attitudes and behaviors and never developed his own.

Although he loved Monica, Richard was threatened by her. She represented those free-spirited qualities in himself he wanted to express but was unable to. Because of his unconscious identification with Monica, he began to treat her as his parents had treated him.

Often, we are attracted to parts of someone we would consciously or unconsciously like to emulate. This tendency can be reflected in the way the couple interacts with money. For example, a Safety Player may be attracted to an Entrepreneur because Entrepreneurs have the confidence and ability to go after their goals, and a Safety Player typically represses talent and ambition. Or the Entrepreneur might be attracted to the High Roller because of an unfulfilled desire to seek thrills and excitement with money—a desire that Entrepreneurs have to harness because they need to remain focused on goal attainment.

However, often that very trait that draws and captivates someone becomes a significant irritant, as it did in the case of Monica, who was enticed by Richard's obvious control over his money, his confidence in making financial decisions, and his ability to earn a good living. What she didn't realize and admit to herself was that she also wanted control; she was frustrated and depressed by having a husband who wanted to control money with an iron hand. After all, she said she was bright and could learn to become a capable financial manager. She was in charge of budgeting their money so why couldn't she learn to spend it without constant surveillance from her husband?

Monica made the mistake of not examining her money style and deciding what was important to her. She had gone along with Richard's program ever since they were married. He wanted her to leave her job so she could take care of their home; he wanted her to come into his office and help out when he worked on weekends; he wanted her to pay all the bills and keep the checkbook balanced. Monica had agreed to all of Richard's requests, usually because he promised some financial reward—a vacation, new furniture, an evening out on the town. However, the rewards were usually delayed or never appeared. Even as the disappointments piled up, she never asserted herself but allowed Richard to continue to make promises he didn't intend to keep. Richard assumed she was happy to relinquish most major decisions to him and didn't realize that Monica felt like a nonentity in her marriage, that she was bored and depressed by being at home.

Monica understood that the abundance of free time and lack of excitement in her life only increased her frustration. She had sold out, thinking that money was the cure-all that would give her a greater sense of personal worth. Money was being used as an external bandage, but it could never cure her internal emotional wounds, namely her lack of self-esteem and feeling of value and entitlement.

Despite these problems, the situation for Richard and Monica was not hopeless. Richard admitted that he wanted more out of life but didn't know how to get off the work treadmill nor change his money attitudes. Monica realized that if she wanted a partnership role in controlling their money, she would have to become more assertive and directly involved with money management.

Once Richard and Monica had gained insight into their respective money styles, the next step was to develop a plan for changing their present modus operandi. This included developing new strategies for investing their money that would allow the greatest financial and psychological growth as well as formulating a money management system that included the process of negotiation.

The negotiation process began with the selection of a new home. They purchased a duplex in a beach community that was ideal for renovation and expansion. This pleased Monica because she had a more comfortable home that she could redecorate, and it satisfied Richard's desire for a sound, appreciable investment with a reasonable monthly payment.

Monica started to keep records and manage the books on this and other investments. In addition to paying the monthly bills, she monitored their new spending plan, which they jointly designed and negotiated. This helped her to understand their cash flow situation more clearly and actually helped her curb her consumption desires and emotional spending.

Monica also enrolled in classes at a local community college and attended several free seminars given by local financial institutions in order to give her more confidence and skills in financial matters. Initially, she felt somewhat intimidated by her new course work and perplexed by the financial jargon, but she found that the benefits certainly outweighed the drawbacks. She discovered that she had a vast new area to share with Richard and felt she was contributing at last in a meaningful way. Since she was reluctant to go back into the work force after so many years as a housewife, Monica welcomed the opportunity to be actively involved in managing their duplex and other investments.

In addition to the duplex, Richard and Monica made some other real estate investments, to capitalize on Richard's expertise in that area. Richard had dabbled in real estate since he got out of college. He, like other Achievers, preferred the perceived sense of control he had in the real estate market. Owning a rental property gives you control over insuring it, painting it, having the roof fixed, raising rents, controlling expenses, and so forth. On the other hand being a limited partner in a real estate project gives you essentially no control; you are inactive as far as management goes. However, the whims of the marketplace can have a dramatic impact on either investment.

A percentage of the price movement of individual common stock can be attributable to the volatility of the stock market as a whole and not necessarily to the performance of an individual company or the current conditions in the company's industry; the payoff on an investment in a rental unit will be as much or more determined by inflation, market conditions, and changes in the tax laws as by the upkeep and condition of the building. However, owners of rental properties frequently feel they have much more control than owners of common stock investments of equivalent value.

Let's look at a good matching of money and investments for Richard, the Achiever. Advising Richard, a lawyer with many clients in the real estate and construction industries, to invest in real estate was analogous to telling an entrepreneur to invest in his own company. Richard's risk would be substantially reduced because of his business affiliations and access to crucial information. Thus, Richard and Monica purchased a couple of residential properties for investment purposes, including a four-unit apartment building.

Of course, investing primarily in real estate created a diversification problem for Richard and Monica. After all, bad times for Richard's major clients in the real estate business could be coupled with bad times for his real estate investments. So the couple also began a search to buy stocks and bonds. They subscribed to a reputable market periodical, started following some stocks, and after three months felt confident enough to make their first investment. Many Achievers find investing in the stock market satisfactory, particularly when they invest in blue chip stocks with good track records. Achievers feel comfortable with new investments when they develop a level of expertise that allows them to gain control and not rely solely on the advice of an investment adviser. Remember, Achievers have difficulty trusting others with their money and that certainly includes financial advisers.

Besides these investments, Richard and Monica created a special fund earmarked for individual luxuries and opened a joint checking account and a joint money market account. Richard always had an individual checking account, but Monica, who never had her own account, opened one for herself so she no longer had to get permission from Richard to make most purchases. They negotiated a spending plan and set priorities based on individual as well as joint needs and desires.

Finally, Richard and Monica decided to set aside some time and money for travel. They agreed to take a weekend trip every two to three months, contingent on Richard's work schedule. This was a high priority for Monica because it was the only time she could get Richard away from the stress of his work. Next on the list was a two-week vacation to Tahiti, Monica's original honeymoon choice, which Richard had vetoed when they were married.

Within a three-month period, Richard and Monica had overcome many of their individual and joint mind sets concerning their money. They were well on their way to communicating with each other about the money issues that had previously caused much discord in their marriage.

Richard had been a hoarder. Because of his compulsive savings habits, he used his talents and expertise to advise clients and friends about money, but didn't give himself the benefit of his knowledge. Monica had lived her life entirely through Richard, who was a totally different person with a very dissimilar money style. Neither money style was entirely right or wrong, and the two of them needed to meet somewhere in between and function bilaterally instead of unilaterally. Subsequently, they developed common goals that took into account their different money attitudes and reinforced personal strengths instead of playing off weaknesses. They found investments that not only satisfied their individual Moneymax Profiles but also suited them as a couple.

The money game is always more complicated and more interesting if more than one money style is involved. Married couples frequently encounter problems when the spouses have very different viewpoints and both want to be involved in managing money.

MISMATCHED MONEY PERSONALITIES

One of the most combative combinations in marriage is an Achiever and a High Roller. Bill, an Achiever, was a vice president of a pharmaceutical company and his wife, Toby, a High Roller, had left her job as an account executive in an advertising agency to sell real estate. Throughout their five years of marriage, Bill was solely responsible for financial planning and money management. Toby, an assertive, spirited woman, wanted to play an active role in deciding how their money should be invested but whenever she suggested that they talk about money, Bill became withdrawn and angry. He quizzed her about any investment she recommended, and since her financial knowledge was limited, Toby usually ended up feeling like a foolish, uninformed female.

Toby's first big real estate sale netted her a profit of $18,000 and she excitedly proposed to Bill that they look for an investment that would quickly multiply her money. He refused to participate, didn't want to set a precedent for involving both of them in money matters, and told her to go off on her own and see how well she could do in the investment world. Before long, she was led into commodities trading by a very persuasive salesman. The result was a quick and painful $18,000 loss. While the direct cause of Toby's loss was gambling in the commodities market, the indirect cause for the loss was the failure of a High Roller and an Achiever to communicate about money, to share responsibility for managing money, and to find investments that satisfied both of them.

Suppose, after discussion and education, Bill and Toby developed a program for investing in high quality convertible bonds (bonds that can be converted into the company's common stock; this can be profitable if the stock price rises). The safety offered by the bonds would have appeased Bill's conservative nature and need for control as a Moneymax Achiever. The stock aspect would have met Toby's desire to analyze investments and become involved and her High Roller need to take a chance at making bigger profits.

The High Rollers are clearly at one end of the continuum of thrill-seeking and risk-taking with money while the Achievers are at the other extreme, clinging to certainty and predictability, avoiding risks and anything unfamiliar. The High Rollers are hungry for excitement and novelty whereas the Achievers protect themselves with routine and tradition. The High Rollers are adventurers who seek sensation with their money wherever and whenever they can find it or create it. They prefer uncertainty, unpredictability, novelty, a lot of variety, low structure, high intensity, and high complexity. On the other hand, the Achievers are practical, rational, utilitarian with money. They prefer certainty, predictability, familiarity, little variety, high structure, low intensity, and low complexity.

The blending of these two money styles is not as easy as combining other Moneymax Profiles with more similar styles, such as the High Rollers and the Entrepreneurs. The danger with that mix is the temptation the High Roller might place before the Entrepreneur, who already has a blind spot for assuming too much risk. The Entrepreneur might be tempted to follow the High Roller down the lane of thrills and excitement and might stray from a defined, focused goal. Nonetheless, High Rollers and Entrepreneurs typically would have less tension than High Rollers and Achievers. The union can be achieved successfully, however, as evidenced by Toby and Bill.

For the first five years of their marriage, Toby and Bill fought about anything that was remotely connected to money. After discovering their money styles and comparing their scores on various money traits, they began to understand, for the first time, why they locked horns on money issues. They also began to develop a mutual respect for one another's individual money attitudes without judging them as right or wrong.

Bill now knows that Toby is likely to make impulsive financial decisions so he will try to help her adopt a more reflective style. If she suggests an investment, or buying a household item that is costly, he can help her explore the pros and cons of the purchase and weigh their options.

They tried this system when Toby decided to buy a car phone for her business. Bill accompanied her on the first shopping trip, asked questions, avoided the salesperson's manipulative tactics, and walked away with a pretty good idea of the bottom-line price. On her own, Toby then started to explore other available brands and models. She knew exactly what questions to ask, how to manage the salesperson, and ultimately found what she considered to be the best deal in town. Her husband agreed that she had made a wise choice and commended her efforts. Toby was elated with her performance and the great deal she found for herself. She had always been assertive, but this time she also felt in control.

While the Entrepreneurs' blind spot is a tendency to seek too much risk with their money, the Achievers' blind spot is oftentimes their inordinate need for control of money and the fact that they don't trust others with their money. This often prevents them from using financial advisers who may be a lot more knowledgeable about investments which could give them greater return. The lack of trust and need for control also prevent Achievers from sharing stressful financial decisions with friends, relatives, and coworkers who might lend valuable advice and support. Many a stockbroker and financial planner have torn their hair out trying to talk money with the Achiever, not to mention the Achiever's spouse, siblings, parents, or children.

This blind spot for control and close scrutiny of money is also what aids the Achiever in making and accumulating money, just as the comfort level with risk helps the Entrepreneur in goal attainment. Let's look at a profitable use of this trait in the investment game. Imagine an engineer with a strong need to succeed and to control his money in the process. By nature he likes to figure things out for himself and prefers investments that allow him to apply his mathematical skills and develop precise calculations for returns.

He might buy 100 shares of common stock, but unlike some investors, he decides to sell a call option against his stock. In doing so, he has contracted to sell his 100 shares of stock at a certain price (strike price), for a given length of time (expiration date), for a fee (premium). This premium will be credited to his account immediately and will increase his yield over and above the straight price of the stock. If the stock goes up beyond the striking price, he will sell the stock; if it goes down, he will be protected up to the amount of money he has taken in as a premium. Even though the transaction may limit his gain, it will decrease his risk and increase his yield. Mathematical calculations might not be for every investor, but the engineer might be able to develop a very profitable and satisfying investment program for himself.

Many Achievers can learn to increase their comfort level with risk if they can perceive some control in the situation. Because the engineer is highly involved in the investment process, he assumes more risk. Achievers find this to be true when investing in the stock market, and many of them prefer discount brokerage houses which allow them to execute their own trades. Other Achievers who use stockbrokers have searched until they found a broker who deserved their trust and confidence—who presented them with alternatives and allowed them active participation in financial decisions.

SEEKING FINANCIAL ADVICE

Rosemary, a very successful pediatrician, was an example of an Achiever who was paired with the financial planner. A member of a local women's networking association, she knew a number of financial planners and stockbrokers who also belonged to the association. After serving on a joint committee with a financial planner who worked close to her office, Rosemary decided to take the plunge and trust someone else to manage her money. She had a real tax problem now that she was in her fourth year of private practice and earning a considerable amount of money. She owned her own condominium, had no other investments, but had $80,000 to invest. After meeting with Rosemary, the financial planner developed the following assessment and priority of her needs:

1 Tax savings
2 Growth opportunities
3 Other-directed investments (desire for others to manage her
    money)
4 Moderate to high risk investments

It was perfectly reasonable to develop that proposal of prioritized
needs since Rosemary initially made the contact because of the high
taxes she was paying. Rosemary also expressed a concern about building a nest egg for the future and getting a better return on her money,
more than the bank was offering on her CDs.

When asked how much risk she was comfortable taking, Rosemary
responded that she was a moderate to high risk-taker. After all, she
decided to become a doctor when everyone in her family told her to
become a nurse. Her parents always saw the glass as half empty, instead of half full, and Rosemary felt she was much more daring and
competitive than her family. In fact, Rosemary was not different from
the majority of people who like to see themselves as greater risk-takers
than they really are. Because risk-taking is seen as a socially desirable
trait, people generally like to portray themselves as comfortable with
risk even if they are not sure how they feel.

Based on the presumption that Rosemary could tolerate moderate
to high risks and that she was a busy professional concerned about tax
savings and income for the future, the financial planner made the
following investment recommendations:

Exploratory oil wells	($20,000)
Common stocks	(40,000)
Mutual funds—emerging growth companies	(10,000)
Real estate partnership—growth	(10,000)
Total	($80,000)

When Rosemary left the office, she was very agitated but didn't
know why. Personally, she liked the financial planner but was apprehensive about making a commitment to the plan. She thought she'd
give it some time, think things over, but didn't know how to figure out
what was bothering her. The financial planner called several days later

and Rosemary said she would talk to her at the next women's network meeting. However, Rosemary did not attend that meeting because she had nothing to say to the financial planner. She was embarrassed to admit that she did not want to go ahead with the financial plan without a valid reason for refusal.

When Rosemary took the Moneymax Profile, she discovered that she was an Achiever. It then became obvious why the financial plan failed: too much risk, not enough perceived control, diversification not well developed, lack of client involvement in the implementation process, and no provision for safety.

Rosemary was indeed an Achiever with the following prioritized needs: self-directed investments, low to moderate risk investments (safety important), growth opportunities, and tax savings. Interestingly, tax savings was the number-one priority in Rosemary's first financial plan when it should have been last, according to her particular money attitudes and style.

After learning more about her Achiever profile, Rosemary returned to the financial planner's office to negotiate a new investment strategy. Unfortunately, the planner was resistant to changing the original plan. After a few telephone calls, Rosemary concluded that the planner was unwilling to spend much time with her and explain various investment strategies. She was disappointed but immediately decided to find another financial adviser.

She needed a professional who would address her need for involvement and control, explain thoroughly the element of risk in any recommended investments, and expose the downside of investments as well as the appealing aspects. Because Achievers are very concerned about protecting themselves against potential loss, it was very important that Rosemary find an adviser who would involve her in the decision-making process, regardless of how busy she appeared to be. Because Achievers have a difficult time trusting anyone with money, Rosemary needed to find someone who was willing to answer all of her questions and proceed at a pace that was nonthreatening.

After asking for recommendations from friends and business associates, Rosemary found a financial planner who met all of her requirements. He presented her with a variety of options from which to build a financial plan: a growth-oriented family of funds (moderate growth) which would give her the involvement she wanted (she could follow the market and maneuver her funds accordingly); blue chip common stocks for growth with safety; limited partnerships in real estate, equipment leasing, or gas drilling in order to satisfy her need for reducing taxes and/or give her the opportunity for gain; U.S. Government securities, again for safety. Rosemary chose the following recommendations after discussing the pros and cons of each investment:

Family of mutual funds—moderate growth	($30,000)
Common stocks—blue chip	(20,000)
U.S. Government securities	(24,000)
Real estate partnership	(6,000)
Total	($80,000)

Rosemary was very satisfied with the plan. She felt she had found a planner she could trust who didn't want to manage her money unilaterally but would allow her to have the ultimate control. She also learned that she was willing to risk more as long as the potential return justified the risk.

She was on her way to preparing for the future and was surprised that not only was she comfortable but she was enjoying the process as well. No longer paralyzed by her inability to change the way she had been managing her money, Rosemary became a profitable client for the financial planner. He got a long-term, satisfied client, and Rosemary referred her colleagues in the hospital and her medical corporation to him. The planner's commitment of time and personalized service turned out to be a good investment for both of them.

MONEY MANAGEMENT STYLE

1. The Achievers have a preference for income real estate (residential); they use it and they like it. This is probably because they can be as integrally involved as they choose—even becoming their own property managers (a hands-on approach). This is an investment that can be seen and touched, unlike many other investments. There are a smaller number of Achievers who invest in commercial property and they express a high degree of satisfaction with it as well.

2. They have been more satisfied with their commercial property investments than with common stock. This seems to be because they believe that they have more control with real estate. In addition, a loss in property value is not as visible as a loss in the stock market.

3. The Achievers are great users, and more satisfied users, of government securities—like T-bills, T-notes, and government bonds—than the Entrepreneurs. While Achievers are willing to sacrifice greater returns in order to fulfill their need for safety, the Entrepreneurs are willing to risk more for a chance at attaining a goal.

4. They are third among the top three investor groups in the stock market along with the Entrepreneurs (first) and the Money Masters (second).

5. Achievers are the number-one users of IRAs and Keoghs.

6. The Achievers are more satisfied with whole life than universal or variable life insurance, probably because of the safety factors inherent in whole life, and the fact that it has more than fifty years of reliable performance to its credit. Universal life has only been around for about seven years and variable even less than that. Thus, they are relatively new products and their performance is very sensitive to interest rates and/or market conditions.

7. Even though they rank seventh out of the nine profiles in the sixty and over bracket (23.7 percent), the Achievers are the second of all nine profiles in satisfaction with annuities. This appears to confirm their strong interest in the significant safety features that are included with fixed annuities such as guaranteed principal, periodic interest guarantees, and guaranteed monthly income during their later years when the income stream is very important. In my practice I have known many Achievers who, once introduced to variable annuities, came to the realization that they could satisfy multiple financial objectives with this instrument. Since the Achiever money personality requires a high degree of perceived control, the multiple investment options available with variable versus fixed annuities—such as guaranteed accounts, stock and bond accounts, and money market options—appears to allow them flexibility, opportunity, and safety to the degree they desire.

8. Of the three affluent profiles, the Achievers are the least satisfied with limited partnerships, probably because they believe there is less personal control with this investment.

9. Commodities/options and futures contracts are rejected the most. More than 70 percent of this group are not interested in these investment vehicles.

THE ACHIEVERS—FINANCIAL STATEMENT

The Achievers rank second in income and assets of all Moneymax groups. They are the most married, highly educated, and are predominately in professional/managerial careers. Of all the profiles they rank number one in pride and reflectivity. They are extremely proud of their accomplishments and the way they have handled their money, and they ponder fast financial decisions and behaviors before making current decisions.

The Achievers want and need control over their money. They tend to distrust the honesty of others in dealing with money and feel more comfortable with a decision-making role in money management. They believe they are fully responsible for their financial fate—attributing financial success to their own efforts rather than to luck.

They believe wholeheartedly that hard work brings them financial success. The Achievers like to keep the money they earn and watch it accumulate. They avoid risks with their money (lowest of all groups in risk-taking). They also tend to feel that providing for one's financial welfare is a highly individualistic matter; they tend not to be proponents of altruistic behavior. The Achievers tend to keep a low profile with money, not seeking prestige or public recognition.

10

---◁►◁◦►---

Perfectionists

Whoever thinks a faultless piece to see,
Thinks what ne'er was, nor is, nor e'er shall be.
—Alexander Pope

GUIDELINES
Perfectionists

. . . Often become too critical in the way they make financial decisions and manage their money.

. . . Experience tremendous anxiety and worry about their money management.

. . . Unknowingly allow their skeptical nature to impede their financial progress.

. . . Are frustrated and discontent with their financial status in life.

. . . Lack trust and pride in themselves because of the way they have handled their money.

. . . Are very distrustful of other people dealing with their money.

. . . Believe that others will be generous in helping those less fortunate.

The Moneymax Perfectionists, the overly critical, are the first cousins to the overly cautious Safety Players. Both profiles ultimately wind up not using their money as effectively as they are capable of using it. The Safety Players cannot take risks comfortably, and the Perfectionists are so afraid of making a mistake that in order to avoid making a wrong decision, they oftentimes make no decision.

Maxims like "If you want something done right, do it yourself" and "If you can't do something right, don't do it at all" are central to the belief system of the Perfectionists. They can become almost compulsive about doing a job "just right." They believe that whatever they have achieved is a result of their high personal standards and willingness to always go the extra mile. They wash a car and mow the lawn with the same perfectionist standards as they write a report or undertake a project at work.

Perfectionists allow for no gray areas when evaluating their performance; the rating system is A or F, success or failure, all or nothing. While this unwavering scale can produce enormous anxiety and frustration, the Perfectionists think it is the price they must pay for any success. They truly believe that if they stop or alter their basic methodology, they will slip from good to average, or even worse into mediocrity.

If a Perfectionist student thinks he got an A on a report because he spent three weeks writing it, revised it five times, and had two friends critique it, it is unlikely that he will spend less time and effort on the next report. If a fellow student with the same assignment got an A on the report after writing it in four days with no revisions, the Perfectionist would not think that perhaps there was a more efficient way to tackle the assignment. Instead, he would think that his fellow student was smarter, had more self-confidence, had a flair for writing. The same holds true for the Perfectionist who visits six department stores before buying the right dress for a cocktail party. If she found a beautiful garment at the first store, she would probably continue on to the other five stores just in case they had something better. Even if she finally purchased the dress in store number one, the Perfectionist would feel satisfied that she had considered every possible option before spending her money.

When Perfectionists make mistakes, they are very critical of themselves. Instead of accepting a mistake and learning from it, they berate themselves for being less than perfect and zero in on their flaws and shortcomings. "I should have" and "I could have" are part of the Perfectionists' everyday dialogue.

Striving for excellence and success is an admirable goal and sometimes "going the extra mile" is necessary. But the Perfectionists believe that the extra mile is not an option but a requirement. Unlike the Achievers and the Entrepreneurs, who enjoy putting forth additional effort, there is no pleasure for the Perfectionists. The extra effort hangs over them like a threat; if they don't try harder and harder, then they fail themselves as well as others. The stress to continually outperform themselves can become very debilitating.

If Perfectionists have to paddle their canoe at 110 percent just to stay in the race, how hard must they paddle to get ahead or to win the race? They keep upping the standards until the goals reach into the area of impossible. When the goals seem impossible, they choose not to play in the game for if they can't win, why try? Failure and rejection only reinforce their belief that somehow they didn't do their best.

Perfectionists have a hard time believing that some of their hard-earned success has come about in spite of their high standards instead of because of them; that in many endeavors 20 percent of total effort yields 80 percent of the results. They are their own worst critics, not allowing themselves to accept imperfect products, imperfect performances or game plans. They often waste valuable time and energy in self-defeating patterns and their ambition and work ethic bring them anxiety and self-doubt instead of confidence, success, and personal growth.

One of my clients, when evaluating the pros and cons of being a Perfectionist, wrote the following: "Plus side—1) If I try to reach a 10, I'll at least hit a 7 or 8; 2) I'll never feel like a total loser and won't be embarrassed by my work. Minus side—1) Sometimes I'm so nervous, I can hardly get my work done; 2) My life seems boring and dull because I'm afraid to try new things; 3) My friends say I nit-pick everything to death; 4) I can't seem to relax even on vacation because I'm worrying about what I have to do when I get back home; 5) Trying to do everything to perfection is just plain exhausting and frustrating; 6) I'm tired of criticizing myself—the way I think and look and act; 7) Being a Perfectionist doesn't seem to be getting me anywhere since I don't have the greatest job or salary; 8) I don't have a good personal relationship because I'm always finding fault with my dates; 9) No matter how hard I try I'm not usually satisfied with my performance."

Obviously, the minus side of the evaluation far outweighed the plus side. Nonetheless, breaking out of perfectionist habits can be difficult because the habits have been reinforcing even if in a negative way. Perfectionist standards have created a safe haven and a bench mark by which to avoid failure.

The Perfectionists have a difficult time trying to plot the perfect money game. In terms of investments, the Perfectionists set up many different criteria. Finding a completely suitable investment, one that meets all their different criteria, is a task that often is long and laborious. Perfectionists look at every different angle and say, "Oh, that will never work," or "That is too risky," or "If I'm really not convinced, I'd better say no." They don't allow themselves to see a balanced picture of money alternatives and have a tendency to talk themselves out of many opportunities that come along. They can find fault with any kind of financial involvement. They have a negative bias toward money and investments to such a degree that no matter how small the fly in the ointment, they will pluck it out as proof of imperfection.

Conservative with money, the Perfectionists tend to invest in very safe investments even though they express dissatisfaction with those investments. Their number-one financial goal is current income, followed by safety, growth/appreciation, and tax advantage. Because Perfectionists are so difficult to please, financial advisers often have a hard time talking money with them. Following is a typical investment dialogue between a Financial Planner (FP) and a Moneymax Perfectionist (MP):

FP: I can appreciate your concern about taking risks, but have you ever considered that keeping all your money in the bank is an even greater risk than you imagine? For example, let's assume that you're earning 7 percent on your CD and that your tax bracket is 33 percent; that means that, before adjusting for inflation, your after-tax return is about 4.7 percent. If inflation is low, let's say 5 percent, your inflation-adjusted return will be a negative .3 percent. Yes, the money will still be in the bank but its earning power is being eroded by taxes and inflation, factors over which you have no control.

MP: Yes, I know, but at least my money will be safe.

FP: You should consider other options that will provide you with as much safety as you desire but will yield you a positive return along with growth opportunities to fight inflation.

MP: I don't really care about fighting inflation anymore because

I've tried that over the years and it just doesn't work. I've lost money in everything I've ever invested in—stocks, bonds, commodities, and mutual funds. You can't tell me that there's anything as safe as keeping your money in the bank. I'd just rather know that the money will be there regardless of what happens.

FP: Yes, but you're losing money without even making an attempt to improve your financial condition. You're just giving money away by throwing in the towel and you're basing it all on your past negative experiences. You can have the opportunity for reversing that trend if you will allow yourself a different point of view by becoming aware of other possibilities. For example, you could invest as little as $2,500 in a partnership that is a pool of residential mortgages and have the principal and interest guaranteed by the U.S. Government. You'd receive cash flow on a quarterly basis, starting at about 6 percent in the first year and increasing by one half of 1 percent per year, plus an equity position in the appreciation of the real estate. The average annual rate of return, considering cash flow plus equity, could be about 12 percent—not bad considering the low risk nature of the investment.

MP: Yes, but you can't get at your money if you need it and there's got to be some risk.

FP: There is risk, but it is less risk than keeping all your money in the bank because you have steady reliable cash flow, growth opportunity—that doesn't exist in your bank account—and it's backed by the government.

MP: Yeah, but how much risk is there—2 percent, 3 percent? That counts for something. By the time you eliminate that 3 percent, you're back down to 9 percent and then that's only 3 percent or in some cases 2 percent more than what I'm making now on my money and all I have to do is leave it in the bank. Oh, and we haven't mentioned your commissions that would also come out of that investment, so we're talking about even less than 2 percent.

FP: If you assigned a 3 percent risk factor to this investment, you should assign the same risk factor to your bank account. As for the commissions, it is a no-load investment. That means that your entire $2,500 is working for you and commissions have not been deducted from it before it was invested in the mortgages.

MP: But you must get paid somehow?

FP: Yes, that's true. I do get paid a commission but it's not deducted from the amount you invest. If you feel that it isn't worth trying to make 6 to 8 percent more per year net after taxes as opposed to keeping your money in the bank, I'm not sure what else I can say to convince you to consider other investments.

MP: Well, I guess you can call me a cynic, but you haven't convinced me.

On the job, the Perfectionists' need to perform up to the highest standards can thwart their productivity and efficiency. If they work on an hourly basis like most professionals or skilled workers, they might put in a lot of extra time to ensure that every project is worthy of their seal of approval. Too much time invested in one assignment may cause them to miss a deadline or lose valuable hours that need to be allocated for another assignment. Instead of gaining a reputation for being dedicated and meticulous, they may be viewed as high strung and unable to budget their time efficiently. When passed over for a promotion or denied an adequate salary increase, Perfectionists are disappointed, resentful, and perplexed. Instead of reevaluating work habits and allocation of time, they pledge to work harder and produce better results, and the self-sabotaging cycle begins again. The unreasonable goals and demands they inflict upon themselves are only exacerbated by frustration and defeat. If their goals and work habits were reasonable, they wouldn't find themselves continually in the same trap.

WHEN HARD WORK DOESN'T PAY OFF

One of my clients, a Perfectionist, was aware that he wasn't living up to his potential but was at a loss to explain why. Charles was a tax lawyer who had worked for the IRS for eight years before going into practice for himself. He stated that he had only one goal: he wanted to earn more money. Charles emphatically claimed that he was a hardworking, ambitious man with a solid career and client base, yet he wasn't making as much money as other tax attorneys; he was always trying to catch up with himself financially.

Not only was Charles overly critical in describing his inability to earn money, but he was also highly critical when talking about his personal life. A single man, he dated frequently but hardly ever saw any woman more than two or three times. Over the last two years his longest relationship with a woman had lasted for three months. In addition, he said that neither his family nor friends had been very supportive when he opened his own law office; some of them took their tax business to other attorneys or accountants. At one time or another, just about everyone who mattered to Charles had let him down, had failed to come through for him.

The key to the Perfectionists' self-deception lies in the way they cover up insecure feelings and their reluctance to take a risk, whether the risk is personal or professional. They always manage to find a "good" reason or excuse for avoiding whatever makes them feel uncomfortable or afraid.

Charles was extremely conscientious, but his diligence was costing him a lot of money. He told his clients that they could call him anytime during the day when they needed advice. He often talked to each client for thirty minutes, maybe forty-five minutes, and never billed any of them for counsel given on the telephone. His fear that he wasn't giving them the very best advice caused him to volunteer hours of free service. Not only was he losing money in not billing his hours, but his office paperwork was backed up and some of his projects were more than six weeks overdue. Most weekdays he stayed in the office until eight or nine o'clock in the evening. It was an exhausting schedule that he blamed totally on his clients. He said, "If I don't do the work right, they'll leave; I have to give them what they want."

Underneath Charles's rationale was a feeling of abandonment. He projected his own critical nature onto his clients and thus saw the world as full of people who were waiting to judge him. If he didn't live up to his clients' expectations, they would no longer hire him and he would be abandoned. What Charles didn't understand was that the expectations, the high standards of performance, were designed not by his clients but by him.

Another reason that Charles was having a cash flow problem was his fee schedule. His hourly rate was well below the amount charged by other lawyers with his expertise. While he acknowledged that his fees were not high enough, he was afraid to raise them and risk losing clients. But he resented the fact that he couldn't always afford the few luxuries he allowed himself like buying fine wines, taking a weekend gambling jaunt to Reno, or vacationing in Hawaii. He didn't, however, allow his pleasures to drive him into debt and was quite skillful at budgeting his money. Yet he always had to prioritize his luxuries because he never had enough money to pay for everything, a fact that depressed him even though he insisted that he was used to making sacrifices.

Most of Charles's money was in a savings account and a money market account. He said he planned to buy a house one day and wanted quick access to his money. The only investment he had been tempted to make was one that he stumbled upon five years ago while on a one-week vacation in Hawaii. He had discovered a condominium complex on the island of Kauai that was greatly undervalued. The units were selling for $36,000, a price that astounded Charles. After thoroughly scrutinizing the condition of the units and checking on nearby land values and housing, he was convinced that he had found a fabulous investment, one that he would buy and rent out. He even entertained the thought of moving in himself, moving his business to Hawaii.

When Charles returned home, he told clients and friends about the condominiums and recommended that they consider buying into the complex. Several of them did follow up on his advice and purchased units. At the last minute Charles changed his mind and decided not to buy the condominium. When he was on vacation, his guard was down and his normally cynical self was tempered by an impulsive desire to make some changes in his life—buy some real estate in Hawaii and perhaps move there. When he arrived home, his old Perfectionist role slipped back into place, and he found enough good reasons to stop himself from making the investment. As he related the story to me, he concluded by saying that since he first saw the complex, the units had escalated in value to just under $200,000. Charles said he was somewhat angry with himself for letting such a good deal get by him but that at least some of his clients had profited.

Clients came to Charles to analyze their business deals and learn how to obtain the best tax advantages. His IRS experience and his legal background enabled him to give sound, expert advice. However, despite his admirable track record for others, he never structured a business deal for himself. When it came to advising himself, he was so self-critical that he didn't see how he was getting in the way of his own financial success.

Like Charles, none of us set out deliberately to mismanage our careers or our money. People often make decisions that unknowingly are self-destructive, not because they want to fail but because they don't have a clear idea of who they are and what they want to accomplish. It's easy to mismanage the truth, if the truth is elusive.

No matter how inflexible a person appears to be or how rigid a behavior, there is always an escape exit somewhere. No matter how compulsive people are about their lives, there are times when patterns are broken and the trace of a new identity appears. When Charles tired of his self-critical nature, he escaped by gambling in Reno, which was inconsistent with his usual handling of money—a safe, careful, prudent style. The overly cautious Safety Player might suddenly buy a Porsche. There are always a couple of instances when impulse wins out and the Perfectionists go for broke. Unfortunately, the money escape exits are too often a disaster—desert acreage schemes, walnut and avocado groves enticingly displayed in four-color brochures. Charles's impulsive trips to Reno were justifiable to him yet he couldn't justify his impulsive desire to buy a condominium in Hawaii.

Once Charles examined his Perfectionist profile, he was able to see how his critical attitudes affected his work and his investment style. He was willing to develop new work and money systems to increase his productivity and prosperity.

There was nothing wrong with Charles's policy of keeping his clients satisfied and happy. It is the long-term satisfied client who is the most profitable and cost-effective for professionals like Charles who rely on a steady and ever-increasing caseload. Satisfied clients not only bring repeat business but are the source of referrals. However, Charles was giving his clients entirely too much free time, and ultimately people don't particularly prize what they get for nothing. As standard policy, Charles advised his clients that he had reorganized his time schedule and would be taking phone calls in the morning between eight and nine o'clock, allotting a maximum of ten minutes per call. If a question or problem required more than ten minutes, clients would have to schedule a meeting in his office. He would be available again in the afternoon from four-thirty to five-thirty.

Charles also decided to hire a full-time assistant to replace his part-time secretary. Up to then the only time he'd hired full-time help was during his busiest times of the year like tax season and tax planning. His assistant would be trained not only to do the clerical work but also to interact with clients and act as a troubleshooter. Charles would have to train the assistant to handle problems, not just to pass them along to him. The assistant needed to become proficient in building and reinforcing client relationships and in screening Charles's calls. In time, his assistant would learn which calls should be handled during Charles's designated telephone hours and which should be handled immediately.

The important issue for Charles was that he not fragment his time and distract himself from those duties that had to get done every day. He needed to adopt more organized work systems in order to maximize his efforts and learn the difference between compulsiveness and proficiency. He set up a systematic filing system which kept his work organized on a daily basis. He had file folders for each day of the month that included the day's scheduled tasks. He budgeted his time on those projects so that he could complete a day's work within one day and not carry one day's work forward into the next day.

Once his calls were targeted for certain hours of the day, Charles found that he was able to get a lot more work done. Since Charles needed a great deal of concentration while working on complex tax matters, he could not afford the constant interruption of phone calls in the middle of his peak, productive time.

Utilizing work systems that facilitated productivity, hiring a capable person to assist him, and analyzing and altering his overcritical nature were objectives Charles had to achieve before he could become more financially successful. His current style was not the least bit pleasurable, exciting, or challenging, but created resentment and anger. Also, he was experiencing a lot of anxiety in making the smallest of financial decisions, a common trait of the Perfectionists, who generally agonize over money problems.

Charles was initially resistant to hiring an assistant, thinking only of the money he'd have to take from his already sparse budget and what luxuries he'd have to sacrifice in order to pay a full-time salary. He was very shortsighted in his thinking because he didn't consider that, with steady help, he'd be free to go after new clients or to pursue new opportunities with existing clients. Charles had never planned to expand his business because he was always worrying about finishing the work at hand. Thoughts of expansion made him nervous even though he wanted to make as much money as he possibly could.

His reluctance to hire an assistant was not solely due to the monetary cost, but was also tied into his money personality. Because Perfectionists are low in trust, Charles wasn't sure he could find exactly the right person to depend upon. Also, because Perfectionists carefully control all situations, Charles was not inclined to delegate responsibility. Giving up some control and incurring an extra expense was a combination that was alarming to him. However, he believed that the time and money he invested in the short-term would bring him much more in the long-term.

Although it required a lot of effort, Charles successfully altered his work style and curbed his highly critical ways. He doubled his income in just short of two years. He currently makes $120,000 in annual gross income and has been able to keep his expenses and overhead down. His assistant averaged out to a cost of about $30,000 a year, including benefits, but she was worth much more in the long run.

It's difficult to generalize about the Perfectionists and whether their criticalness appears to affect all areas of their lives. It certainly affects their financial lives since they have such a difficult time choosing investments that will bring them both profits and peace of mind. If they have a chronic tendency, like Charles, they will be critical whether choosing a job or choosing a mate. Yet Perfectionists will have areas that may not be affected. In his accounting and legal work, Charles exemplified perfection, right down to every comma and semicolon. His apartment, however, was a disheveled mess, and he had no interest in changing his living conditions. The disorderly apartment provided a release, a letting off of steam, a breakaway from the control he experienced in his professional life. The same kind of release mechanism is sought by the overly cautious Safety Player who drives a Porsche full speed down the highway.

Of all the Moneymax groups, the Perfectionists are the least content with the personal happiness that money has brought them. However, they are willing to accept personal responsibility for their financial status, even though they experience great confusion in determining the causes for their lack of financial success.

They score very high in self-determination, in third position after the Money Masters and the Achievers, yet have little to show for it. The Perfectionists rank eighth in income and ninth in assets. Despite their overall low ranking in income, 13 percent of them earn between $30,000 and $40,000 a year, and 11 percent earn in excess of $40,000. They are mostly middle-aged, and on the average are forty-five years old. As a group, they have an above-average number of divorced people, and 54 percent are married with dependent children living at home.

The Perfectionists lack positive self-esteem, particularly with their money. Of all the Moneymax Profiles they experience the least amount of pride in the way they handle their money. Their negative sense of themselves significantly impacts their financial status because they feel they have little about which to feel proud. They do not impulsively and destructively act out their feelings by emotional spending. Rather, they state that they prefer saving money to spending it, perhaps as a reaction to their tight budgets. The significant point here is that they don't foolishly wait for a rich fairy godmother to rescue them. They accept responsibility for their fate, yet at the same time attribute too much of their perceived financial failure to their own lack of abilities and skills, thus damaging positive expectations for future success. It is as if they are resigned to their financial stations in life, ambivalent about motivating themselves to strive for greater financial gain.

Perfectionists are very deliberative about financial decisions. Second-highest in reflectivity (tied with the Money Masters), they carefully assess what they have done in the past, but they are perhaps too reflective for their own good. Unlike the Money Masters and Achievers with similar scores in reflectivity, the Perfectionists use reflectivity as a stalling mechanism, a way to procrastinate and keep themselves from taking action. Reflectivity, which is a very positive financial trait, is not properly used by the Perfectionists to foster personal and financial well-being and confidence. Perfectionists can deliberate until they talk themselves out of risking change in their style of operation and thinking. They can stay on the same job, function with unprogressive beliefs and attitudes, remain in unhappy personal relationships, manage money in an unproductive manner. In short, they are reluctant to move away from anything that symbolizes security.

They tend to accept their financial lot in life rather than fighting assertively to change it.

NO DEAL IS EVER PERFECT

Murray was a Perfectionist who took three months to decide where to put his $2,000 IRA. His wife Beth explained his dilemma: "He wants a ton of money without any risk." He finally invested his IRA money in a real estate limited partnership, feeling that it had a good balance between safety and return.

Murry took even longer to decide what house he wanted to buy. He and Beth searched at great length for the perfect house for almost a year while interest rates were climbing. Between Beth's high standards for the home's necessary amenities and Murray's difficulty in making financial decisions, it was a frustrating experience. While they both described themselves as "fussy," they also agreed that Murray was the more difficult one to please. Beth described Murray as "somebody who can't make a financial decision. He will sit and analyze the situation from now till doomsday." Included on Beth's house requirement list were a large kitchen, a lot of storage space, an outdoor area for entertaining, and three bedrooms. Murray's concerns were strictly financial. He wanted to be sure that the property would be resalable, that it would appreciate; if they wanted to sell the house in five to seven years, he wanted to feel certain that they would reap a profit. He also wanted to live in a strong, viable community.

Beth finally found the house that she wanted to buy and urged Murray to agree to the purchase. Real estate was still selling well even though the interest rates were beginning to climb. Still, rates had not been that low for a long time. Their real estate broker called several times to tell them that they had no further time to deliberate. Murray said the broker was trying to manipulate them, and he wouldn't be manipulated. Tired of being patient and understanding, Beth gave Murray an ultimatum—this house or no house.

The only drawback for buying the house was the railroad tracks that lay 100 feet behind the house. The owners and the broker told Murray that the train in operation on those tracks only came by once a day between ten-thirty and twelve-thirty Monday through Friday and at noon on Sunday. Murray verified the schedule by calling the Southern Pacific Railroad and had an attorney check to make sure that there were no plans to change the schedule or increase traffic on that line. With that information, Murray consented to buy the house; they closed escrow, and moved in.

They were content in their new home until six months later when the doorbell rang. It was a neighbor, who informed them of an upcoming public forum with city council members to discuss the "light rail" issue. According to the neighbor, many of the people in their community didn't know anything about the light rail.

Apparently, the light rail was an aboveground railway line which was part of the Metro Rail, the proposed new subway system for Los Angeles. As planned, a light rail portion of the Metro Rail would run on the tracks outside of Murray's house. A trolley would roll by their house every three minutes.

Murray became extremely agitated, and for the next two weeks he walked around in a state of frenzy. He knew it was a mistake to buy the house; he shouldn't have let Beth force him into a decision; he was sure the rail system would be approved and the value of his house would plummet. Beth said he was wasting a lot of energy by worrying and he should expend the energy by opposing the railway line.

Murray finally decided to take charge of the situation and joined a coalition of homeowners, schools, and other groups that opposed the light rail. Beth and Murray have played a major role in raising public awareness of the light rail and its adverse effects on their community. They are convinced that they will stop the proposed line, and in any event, they are not giving up. The coalition, which started out with 35 members, has increased to 1,200. Murray felt very good about the part he was playing, the actions he had taken on his own behalf as well as on behalf of the community.

In this case, the Perfectionist's close scrutiny did not pay off, but not due to his negligence. Murray thoroughly evaluated the house before purchasing it but could not have known about the proposed light rail system. Instead of endlessly denouncing himself for buying the house, he decided to take action and try to change the situation. He has made a major contribution to himself, his wife, and their future financial well-being. Murray is proud of himself, a trait which is often lacking in the Perfectionists.

STEPPING AWAY FROM THE SAFETY ZONE

Ben was in his early forties, divorced, and the father of a sixteen-year-old daughter. He was raised to believe that money is indeed the root of all evil and that the pursuit of money would bring unhappiness and pain. His parents resented people with more money than they had and said that rich people got rich by being dishonest, not by working hard. The messages were so strong and so persuasive, that despite how hard Ben tried to ignore them, he became apprehensive about money and its meaning in his life. Ben's mother told him that "money kills" and used his grandfather's death to prove her assertion. On many occasions, she related the details of her father's life: how he worked long hours; how he was consumed with accumulating more and more money; how he died at age forty-eight from a heart attack.

As the manager of a small art gallery, Ben worked sixty hours a week for a very low salary. His friend Anthony owned the business and had convinced Ben that he was the man to turn a small business into a huge success. Anthony promised Ben a share of the gallery as soon as it started to show a reasonable profit. An aspiring artist, Ben refused to show his paintings to anyone. While he believed in his talent and intelligence, he was unable to set financial goals for himself. Not only was he reluctant to market his art work, Ben was also unable to ask Anthony for a much deserved raise.

Ben had many excuses to explain why he had not exhibited his painting anywhere, including Anthony's art gallery. All of the excuses were a camouflage to hide his highly critical judgment of his work and fears of rejection. He described himself as a person with high standards and said he found it difficult to join artists' associations because his work might not be judged superior.

Ben lived in a studio apartment in a beach town on the West Coast. He had a spartan lifestyle, saved his money to send to his ex-wife for child support, and spent what little he had left to buy art supplies and pay for an occasional date. He knew some very interesting women but found it difficult to move from friendship to romance. After all, what woman would want a serious relationship with a struggling artist?

I first met Ben in the art gallery. He was intrigued by the Moneymax Profile and asked if he could barter his paintings for my services since he was short of funds. He had placed himself in a position where he was forced to show a stranger his art work. When I saw his paintings, I was surprised by his talent because he had described himself as an amateur and his work as the kind of art displayed at local art fairs and bazaars. Quite the contrary, he was an exceptional artist. Our exchange would certainly be mutually beneficial.

When Ben learned that he was a Moneymax Perfectionist, he said it made sense since he reminded himself of his overly critical father, who never gave anyone a real chance. Ben had difficulty coming to grips with the fact that he was his own worst enemy and that his money style reflected self-imposed barriers. At first he stated that he did not want to make significant changes in his life; he just wanted his fair share of Anthony's business. He felt frustrated because he seemed to care more about the gallery's success than Anthony did. In fact, Ben wondered if Anthony only wanted the gallery as a tax shelter, while he purchased art for his personal collection. It appeared that Anthony cared very little about whether the gallery did, or did not, make money.

Ben was a Perfectionist whose overly critical style prevented him from asserting himself financially. He lacked the self-esteem to risk marketing his paintings because he was afraid to have them evaluated by gallery owners and the public. It was easier to remain a struggling artist, waiting to be discovered in his one-room apartment over a garage. However, as he got older he became increasingly frustrated that no matter how hard he worked, he was always surrounded by financial constraints.

Ben ultimately discarded the belief that going after money would bring him misfortune and instead saw money as a means to provide personal freedom and financial independence. He had not realized how his family's messages about money being evil had infiltrated his attitudes. Even though he valued his talent and took his work very seriously, he had conducted his career and personal life in a robot-like fashion. He began to develop both short-term and long-term goals to improve his financial situation and put his career back on track.

Ben began by talking to Anthony about his future at the art gallery: when could he expect to receive a share of the business; what kind of salary increases could he expect; what plans did Anthony have for expanding the gallery? When confronted, Anthony admitted that the gallery was not a high priority in his life and he was unwilling to put any more of his money into expansion; he would give Ben a small salary increase every year, but could not predict when Ben would get a share of the business. With that information, Ben decided to take the salary increase and keep his job until he could get a better position, but he had no illusions about becoming a partner in the business. In addition, he decided that it was time to start selling his own paintings.

Initially, Ben was very disappointed by the reaction to his work. After taking his canvases to a number of galleries, he received only mild encouragement, and only one gallery owner was enthusiastic. She agreed to display his work but chose only one painting. She did, however, spend a considerable amount of time analyzing his work and making suggestions as to how he could improve his technique. Rejection and criticism were a hard combination for Ben to endure. But, after admitting that her suggestions had some validity, he decided to follow her advice. When he returned to her gallery with two new paintings, she was delighted with the results and accepted both of them.

As Ben learned to deal with rejection, it became easier to approach more galleries and risk being turned away. He was selling his work and making some extra money and moving forward toward his goals. He learned the hard way what is often easy for profiles like the Entrepreneurs and the Achievers.

A year after selling his first painting, Ben moved to New York City where he took a job as an assistant manager for a very reputable art gallery. He asked for, and received, a salary that was a third more than Anthony had paid him; he also got employee benefits and a promise that he could travel, at company expense, to shop for art for the business. His last dilemma was to set higher prices for his paintings; he had reached a point where he could start demanding much higher prices for his work. When Ben showed his paintings to his new boss, he was advised that his $250 and $350 price tags were far below market value. With as much apprehension as excitement, he began charging four and five times those amounts.

I last heard from Ben when I received a postcard announcing his one-man show in a gallery in Boston. He signed it: "Sincerely, Ben—former Perfectionist, now my own biggest fan and supporter." Ben had accepted the fact that he was primarily responsible for fulfilling his career and financial aspirations. He also realized that he had a great talent that could bring him tremendous personal satisfaction as well as financial security. In addition, if he continued to revise his money thinking and style, he could structure a life which allowed money to bring him peace of mind and the luxury of creative freedom. He had learned to trust, a feat which is not easy for the Perfectionists.

FINANCIAL REFRAMING

The Perfectionists have a significantly low level of trust in how other people deal with money. Because they are so self-critical and project their critical natures upon others, it follows that Perfectionists not only expect to find fault, they look for it. They tend to be negative, suspicious, and cynical of anyone's motives, attitudes, and behaviors concerning money. If Perfectionists don't trust themselves, it follows that they may not trust other people.

Unlike the Safety Players, who believe that economic conditions can be changed if luck intervenes, the Perfectionists are more realistic, believing that a willingness to accept financial responsibility does make a difference. The point is just that: they continue to reflect hard work in their careers instead of smart work. As long as they stay locked in a pattern of criticizing and blaming themselves instead of sizing up reality and making changes, they will continue to work hard instead of smart and be frustrated with their money status. Like Ben, who wasn't making the money he wanted or deserved, the Perfectionists are apt to analyze what they are doing wrong instead of looking at the entire situation and everyone involved to find the answer and rectify the situation. When they feel unappreciated and unrewarded, they are the last ones to ask for a raise or seek a new job. Instead, they tend to keep running in place and passively accept disappointment rather than assert themselves. They need to believe that they deserve financial success instead of looking at themselves as second-class citizens who are lucky to have a job. They need to reevaluate their skills and talents because many Perfectionists are under challenged and have much greater potential than they realize.

Perfectionists are not likely to gamble their money away, spend it emotionally, or steal it from someone else. In fact, they hold the strongest belief in the financial generosity of others. Since they are altruistic thinkers, it is likely that they are financial good samaritans and are much more comfortable giving money away than receiving it. However, an inability to receive money, as well as advice, can cause Perfectionists to pass up career and investment opportunities.

What the Perfectionists do with their money is dependent upon the meaning that they attach to money. We tend to view things, like money, based upon how we have perceived them in the past. By changing habitual perception patterns, we can create greater choices in our lives, as Ben was able to do. If we perceive money as a liability, that's the message we deliver to our brain and the message that comes to mind when making financial decisions. If we change our frame of reference by looking at money from a different point of view, we can change the way we respond.

One technique used with Ben and other Perfectionists is called financial reframing. In its simplest form, it means changing a negative statement into a positive one by changing the frame of reference used to perceive a money experience. There are two types of reframing: context reframing and content reframing.

Context reframing involves taking a behavior or experience that seems bad or undesirable and showing how the same behavior or experience can be seen as an advantage in another context. For example, Ben believed that his grandfather's ambition and quest for money was detrimental because his grandfather died at forty-eight. After discussing his grandfather's life, Ben admitted that his grandfather was a businessman who thrived on hard work and was very proud of his accomplishments. Also, his grandfather was a man who enjoyed making and spending money; money had enabled him to travel to Europe, put his children through college, and buy peace of mind and security for him and his wife. Had his mother not constantly tied ambition and money to his grandfather's death, Ben would have believed that his grandfather was a happy, satisfied, successful businessman.

Content reframing involves taking the exact same situation and changing what it means. For example, Ben's mother might say that "all rich people don't work very hard and are lazy." After content reframing, we might conclude that "rich people are fortunate to have so much free leisure time to really enjoy their lives and their money."

There are multiple meanings to any experience. The meaning is whatever you choose to emphasize, just as its content is what you choose to focus upon. One of the keys to financial success is finding the most useful frame for any money experience so you can turn it into something that works for you rather than against you.

MONEY MANAGEMENT STYLE

1. Perfectionists perceive commodities/options, futures contracts, and limited partnerships as the highest in risk of all investments.

2. Of those investments they believe are high in risk, they have been least satisfied with limited partnerships.

3. At the other end of the spectrum, annuities and life insurance receive their lowest scores in levels of perceived risk.

4. Real estate, IRAs and Keoghs rank at the top of the list of the investments with which they are the most satisfied.

5. The Perfectionists perceive owning individual shares of common stock as a risky investment—more so than any of the other Moneymax groups. However, they also tend to perceive many investments, which by comparison are not inherently risky—like municipal bonds, government bonds, and whole life insurance—as having moderately high risk.

6. Perfectionists can have tunnel vision. They are hard to get through to, and because they are so fearful, they are not able to distinguish money truth from money fiction. They have a difficult time trusting financial advisers, and probably prefer to make investment decisions themselves. However, they experience high levels of anxiety when making financial decisions, so they could benefit from professional support and education, but they must learn how to take some risk in the process; otherwise, nothing will change. Since they would immediately reject any high pressure sales approach, they should seek out and select a competent, low key adviser. Perfectionists often feel

most comfortable attending seminars which give them an opportunity to observe without making a personal commitment and to be in an environment where they can be anonymous. Their skepticism impedes expanding their awareness and knowledge and therefore stymies greater financial growth. Many Perfectionists, once aware of their Moneymax Profile, will be able to transform their high level of skepticism into a more rational approach. Perfectionists can learn to utilize their analytical money personalities to make well-informed financial decisions which will lead to profitable investment results. When this occurs, their confidence in themselves, as well as their trust in others, will increase.

THE PERFECTIONISTS— FINANCIAL STATEMENT

The Perfectionists have similar scores on the traits that have brought great financial gain to the Achievers and the Money Masters—low emotionality, high reflectivity, high self-determination. Yet, of all the Moneymax groups, the Perfectionists are the lowest in both contentment and pride with their money. In addition, they rank eighth in income and ninth in assets.

Their overly critical nature and fear of taking risks prevent them from being better money managers. They do believe they are responsible for their financial lives and are very reflective when making money decisions. However, their reflectivity loses its effectiveness because it tends to reinforce the Perfectionists' highly critical nature and prevents them from taking action with their careers as well as their investments.

Overall, the Perfectionists' average age is forty-five, making them the third-youngest of the Moneymax groups. The Perfectionists' money style inhibits progress and assertion with money. They distrust themselves and become self-punitive with their money. They get more satisfaction by saving money rather than spending it and believe that people are basically dishonest when handling financial transactions.

They are very altruistic, believing that most people are willing to help others in financial difficulty.

When Perfectionists analyze and alter their self-sabotaging traits and become active, rather than passive, in the money game, they not only parallel the affluent Moneymax groups in trait scores, but they begin to compete in terms of income and assets.

11

Money Masters

He who knows much about others may be learned, but he who understands himself is more intelligent. He who controls others may be powerful, but he who has mastered himself is mightier still.

—Lao-tzu

GUIDELINES
Money Masters

. . . Are successful in accumulating assets.

. . . Are confident of their future financial security.

. . . Are very content with their money.

. . . Like to be highly involved in managing their money.

. . . Are proud of their financial accomplishments.

. . . Are wise financial decision-makers.

. . . Trust that other people are honest when dealing with their money.

The Money Masters are just that—masters of themselves and their money. While they're third in income, surpassed by the first-place Entrepreneurs and the second-place Achievers, the Money Masters are first in assets. On the average, they're only four years older than the Achievers and the Entrepreneurs (average age of forty-six for the Achievers and the Entrepreneurs; average age of fifty for the Money Masters), so age doesn't appear to be the major contributing factor for the difference in asset accumulation. The Money Masters do have fewer dependent children under twenty-five years of age (32 percent) as opposed to 40 percent for the Achievers and 38 percent for the Entrepreneurs. Thus, the number of dependent children could be a determining factor that allows the Money Masters to accumulate more; however, the percentages do not differ that significantly.

More of the Money Masters are retired or near retirement—38 percent of them are sixty years and older—compared with 27 percent of the Entrepreneurs and twenty-four percent of the Achievers in the same age category. In addition, 53 percent of the Achievers have two spouses contributing to the family income while the Entrepreneurs have 50 percent and the Money Masters have only 46 percent. Those two factors, fewer two-income families and a greater number of older, retired members, might explain why the Money Masters are third in income.

One might argue that higher education is a direct link to higher income. However, we have already seen that the Entrepreneurs, who are first in income, are only fourth in education behind the Achievers, who are tied with the Hunters for first place. Interestingly, the educated Achievers are second in income and second in assets while the educated Hunters are fifth in income, sixth in assets. The Money Masters rank third in the number of college graduates and it is likely that, like the Achievers, the Money Masters have reaped tangible profits from their education.

If the demographics only partly explain the Money Masters' superior wealth accumulation, then the reason lies in their attitudes and feelings about money. And indeed, their money personalities do eliminate a lot of the mystery and explain the variance in wealth accumulation between the Money Masters and the Moneymax high income earners, the Entrepreneurs and the Achievers. The superior financial assets of the Money Masters are more attributable to their money attitudes than to age, education, income, and dependent children.

The Money Masters are in control; they know themselves and their money styles. They are aware of who they are, where they have been, and where they are going. Their money sense of themselves is both positive and secure. Of all the nine Moneymax groups, they rank the highest in involvement and contentment, are tied for first position with the Achievers in self-determination and pride, and are tied for first position with the Producers in work ethic and trust. Of all the groups, the Money Masters are the lowest in two traits that handicap wise and fruitful money management: emotionality and anxiety (tied with the Optimists in emotionality and anxiety scoring).

While even the Money Masters can fall short of total financial satisfaction, they have discovered the formula for both using and enjoying their money to their greatest benefit and pleasure. They have found the optimum balance between the control and mastery of money and the contentment and sense of security they reap from it. After making a decision to alter their money styles, many of my clients choose to model the Money Masters because they make optimal use of all of their personal financial traits. Likewise, they have nothing working against them to prevent a constant, steady climb to the top of the financial heap.

Master is defined as "a person with the ability or power to use, control, or dispose of something." In terms of money, this Moneymax Profile epitomizes the definition. The Money Masters not only have the power to accumulate their money better than any other Moneymax group, but also they are able to use their money to provide self-satisfaction and contentment better than any one else. It makes no sense to have wealth if you can't enjoy it and make it work for you. It makes no sense to work hard for money but wind up feeling insecure because you have no accumulated assets like some of the Moneymax Profiles, the Producers and the Perfectionists to name just two. Because the Money Masters exemplify an ideal blending of the thirteen financial traits, it is worthwhile to take a look at how they score on each trait and to compare and contrast those scores with the scores of other Moneymax groups:

Involvement—the degree you desire to be personally responsible and involved in managing and investing your money (first place). The Money Masters desire involvement with their money to an even greater extent than the Achievers. The Money Masters are involved and remain in control because they enjoy money management, while the Achievers have to be highly involved because they don't trust others with their money. The Moneymax groups lowest in involvement are the Safety Players and the Optimists.

Trust—the level of honesty you believe people have in dealing with money (tied for first place with the Producers). While both the

Achievers and the Money Masters have confidence in their money management skills, the Money Masters would trust someone else's financial advice long before the Achievers would. Since the Achievers score second-lowest in trust (the Safety Players trust even less), they tend not to relinquish control of money and investments, while the Money Masters have a much easier time listening to others, be it a knowledgeable broker, accountant, financial planner, banker, or friend. This does not mean in any way that Money Masters can be victims of blind trust; they are savvy with money and scrutinize all angles before making decisions. Even though the Achievers and Money Masters might use a discount brokerage house to execute their own trades, Money Masters are more likely to use the services of a broker who has won their confidence by making sound investments. While the Money Masters would not allow a broker or financial planner to make a unilateral financial decision, they do not turn a deaf ear to advice that might be profitable for them.

It should be noted that this difference in trust does not imply that the Achievers never employ brokers or financial planners. They certainly do, but Achievers are more skeptical than Money Masters and have a more difficult time sharing control of their money. It is likely that Money Masters can trust others because they trust themselves. It is much easier to trust others when you trust yourself, no matter what the currency of the transaction. Because the Money Masters count on themselves to treat everyone else's money as if it were their own, they believe that the money road runs two ways. After the Money Masters and the Producers, the other Moneymax group that scores high in trust is the Optimists.

Reflectivity—the extent to which you reflect upon past financial decisions while making current decisions (tied for second place with the Perfectionists). The only group that outscores the Money Masters, and not by a significant difference, is the Achievers. While the Money Masters and Achievers use reflectivity for solid financial gain and growth, the Perfectionists use it to overly criticize themselves and whatever financial opportunities are presented to them. The lowest scores on reflectivity belong to the Safety Players and the Optimists.

Self-determination—the extent to which you feel in control of your financial destiny (tied for first place with the Achievers). The Money Masters do not rely on fate to help them make money. They believe that their talent, knowledge, and skills will ultimately lead to financial success. Long-term as well as short-term thinkers, the Money Masters analyze what they want and then determine the most expedient, efficient way to fulfill their goals. Other groups that have high scores in self-determination are the Perfectionists and the Producers. The two groups most likely to believe that financial success is primarily due to good luck are the Optimists and the Safety Players. While the Entrepreneurs have average scores in this trait, they are so convinced of eventual success that they believe in good luck not bad luck. While a low or average score in self-determination tends to be a handicap in the money game, it does not negatively impact the Entrepreneurs, who are the number-one Moneymax wage earners.

Risk-taking—the level of comfort you feel in taking risks with your money (eighth place). The only group that takes less risks with money is the Achievers. The Money Masters turn a very calculating eye on money because they want to be assured that it always works for them, not against them. They calculate each money step as part of a meaningful strategy that will ultimately lead to the accumulation of more wealth. The Money Masters do not take risks unless they have covered their bets. They like to know that whatever money moves they make will be profitable as well as bring them contentment and peace of mind. Unlike the Entrepreneurs, the Money Masters do not feel compelled to take risks in order to be successful.

Of all the Moneymax groups, the only two that take high risks are the High Rollers and the Entrepreneurs. If they aren't very careful, the Entrepreneurs can find risk-taking to be a money trap. Their zealous commitment to their vision and goals can lead them to assume more risk than they can afford. However, while risk-taking doesn't restrict the earning power of the Entrepreneurs (first in income), it might influence their asset accumulation (third place, behind the second-place Achievers, who are the lowest risk-takers). For the High Rollers, risk-taking can be a financial disaster, causing them to rank overall seventh in income, eighth in assets.

Emotionality—the degree of emotion you feel in dealing with your money (tied for last place with the Optimists). The Money Masters have no emotional attachment to money but use it in a rational manner, as a tool to buy them security, happiness, and peace of mind. Besides the Money Masters and the Optimists, other Moneymax groups who do not allow feelings to guide financial decisions are the Achievers, the Safety Players, the Perfectionists, and the Entrepreneurs. On the other end of the emotionality scale are the Hunters and the High Rollers.

Spending—reflects your attitudes for spending versus saving your money (tied for second to last place with the Achievers and the Producers). The Money Masters feel better when they save money instead of spending it. That is not to say that they don't spend money and don't enjoy spending it. However, they tend to spend money on appreciable items and are greatly influenced by the value of an item before making a decision to purchase.

Money Masters prioritize their goals and objectives and develop a spending plan that reflects their priorities. That spending plan guarantees that they will remain in control of their money and continue to accumulate assets.

The Hunters, the victims of emotional spending, can benefit greatly by adopting the spending style of the Money Masters. The imbalance between spending and saving (accumulating assets) makes the Hunters feel out of control with money. The Hunters spend money without any real awareness that they may be sacrificing future security for the pleasures of the moment. One of the reasons the Money Masters have so much contentment with money is due to the fact that they know how to accumulate money for themselves, by themselves. The Hunters, unfortunately, are too ambivalent about taking care of themselves. Too often the Hunters do not try to influence their financial results and instead choose to remain powerless at making changes in the results on their financial scoreboard.

Anxiety—the degree of anxiety you feel in making financial decisions (tied for last place with the Optimists). The Money Masters are confident, steadfast, and resilient when working with money. Their lack of emotion and anxiety results in levelheaded, sound money management styles. A financial mistake does not cause them to doubt their abilities. Other Moneymax groups low in anxiety are the Entrepreneurs, Achievers, and Safety Players. The groups that tend to get nervous about money and money decisions are the Producers, the High Rollers, the Perfectionists, and the Hunters.

Power—the extent that the desire for power drives your behavior (tied for last place with the Optimists). Contrary to popular opinion, the segment of American society with the most assets, the Money Masters, is very uninterested in receiving public recognition because of their money. While the Moneymax groups as a whole reflect a low desire for power and prestige, there are some profiles that tend to shift toward the power end of the spectrum: the High Rollers (seventh in income and tied for seventh in assets); the Producers (ninth in income and tied for seventh in assets); the Hunters (fifth in income and sixth in assets).

Altruism—the extent to which you believe in the financial generosity of others (third place). The three top profiles in this trait—the Perfectionists, the Producers, and the Money Masters—have very close scores. It is interesting to note that while the Perfectionists and Producers are both low in income and assets, the Money Masters, one of the wealthiest groups, is also one of the most altruistic groups. Obviously, they don't accumulate more money because they refuse to give any away. Their practical, rational money style may cause them to hold on to their money, but they are not hoarders and they are not lacking in financial generosity. It's a common fallacy to assume that people who have money and assets get them because they are tight-fisted and contribute very little to others who are less fortunate. While it may be true that the Money Masters can afford to be altruistic, it is also true that people who can afford to give money to those in financial difficulty don't necessarily do so. Since the Money Masters don't have a need to impress others with their money (tied for lowest power motive), they don't use their charitable contributions to buy entry into elite society. Rather, they donate their money to causes and organizations which they truly want to support. The group that scores lowest in altruism is the Safety Players.

Work ethic—your views of how the work ethic relates to your financial success (tied for first place with the Producers). The Money Masters worked hard to get where they are and refute the assumption that the wealthy get wealthy by inheritance, nepotism, or dishonest means. After the Money Masters and Producers, the groups that score the highest in work ethic are the Achievers and the Entrepreneurs.

Pride—an index of the personal satisfaction you have attained in the way you have handled your money (tied for first place with the Achievers). Other groups with high pride are the Entrepreneurs and the Optimists. The lowest scores in pride belong to the Perfectionists.

Contentment—the degree of personal happiness money contributes to your life (first place). The Money Masters have positive, healthy, and profitable attitudes on all of the above financial traits. Thus, it is logical that of all Moneymax groups, the Money Masters have the highest contentment with money and have secured peace of mind with their financial status in life. Other very content groups are the Optimists and the Achievers. In the middle, with average contentment scores, are the Entrepreneurs and the Producers. The groups that are the most discontented with their current financial condition are the Safety Players, the Hunters, the High Rollers, and the Perfectionists.

When using the Money Masters as a model profile, it is pointless to isolate one or two traits to emulate. For example, it is counterproductive to think that if you can learn to trust the financial advice of others, you can become a Money Master. It is the combination of traits that works to their benefit. Because they are so knowledgeable, so involved, so in control of money, the Money Masters can trust others because they know who to trust, who is deserving of their trust.

When we look at the Money Masters and determine the reasons why they have accumulated so much, we find that it isn't so much that they have a magical investment formula as it is that they possess the basic money attitudes that foster financial success. They are practical; they don't need a lot of prestige and public recognition; their financial decisions are usually good ones. Most of the time their investment decisions have been profitable because they have been thoughtful and have avoided high risks, settling instead for steady, reasonable returns. Often the need to pursue high risk, the big kill with big returns, is more of a power play than a money motive. The fact that the Money Masters don't need prestige or recognition from anyone else enables them to analyze all financial options before committing themselves.

The Money Masters, in total control of money, are also the masters of self-esteem. They not only possess great confidence and a sense of accomplishment but also have significant contentment and feelings of personal worth. Their tremendous personal power earns them security and the belief that they can excel at whatever they set out to accomplish. The security and confidence that come from knowing they are in control give them high self-esteem and a high level of trust in their fellow man.

The Money Masters, third in income, are first in assets because of their healthy money personality and good, sound financial decisions. They dispel the notion that you have to make a lot more money in order to accumulate more assets. Instead, they prove that you have to use your money more wisely to assure continued financial success and security.

The Money Masters rank the four Moneymax financial goals in the same order as the Achievers and the Entrepreneurs: 1) growth and appreciation; 2) current income; 3) safety; 4) tax advantage. The Money Masters have done well in the real estate market and own single and multifamily rental properties; they consider both to be very satisfactory investments. The Money Masters also like whole life insurance, which gives them good, sheltered growth and fits their goal of accumulating assets conservatively. Its cash value is like buying a home and getting the equity versus buying term insurance (like renting) and receiving nothing if you live. Since the Tax Reform Act of 1986 was passed, many Money Masters, as well as financial advisers, feel that high quality cash value life insurance is one of the best financial vehicles for accumulating money for the future because all growth is sheltered from taxation until you take the money out.

For those Money Masters who are more interested in current income than growth, municipal bonds or bond funds are one of the preferred investment choices. The bond funds allow them greater diversification of risk and the professional management the funds provide appeals to their practical, low risk attitudes. There is, however, a case for purchasing individual bonds as well.

What I have found the most interesting about the Money Masters is that when I've asked them if money provides a sense of security, they have replied that confidence in themselves is what makes them feel the most secure. If they had to start all over again—make money and accumulate it—they are convinced that they could duplicate their success. That high level of confidence comes more from their sense of themselves than it does from the money they have earned and saved. It is obviously difficult to predict how the Money Masters would feel if they had substantially less assets. Would they be as content, feel as secure? A great number of Money Masters answer in the affirmative. They are emphatic in stating that money alone doesn't buy contentment nor does it buy security.

MANEUVERING A TWO-PARTY JOURNEY

As stand-alone money managers, Money Masters maneuver their financial lives quite skillfully. However, when matched up, in business or personal relationships, with people who have different money attitudes, the Money Masters can encounter difficulty.

Julia (a Money Master) and her fiancé, Roger (a Safety Player), were unable to resolve some critical financial issues that stemmed from a wide disparity in their incomes and assets. Both Julia and Roger had been previously married. She had experienced few financial problems in her former marriage because she and her ex-husband had no children and, for the most part, kept their money separate. However, there were two properties that they jointly owned, a vacation home in Santa Barbara and a condominium in Los Angeles. When they divorced, Julia kept the Santa Barbara house and her ex-husband kept the condominium. All other assets purchased after their marriage were shared equally.

Roger had quite a different situation with his ex-wife and family. He had been the only breadwinner for the family, and his divorce "wiped him out," as he put it. His ex-wife was entitled to live in their house until their daughter was of college age, so he would not reap the benefits of the equity in the house for several more years.

Julia was the owner of a successful travel agency that managed not only to survive the lean days since deregulation of the airlines but also was growing substantially each year due to the addition of some lucrative corporate accounts. Roger was a builder whose small business provided an adequate, but erratic, income. He always seemed to underestimate the time necessary to complete a job, so cash flow often became a problem. Roger was a hard worker but never appeared to be able to save as much money as he planned; his business expenses and child support payments consumed much of his income. He had few investments and kept his money as liquid as possible. However, he felt that he handled his money well because he was frugal and managed to support his business without ever defaulting on a loan or without any major financial difficulties with contractors and suppliers.

As the wedding date approached, Julia asked Roger to agree to a prenuptial contract. In Roger's previous marriage, the money had always been in one big pot; there was no such thing as your money and my money. Now the woman who supposedly loved him was asking for a legal separation of money. Since Roger felt that two people who were married should be able to trust one another and help one another during bad times, he had a difficult time understanding Julia's request.

They were also having problems working out a living arrangement. Both lived in apartments in the suburbs of Los Angeles; both lived close to their offices. Roger wanted to buy a lot on the beach and build a new home for them, but Julia felt they couldn't afford it and didn't want to have to travel a longer distance to work. Roger proposed that Julia pay for the lot and he would build the house. Julia said that when his former house was sold and he had some money to contribute toward the purchase price of the lot, she would consider investing in a beach house. But she needed to be close to her office, and it was not practical for them to have two getaway properties, one in the countryside of Santa Barbara and one on the beach. Driving from the beach every day into town and back would add at least ninety minutes to her already hectic day. Roger was very frustrated by Julia's refusal to buy the beach lot, and he grew argumentative, withdrawn, and sullen. Julia felt their relationship was deteriorating and she might have to reconsider his requests or lose her fiancé.

She made an appointment with her attorney, who had initially recommended the prenuptial agreement to protect her assets and future earnings. He concurred with Julia's decision regarding the beach property but advised that the couple resolve their financial differences before he drafted a prenuptial agreement. Obviously some compromises would have to be made by both parties. The attorney suggested that Julia and Roger work with a third party to help them communicate on money-related issues; that is how I met them.

Julia turned out to be a Moneymax Money Master and Roger a Safety Player. Julia made financial decisions in a very analytical way, always looking at the current situation as well as the long-term consequences. It was a style that had always paid off for her. Now she had to make decisions that involved a Safety Player, who has a more impulsive style. Roger did not consider building the beach house as risky since construction was his business. Nonetheless, Roger had not really analyzed the downside of building a house on the beach—the distance and commute time to Julia's office, the advisability of having a house on the beach and a home in Santa Barbara, the work and resources that would be required of him at a time when he was trying to recover financially from a divorce. A couple has enough adjustments to make after marriage without incurring a huge expense to build a new house. Asking Julia, a Money Master, to liquidate some of her assets to buy a beach property that she didn't want or need was outside the boundaries of her money style. In her estimation, they had plenty of time to reconsider the project.

Because she was in the travel business, Julia took frequent trips and whenever possible tried to get Roger to accompany her. Since he rarely had extra money for vacations, Roger thoroughly enjoyed the travel but was bothered by the fact that Julia paid for most of the expenses. He was concerned that she would always be able to afford lavish trips and he would never be able to pay for them. Roger could justify his request that Julia pay for the beach lot because he would contribute his labor and expertise to build the house. While that seemed like an equitable trade to him, he knew there was no trade-off when Julia paid for their vacations. Julia didn't mind paying for the trips because they were usually a business write-off. She didn't like to travel alone and said Roger was a wonderful companion. Even though the travel expenses were not a financial drain on Julia, Roger insisted that the trips be part of their negotiation process.

Julia and Roger had money differences but they also had a lot of similar values. For example, they were both willing to assume responsibility for financial matters. Julia said that when she first met Roger, she wondered if he was attracted to her because of her money, but after getting to know him, she realized that he was too proud to marry a woman for money. It was important to Roger that he convince Julia that he intended to pay his own way. While they were dating, if he couldn't afford to take her out to a restaurant, he cooked dinner at home or packed a picnic lunch for the beach. Roger did all the repairwork in Julia's apartment and in her Santa Barbara house. When he couldn't contribute dollars to the relationship, he volunteered his energy and work.

After an open and honest discussion about the pros and cons of the beach property, Julia and Roger decided to put the project on hold and rent an apartment or condominium that both of them could afford, without Julia having to pay the major share of the rent. The decision would give them some time to adjust to living together before they considered buying or building a house. What initially may have appeared to be a very selfish move on Julia's part, not wanting to buy the beach property, turned out to seem reasonable to Roger once he got rid of his anger and disappointment. At that time the disadvantages of a new house outweighed the advantages. However, both agreed that it would be a viable option for the future. Julia said that she would be willing to sell her Santa Barbara house if she thought that a home on the beach would make them happy and would be a wise investment of their money.

It was very important to Julia that she not begin to resent Roger's lesser income and significantly smaller asset base. In addition, she didn't want to give up her business/vacation trips and she still wanted Roger to go with her whenever he could get away from work. They decided to continue taking trips together but they would budget the trips so that Roger would pick up some of the expenses for hotels and food.

Each agreed that their earnings were to remain their separate and sole property for the time being. Julia made a salary of about $80,000 a year and Roger made anywhere from $50,000 to $60,000. Julia would continue to make her own investments and contribute to her retirement fund from her earnings and would set aside an agreed-upon amount of money for their joint checking and savings account. Roger did the same and said he needed to rebuild his asset base and save some money to cover the erratic cash flow of his business.

They agreed to rent a house on the beach during the following summer to see how they liked living on the beach and to see if the commute from the beach to Julia's office was acceptable or stressful. Julia was very pleased with that arrangement. She always liked to cover her bets and the summer rental gave her the opportunity to evaluate building a house on the beach before making a large financial commitment.

Just as it was important to Julia that Roger not become financially dependent on her, it was equally important to Roger that Julia not resent his financial limitations; he was not about to lose his dignity or pride. They both knew they were in a vulnerable situation because in their marriage the wife would be the major income earner and would have the greater assets. It was a fact they both would have to accept. They appeared willing to be flexible and communicative, knowing there would be many personal and financial obstacles in their partnership.

MONEY CAN'T BUY CONTENTMENT

As a composite picture, Money Masters have excellent scores on each one of the Moneymax financial traits. However, even Money Masters can fall short of total financial satisfaction.

Ronald, age fifty-three, was a very successful account executive for a national brokerage firm. Divorced, he had no financial obligations, since his children had graduated from college. He owned a beautiful home in a beach resort community, and his yearly salary totaled six figures. Ronald personified all the healthy money attitudes of the Money Masters except one—contentment.

Ronald had never liked any of his high-paying jobs, including his current position. Extremely rational, he didn't believe you could actually make money doing work that was enjoyable. For the most part, Money Masters appear to enjoy the way they earn their money; however, there are exceptions like Ronald.

What Ronald enjoyed most was photography. While aware of his talent, Ronald thought he must be mentally unbalanced even to consider leaving his current job to open a photography studio, but that's what he wanted to do. A calculated risk-taker, he knew that starting up his own business would be exciting but there were no guarantees that he could make the business profitable. Ronald had always been a self-starter and whether he managed himself or somebody else, he accepted challenges with optimism and enthusiasm. Thus, he was disappointed in himself because he seemed unable to quit his job and move forward with a new business.

I suggested that Ronald need not quit his brokerage job in order to start his photography business. While exchanging a high-paying job for an uncertain future might suit a Moneymax Entrepreneur, the strategy did not fit Ronald's Money Master personality. A conservative risk-taker, Ronald needed to be able to sleep at night and be at his best to start a new career. He needed to keep his stress level down to a manageable level. If he were to become anxious about making his new business a success, he might set himself up for failure. So we developed a plan for his new business while he continued to work at his full-time job; that way he would still be earning an income while he was planning a new career. At least for the period of time necessary to get his business off the ground, he would have the security of his other job. Ronald never lacked confidence in his professional ability, but he wasn't sure he could support himself by working at his "hobby." However, he was sure that if he devoted enough time and energy to the business, he could make money and perhaps enjoy himself at the same time. It was a risk he was willing to take.

Part of the business development required Ronald to do some marketing research on photographers working in his area—what kind of competition would he encounter, who were the best photographers and what did they charge, who were their clients. To his amazement, there wasn't much competition and he felt his photographs were far superior to most of the work he had seen. In addition, Ronald had worked on a committee for the 1984 Olympic Arts Festival in Los Angeles and had quite a good list of professional and social contacts.

Since the major reasons most small businesses fail are undercapitalization and high overhead, Ronald decided to convert his garage into a studio. He would avoid paying rent, which would allow him to use the extra money for advertising, marketing, or photography equipment. As construction on the garage studio began, Ronald continued to develop his marketing strategy, targeting prospective clients for work on weekends and in the evenings. Since he couldn't leave the office until one, after the Stock Exchange closed on the East Coast, he sought work that would comfortably fit into his busy schedule.

Within a year, his photography studio was up and operational. Using his vast network of business and social connections, Ronald had more clients than he could handle. He quit his brokerage job after five months. His photography studio has now become so profitable that he has hired several employees to assist him. In his free time, he teaches photography at a local community college. He feels his business has given him a whole new perspective on life and continues to be somewhat amazed that work can be both fun and profitable. Ronald feels very fortunate to have successfully changed careers at a time when most people his age are already planning for retirement, not starting a new business.

What Ronald accomplished is not an easy task for most people, including Money Masters. However, if any profile can muster up the confidence and energy to start all over again, it is the Money Master profile. While the Entrepreneurs have the same level of confidence and ambition and are a lot more tolerant of taking risk, the Money Masters are more convinced that they can accumulate money and make it work for them. In general, they are more rational about the chances they take than the Entrepreneurs, who sometimes get ahead of themselves because of their enthusiasm and drive. The Money Masters are more realistic, never assuming that unknown factors, or fate, will intervene on their behalf. They deal very well with a situation as it "is" and do not get carried away emotionally by what they wish it to be.

Ronald was practical in planning his business and executed his plans in a very systematic manner. As a Money Master, he needed to assure himself of success, as much as possible, and to cover his risks, as best he could. Once his new business was successful, he felt comfortable leaving his old job. Entrepreneurs with money in the bank probably would have taken a much higher risk and quit their jobs, figuring that they had enough money to live on if the business failed. High Rollers would have opened up shop immediately and started advertising their services without a business plan. Safety Players and Perfectionists would have a difficult time believing that they could start up a successful business.

MONEY MANAGEMENT STYLE

1. Of the Moneymax groups, the Money Masters are the number-one users of many investments, especially T-bills/notes, municipal bonds, limited partnerships, and money market accounts.

2. They are most satisfied of all Moneymax groups with common stock mutual funds, along with the Achievers.

3. They are the highest investors in municipal bonds and are the most satisfied of all groups with this investment.

4. They are more satisfied than any other group with residential rental real estate.

5. The Money Masters are second to the Entrepreneurs in the own-

ership of coins and stamps. However, the Entrepreneurs and the High Rollers are more satisfied than the Money Masters with these investments.

6. As a group, the Money Masters invest in commercial real estate a lot more than do the High Rollers and the Hunters, but the latter two groups are more satisfied with commercial real estate than the Money Masters.

7. The Money Masters are generally more satisfied with cash value life insurance (whole life; universal/variable life) than most of the groups. Yet, the Money Masters are only moderate users of whole life and one of the top three users of universal/variable life insurance.

8. As a group, they generally desire safety of principal with a high level of tax-sheltered growth and/or tax-sheltered income.

FINANCIAL STATEMENT—
THE MONEY MASTERS

The Money Masters are third in income, first in assets of all the Moneymax groups. They are the second-oldest group, with an average age of fifty. For the most part, they are college graduates and are married with few dependent children. Of all the groups, they are the number-one home owners—84 percent of the Money Masters own their own home.

The Money Masters appear to have it all—adequate income, accumulated assets, excellent work ethic, trust in their fellow man, a generous attitude of giving to others less fortunate, practical spending, confidence in their financial decision-making skills, control and a feeling of power over money, the lowest degree of anxiety and self-doubt, tremendous pride in the way they handle their money, and the greatest contentment of all the groups with their financial status in life.

They care very little about receiving prestige or influencing others with their money. They are cautious and calculated risk-takers, motivated by minimizing their losses and protecting their profit rather than maximizing their gain by taking high risks. In other words, they are interested in maximizing their gain as long as they can calculate the chances of success with some assurance. They prosper with solid, consistent investment plans. It was probably a Money Master who coined the statement, "It's not what you earn that counts, but what you keep." Lastly, even though they are the greatest accumulators of wealth, they feel that it is not their money which brings them the greatest sense of contentment. Rather it is the knowledge that they are capable of controlling their money and making it work for them.

12

---〉·〈---

Producers

The greatest revolution of our generation is the discovery that human beings, by changing the inner attitudes of their minds, can change the outer aspects of their lives.

—William James

GUIDELINES

Producers

. . . Are frustrated that hard work has not brought them greater financial rewards.

. . . Have great difficulty asserting themselves when it comes to getting what they deserve financially.

. . . Desire the feeling of prestige and power that can be derived from accumulating wealth.

. . . Are not particularly proud of their current financial condition—their earning power or assets.

. . . Lack confidence in their perceptions and skills with their money management.

. . . Feel very valuable when they accommodate other people, both in their financial and personal lives.

. . . Have a high degree of trust in the integrity of others when handling money.

Of all the groups, the Producers are the second-highest in altruism; they hold strong to the belief that people are willing to help others in financial trouble. Also, they have the highest degree of trust (tied for first place with the Money Masters), maintaining that most people are honest when dealing with money. And most importantly, the Producers rank number one in work ethic, again tied with the Money Masters for the top slot. Unfortunately, this group that believes so fervently in hard work earns the lowest income and ranks seventh in assets.

Unlike the Money Masters, who are the most confident money managers of all Moneymax groups, the Producers are the least confident of their money management skills. The Money Masters trust themselves and feel powerful because they have successfully controlled their money and accumulated wealth. The Producers lack the personal power to trust themselves to make appropriate financial decisions. The Money Masters have learned through experience that financial power comes from manipulating money, being its master instead of its slave. The Producers don't understand that they can have financial power and change their money status by changing how they view money and how they deal with it. The Money Masters understand the financial maze and look inside themselves for the path through the maze while the Producers look elsewhere.

For the Producers, material possessions are one avenue of escape. They are the second-highest power seekers of all nine groups, the first group being the High Rollers. Since the Producers don't feel the personal power the Money Masters experience, they try to acquire the power by purchasing the goods and services that signify success. They fool themselves into believing that money, and what it will buy, will earn them financial respect. Material possessions make them feel valuable and are one way of rewarding themselves for their high work ethic. Producers are not emotional spenders, like the Hunters, and tend not to buy superfluous, high ticket items. However, when buying necessities, they may choose Vidal Sassoon shampoo over the drugstore brand, Calvin Klein jeans instead of the Sears brand, and hightop Reeboks over Keds sneakers.

Producers don't understand that the process of using their own talents and skills to control their money will give them the sense of power they desire. Research has shown that when people don't have high expectations of achieving their goals, their behavior follows that line of thought, their plan of action is flawed, and they usually fall short of their goals.

As mentioned earlier, the Money Masters are not only masters of wealth accumulation, they are also the masters of self-esteem. They have high self-esteem because their lives work for them. While they encounter personal and financial upheavals, they don't get bogged down in worry and self-doubt; their high level of self-esteem ensures that life will be satisfying—financially, emotionally, socially. The Money Masters are equipped to cope with life's challenges and adversities, including those that are money-related.

For the Producers, self-esteem can be a difficult prize to win. Because they don't know exactly how it feels or how to capture it, the Producers look outside of themselves to find it. Whereas the Money Masters gain greater self-confidence and self-respect with each small but successive money step, the Producers rely more on a system of trial and error. Practical and rational, the Money Masters never stop moving, but they move slowly and cautiously, making every step count. They tolerate a giant step only once in a while in order to maintain control of their money. The Producers believe they have nothing to lose with a more risky strategy. They are moderately content with their financial status, are not particularly confident that they can change it, nor do they have an understanding of how others master it.

Whether they buy lottery tickets, bet on the horses, or play cards, they rationalize that they work hard for their money and deserve to enjoy it. After all, their hard work alone has not brought them a pot of gold. While the Producers do rank third in risk-taking, they are well behind the High Rollers and the Entrepreneurs, who enjoy money risks. Nonetheless, the Producers, like the High Rollers, do not evaluate risks carefully enough and their risk-taking tendencies can sometimes therefore be detrimental to money management.

The High Rollers and the Producers are tied for seventh place in asset accumulation. While the High Rollers earn more money than the Producers, the two groups remain equal in assets because the High Rollers are much higher risk-takers and lose more money than the Producers. Regardless of the numbers and Moneymax rankings, neither group is profiting by taking risk. Both the Producers and the High Rollers may seem to prosper for a period. They may even experience an occasional windfall gain as a result of risk-taking, but suddenly the financial bottom can drop out and result in a loss from which they seem unable to recover.

Emotions and attitudes about money are not to be taken lightly because they have an important relationship to financial success and well-being. They are the very factors that explain the difference in wealth of mind, spirit, and assets between the Money Masters and the Producers. The Producers may work hard but they don't harvest what they sow. They are very frustrated because they believe so strongly that financial success can come from hard work, yet the equation has been disappointing for them. The Producers are confused by a system that allows some people to advance to highly paid positions while others, with equal talent or more experience, are left behind. They don't understand that those who advance not only have skills but believe in themselves and in their ability to succeed. The fears and self-doubts of the Producers sap their ambitious drive and the effectiveness of hard work.

Another reason why the Producers are the lowest income earners and tied as second-lowest accumulators of assets is that they feel more comfortable giving than receiving. If the Producers have low self-esteem, and self-esteem is defined as a feeling of personal competence and worth, then not only would the Producers distrust their ability to cope with financial decisions, but they also don't believe they have an inherent right to be content and happy with money. If they do not feel entitled to money, then their attitudes and behaviors will reflect that feeling. In other words, if you don't feel good about yourself, don't feel entitled to more money, then you may feel better giving away money as opposed to receiving it. Or, you may feel somewhat guilty about taking advantage of opportunities that might result in more money.

ANXIETY—A BLOCK BETWEEN
MIND AND MONEY

Anxiety is a state of uneasiness and distress about future uncertainties. Financial anxiety is a feeling of dread, a fear that distracts the minds of many people, especially the Producers. Of all the Moneymax groups, the Producers are the highest in money anxiety. Their level of anxiety is evidence that internal conflicts regarding money need to be resolved.

Anxiety over one's finances is a condition of life. It's a constellation of uncomfortable, troubled feelings that nearly everyone has experienced in one form or another, in lesser or greater intensity, at one time or another. We live in an anxiety-producing and uncertain economic environment. You would be inhuman not to feel worried, or even terrified, about money now and then. Many people learn to ignore the anxiety, others defend against it, some deal with it, and others wait for it to go away.

Common forms of money anxiety are not usually troublesome. They are aroused anytime you feel unprepared to meet some new or unusual financial experience or decision. This more common kind of anxiety is called "situational anxiety." It is related to a specific event involving your money; it is present when you cannot predict a money outcome. When you negotiate a starting salary for a new job, bargain for the price of a car, fill out income tax forms, haggle over a divorce settlement—you feel anxious. Typically, however, as soon as the outcome becomes apparent, situational financial anxiety can subside in a very short period of time. For most people the anxiety is temporary and does not disrupt the normal flow of their lives.

The Producers, however, can become financially incapacitated by excessive anxiety. It interferes with their ability to concentrate and become more knowledgeable about money. They find it very difficult to deal with financial matters, make decisions, or assume responsibility. Impatient with themselves and their inability to attend to the business at hand, the Producers become unable to improve their performance, and then become fearful over their loss of control.

If they ignore money matters, they can later be tormented by guilt feelings. Their agitation even increases when they try to deny their mistakes or find excuses for why they didn't follow through. Such states of anxiety seem to confirm a self-fulfilling prophecy of financial doom. The fear and anxiety produce more fear and anxiety. At such times, the Producers really need to come to their own rescue with a lot of self-support and encouragement. They need to believe that even the greatest financial anguish can be remedied.

Extreme financial anxiety is usually not suffered by most people. The most common complaint is, "I feel nervous about making financial decisions." The word "nervous" is used to express anxiety about money. Most of the time people ignore or get over the nervous feeling, believing in general that life goes on, that life is good.

When mild anxiety becomes more intense, people say they are "very nervous" about money. The escalation in anxiety causes them to become apprehensive, alarmed, helpless, tense, agitated, or terrified. That is the arena where many of the Producers reside. Their anxiety is a more pronounced, pervasive feeling of continuing financial doom without the possibility of marked improvement. They tend to doubt that things will ever really change for them financially.

The Producers, like many other people, will use the words nervousness and anxiety as synonyms for anger. No doubt you've heard something like this: "I get nervous when my broker tells me my stock went down." Translated into emotional terms, that means: "Sometimes my broker says things about my money that I don't like and it makes me angry. But I can't tell him that I don't like it or that it makes me feel angry. It's not polite to tell people things like that. I don't like to criticize anyone or hurt anyone's feelings. So I just say it makes me nervous. I hope he won't tell me things like that again."

The Producer will choose the word that is more generally accepted —nervous instead of angry. Being angry with a broker is an alarming admission to make, because the Producers fear that the broker may turn around and retaliate in some way, like not giving proper attention to their account. However, they are just as afraid of losing the unrealistic picture of themselves as superbly polite and kind people. Thus, they are doubly angry at the broker who might threaten that image.

When Producers say "I'm nervous" to their brokers, they are trying to convey this: "I hope you feel some responsibility for my nervousness. If you do, you should feel guilty. And if you feel guilty, you will manage my money so well that nothing will go wrong again and I will not have to be nervous or upset." This scenario of nervousness, guilt, and responsibility is often played out by the Producers in the way they respond to other people. Unconsciously, they believe that if guilt pushes their button, it should work on the broker.

Some people, including the Producers, take a very circuitous route in order to deal with their anger and avoid the anxiety that plagues their financial dealings. This route is and has been a well-traveled one by the Producers as well as others high in financial anxiety, like the High Rollers, the Perfectionists, and the Hunters. This is not to say that Producers should seek a total and complete revelation of anger. Openness and honesty in dealing with money can be carried to absurd extremes and cause more harm than good.

When negotiating about money, the Producers must be careful not to use a situation as a dumping ground for their anger. For example, let's consider a situation in which a Producer is angry with an employer because the employer failed to live up to a commitment about a yearly raise. If anger obscures the Producer's judgment, an outspoken Producer may state the grievance, substituting inappropriate frankness for tactful assertiveness. Instead of starting out with, "I thought this would be a good time to discuss my yearly raise," the Producer might begin with, "I can't believe you broke your promise and didn't give me the raise I deserve." Rather than being viewed as assertive and honest, the Producer could be perceived as offensive and threatening. Unaware of the damage that anger might impose, the Producer is puzzled to learn that not only is the raise denied, it may be indefinitely postponed.

The Producers' conflict with anger revolves around: 1) their "right to confront" and 2) their need not to antagonize anyone because of possible retaliation. In other words, they often insist on taking both positions. They want their raise and job, and they want the right to express their anger directly. That would be fine if they could realistically have both. But under the circumstances, they are overlooking an important factor—their two wishes are contradictory and cannot exist simultaneously. They feel they cannot risk antagonizing anyone and still keep their job, yet don't want to relinquish their "right" to express their anger in an uncompromising fashion. This conflict cannot be resolved if both poles continue to repel with equal and opposite force. When they do, the Producers become blocked and their mounting anger feeds into the conflict and intensifies their anxiety.

The Producers have difficulty expressing their anger because of timidity or because it is not in their best interest to express anger directly. They need to find a position somewhere in between suppressing the anger and angry confrontations. If timidity is the problem, they should try to be more assertive. If angry outbursts are the problem, they need to learn how to get their point across with tact and persuasion instead of hostility and fear. I doubt if much business would be conducted successfully if people were always brutally honest, and nowhere is this more true than when communicating about money-related issues.

Many Producers have been raised to believe that they should neither get angry nor express anger. After all, nice people control their anger, don't they? So many Producers remain "frustrated good guys," unable to express or control anger—they get nervous instead. They remain stuck, fixated in their current financial status. The Producers are the men and women who knock themselves out at work, do a wonderful job, and then sit back and wait for a bonus, a raise, or a promotion. When the reward and recognition don't transpire, they agonize over what they did wrong or prepare to go into battle to correct the injustice.

Fearful and culturally bound, the Producers feel compelled to maintain a benign image of themselves, because that image is tied into a fundamental sense of identity. They see themselves as people who don't rock the boat, don't get angry, and don't lash out at other people. Embodied in the image is a certain sense of security that they will not relinquish unless another kind of security takes its place.

Just as anxiety affects health, job performance, and personal relationships, it affects money. If your financial self-image is negative, you tend to feel that no matter what you try to do with money, you will fail. Somehow you will always be the victim of circumstances, the financial struggler who works hard but never seems to get ahead. People like the Producers, who suffer high anxiety, feel that money decisions, like life itself, are forced upon them and they must cope as best they can. Because they perceive themselves as inadequate to deal with money, it is not surprising that even the smallest decision can start the flow of adrenaline.

For example, consider the case of Brian, who received an incorrect bill from the telephone company. Charged to his account were two international long-distance phone calls that amounted to forty-five dollars. His immediate reaction to the bill: "These are definitely not my calls, but how can I prove it? If I call the phone company, I'll probably have to talk to some idiot who won't believe me. When it comes to fighting Ma Bell, I don't stand a chance. If I have to swallow this bill, where will I get the extra money?"

After working himself into a very agitated state, Brian got mad. Then he altered his thinking: "I just won't pay the bill. The phone company thinks they are so damned smart with all that computer equipment, but look at the kind of results they get. They probably make a lot of mistakes like this and get a lot of extra money from people like me who can't afford their mistakes. Well, I'm not going to be a sucker. I'll talk to the president of the company if I have to, but I'm not going to give them an extra dime."

When it occurred to Brian that his telephone service might be cut off if he didn't pay the bill, he returned to his original thought pattern: "It's their mistake but I might have to pay for it." He spent a lot of time and energy agonizing over possible conclusions to his dilemma— all of the conclusions were negative. The anxious money mind thinks that if the situation is already bad (the bill is wrong), then things are bound to get even worse (I'll have to pay for the mistake).

The unconscious mind is a very strong part of our personalities. Stored in its memory bank are your feelings, attitudes, and emotions. While Brian's conscious mind was making the rational decision about whether or not to call the phone company, his unconscious mind was predicting the outcome. When he opened the phone bill and noticed the mistake, he unknowingly hit the alarm button in his unconscious. Since his unconscious mind didn't know the difference between fact and fiction, it only told him what he felt—that he was helpless when it came to money matters and would likely fail again.

Producers find it hard to let go of financial anxiety because: 1) they are afraid of change; 2) they don't believe they can change money attitudes and habits; 3) they aren't sure how to go about changing money attitudes and habits. Change in any area of life elicits fear of the unknown. Predicting a new outcome causes the Producers as much new anxiety as living with the old anxiety. Whether changing an investment style, a job, or a spouse. At least the old kind of financial anxiety is familiar; they have experienced it many times and have developed a way to cope. Also, deep down inside, they don't feel they can change money attitudes and habits. For them, the anxiety about money is a part of life, has always been a part of life, and will continue to be a problem. Finally, if they were to agree that changing their money styles may be beneficial, where do they start?

It is difficult for people like the Producers, who have lived with such an immutable financial image, to leave it behind completely. But change does not have to be complete in order to be effective. In the course of my work I have found that minor changes in financial personality attitudes and behavior result in surprisingly effective strides toward freedom and contentment. The Producers have to develop the courage to venture, cautiously and vigilantly, through the opportunities made by their commitment to change. It is the first few steps which are the most difficult to take. Courage to change one's money self and financial status comes not so much from a position of financial or personal strength as from a willingness to go forward, to alter an unproductive money style and develop better money management systems.

The Producers often confuse assertiveness with aggressiveness. Because they want to be good guys—polite, accommodating, agreeable, nice—they don't want to offend anyone with rude, hostile behavior. While aggression does imply that someone is on the attack—willing to say or do whatever is necessary to win—assertiveness is a different matter entirely. Being assertive means that you are willing to express your thoughts and desires, directly and openly. Unlike aggressive behavior, assertive action is positive, healthy, and reinforcing. It is a constructive way to stand up for yourself, ask for what you want, disagree with others, and say no without feeling guilty.

Carol was a retired schoolteacher who kept herself busy by doing consulting work for nonprofit groups in Los Angeles. While most of her activities revolved around fund-raising, she also did some public relations and marketing. When I met her, she had just completed a year as a part-time consultant to a major philanthropic group that had paid her $10,000—straight consultant fee, no deductions; no benefits. Since the nonprofit group had extra office space, they gave Carol an office and a part-time secretary. It had been a wonderful year for her. Even though the job wasn't permanent, she enjoyed the work and the people she worked with. She knew she was underpaid for the kind of work she did and the long hours she put in, but Carol didn't mind because she had her retirement money and her husband still worked full time.

At the end of the year, Carol's boss called her in to commend her for a job well done and asked if she would like to continue on for another year—same job responsibilities, same consultant's fee. He asked that she accept, or turn down, the offer within a week. Carol was both flattered and perplexed. She knew she had done an excellent job and had been directly responsible for raising a large amount of money through her fund-raising efforts. Not only was she underpaid for her first year's work, but the boss was now asking her to go forth and repeat her success—but with no additional money.

Driving home that night, Carol had another reaction common to many Producers: she began to get anxious and angry. She felt betrayed and was certain that the nonprofit group was taking advantage of her. She had to admit that it had been her decision to work twice the number of hours as her contract specified, but she believed that the extra time and effort were a good investment and would lead to an increase in her fee. Why didn't her boss treat her more fairly? Didn't he appreciate all that she had done for the nonprofit group?

It was obvious that Carol was rationalizing her behavior, placing responsibility on her boss, and avoiding the real issue: What was she going to do about the situation?

Producers, unfortunately, can recognize their talents but too often lack the means to convert personal worth into money worth. Carol knew she had worked hard—and had done a wonderful job—but she didn't have the confidence to say so and state the reasons why she deserved a higher fee. Sitting down with her boss and discussing how her abilities translated into dollars was a thought that made her very nervous. Money negotiation elicits the following Producer reaction: I've never been good at getting the money I deserve; I'll probably say all the wrong things; maybe I should just accept the offer and not have to put myself through the agony—I never win anyway.

Carol's husband seized the opportunity to draw an analogy between her money behavior at work and her money behavior at home. In their marriage, he assumed full responsibility for managing the household finances. Since Carol was a passive money manager, he had given up trying to involve her too much in financial decisions. She always insisted that he was better at dealing with money, he made more money, and therefore he should take care of handling the money. In the case of her nonprofit job, he concluded, Carol would really be doing herself a disservice if she didn't ask for the money she deserved.

When her husband insisted that Carol march into the office and demand her just due, she did an about-face and started to defend the nonprofit group: They did work with a very restricted budget. Some of the full-time managers did not get paid adequately. It was a wonderful job and maybe she shouldn't expect a wonderful job and a wonderful salary. Her schoolteacher's salary had never been great so why couldn't she just accept the money she was offered? Her boss, who was her personal friend, would be disappointed and angry, thinking she was money-hungry.

Carol's turnabout stemmed from two other Producer traits—high trust and high altruism. While both of these traits are admirable, they can put Producers at a disadvantage in the job market and in money negotiations. The trusting Producer money personality usually feels that there will be a fair reward for hard work and dedication to the job. Producers dislike, and are not prone to, self-assertion, but prefer instead to believe that most people share their value system and will do "the right thing"—including anything that relates to money. When financial situations aren't resolved satisfactorily, Producers, like Carol, usually learn to swallow their frustration and disappointment.

Regarding altruism, Producers are very generous with both time and energy. While many people are generous in giving to those less fortunate, Producers do not discriminate. Not only do they give to those less fortunate, but they are often altruistic to those more fortunate than themselves. The same Producers who spend weekends as volunteers for a philanthropic group may also work many overtime hours—with no extra pay—for a boss who has a salary five times their own. Carol's money problems were heightened by the fact that the employer was a nonprofit organization.

After much anguish, Carol did talk to her boss and asked for a substantial increase in pay. She organized and rehearsed her money speech many times. In a calm, straightforward manner, she outlined what she had done in the past year, providing specific numbers and details, as well as a general overview. She let him know how much she loved the job and told him what she planned to accomplish in the second year. At the end of a half-hour, she was comfortable enough to bring up the subject of money. Though a little nervous, she concluded by asking for what she thought was a fair salary.

When she went home that evening, Carol was proud to inform her husband that she had been rehired—and at the fee she requested. Carol's final comment on the matter: "I can't believe it worked. I was scared to death to ask for more money—money has never been my strong suit. But I just told the truth; amazing how it worked."

Besides truth, let's look at what else was an important element in the successful money negotiation: courage. Carol didn't allow her feelings to block her from going forward; she didn't allow her high level of anxiety to sabotage her. When she objectively assessed her talents and dedication, Carol was able to sidestep her Producer tendency to avoid money discussions and decisions because she felt incapable of affecting the outcome. As she continues to face similar issues, Carol will bolster her money self-esteem and reduce the fears and anxiety that prevent her exemplary work ethic from bringing her greater financial rewards.

TAKING THE PATH OF LEAST RESISTANCE

It is very frustrating to realize that the Producers' lack of confidence in themselves and their anxiety and fears prevent them from believing that they have the ability to change their financial status. They do not think that their money and how they manage it can provide more contentment and security for the future. They cling to how things are as predictive of an everlasting financial conclusion. Whether they know it or not they regard themselves as limited instead of unlimited, powerless instead of powerful. Producers believe in the myth of scarcity: money is scarce and no matter what I do, it will always be scarce.

The Producers are reluctant to let go of their money fears. But their fears are only creating smoke screens that prevent them from pursuing financial opportunities. They have a false loyalty to worry, pain, and even resentment. The resentment and anger that have not been overcome keep them from acknowledging what they want out of life. They have to empower themselves because money will not empower them. The Producers have to open the door to wealth and prosperity and become aware of the fact that they are holding themselves back. It is the willingness to allow the door to open that is crucial. Since they do not believe that they are deserving of greater wealth, they shut the door and protect themselves.

Producers can change the way they experience the world, replacing the myth of scarcity with the belief of entitlement. They can give up the fear and anxiety which kill their spirit and motivation. In addition, they can give up the myth that more money will mean that they are selfish, that they care more about dollars than about people.

Producers can learn what it feels like to move ahead financially, but only after changing their attitudes about getting and deserving money. If they remain immobile, they will never allow themselves to become at ease and confident. Instead life will remain a struggle.

MAKING THE WORK ETHIC PAY OFF

Not all Producers close their eyes or put on blinders. Many decide to assume control of their money selves and financial destinies.

One such Producer was Henry. Henry, who was forty-four years old, had been employed by the County of Orange in California for almost twenty years. His salary with the county was approximately $50,000. Henry's wife, Betty, was no longer employed since she chose to be a full-time housewife and stay at home with their three-year-old son.

Henry had been feeling a lot of money stress because he wanted to provide a better life for his family. He and his wife would have liked to have another child, but their two-bedroom apartment was very small. Henry was not in a position to buy a home, and with only one full-time salary, the prospects for buying a home didn't look too bright.

Henry, like many of the Producers (63 percent) rent instead of own their primary residence. They are the lowest group of all Moneymax groups in home ownership; they are also the lowest group with two-income families. In addition, the Producers generally have dependent children at home.

I met Henry at a management training seminar in financial planning which was held at a local university. Since the county paid for its employees to attend, Henry figured he might as well enroll. He was very interested in financial planning but had never approached a financial professional because he didn't think his savings, $30,000, were enough to warrant professional advice. Also, like many Producers, he was embarrassed by the way he had handled his money, since he had no real budget, or goals, or any plans for retirement. Henry and Betty lived from day to day, and even though they were practical about spending money, they had a hard time making ends meet and often had to dip into their savings account.

Henry, however, was the type to ask his friends for money advice and often posed financial questions at lunch. He expressed a desire many times to seek expert advice, but his coworkers laughed and asked if he thought he were a Rockefeller. Also, his friends always brought up the story about their colleague who got involved in a tax shelter and lost a bundle of money. Even though his friends joked about his interest in financial matters, Henry wasn't discouraged. Most Producers want to be more involved in their money management and they are not impulsive when making financial decisions. Henry's instincts and intentions were right; he simply needed some guidance.

At the seminar Henry asked if financial planners would be interested in someone like him who didn't have hundreds of thousands of dollars to invest. He said that he wanted to get smarter about his money but he needed someone to help him map out a plan. The guest panelists overwhelmingly agreed that Henry should seek out some professional help and that he shouldn't hesitate just because he didn't have a lot of money to invest. By the end of the day, Henry was convinced and asked for a referral to a financial planner. He was given the names of a few very good, professional people.

Part of the seminar involved the Moneymax Profile, and in a private discussion that followed, Henry learned that he was a Producer. He was very open about discussing his money style and talked about his immigrant parents who worked very hard to provide for him and his seven brothers and sisters. He said that growing up had been rough—never enough money, always too many bills. While he had a good, secure job, he felt that he would always be at the mercy of money. As he calculated his lifetime earnings and what he had been able to save, Henry concluded that he was just beating inflation and taxes. How could there ever be extra money to buy a house or provide financial security for his family? It worried him a lot.

Henry is not unlike most Producers who are willing to accept the fact that they need a financial plan. However, since they are so disappointed with their current financial status, they usually focus more on the present. For them, first things come first. In their case, the first concern is more current income. Their high level of anxiety and money management style keep them locked into a preoccupation with today instead of planning for tomorrow. They don't seek out professional advice because they are primarily concerned with the present and they are embarrassed about their personal money shortcomings.

Typically, the Producers perceive themselves as capable of tolerating calculated and even higher levels of risks. Twenty percent of the Producers have owned or currently own individual common stocks. While 14 percent have had mutual funds, another 18 percent are interested in owning them. Mutual funds are viewed as having liquidity and can also satisfy the Producers' need for appreciation.

Henry was never comfortable with the stock market. He had heard too many horror stories about people who lost all or nearly all of their savings in the stock market by using brokers who were a little too adventuresome. Even though the Producers do seek out some risk with their money, they are not comfortable with high stakes; they are too responsible and work too hard for their money. Appropriately, they see individual stocks as too risky and mutual funds as a better bet; they also tend to be savers and because they can continually reinvest their mutual fund distributions, they can accumulate more money.

Henry found a financial planner who appealed to him both professionally and personally. After the first session with the planner, Henry realized that he and Betty had multiple needs: they had insufficient life insurance, he had inadequate disability insurance; neither of them had wills; all of their savings were in a money market account. Like the majority of Producers, Henry was primarily interested in more current income, but he was also interested in safety and growth. About twice as many Producers are primarily interested in more current income instead of safety or growth.

The type of life insurance Henry and Betty needed, they couldn't afford, so they bought term coverage for the time being and planned to convert it after they had more income—when their child entered school and Betty went back to work. Upon conversion, the permanent insurance would give them a tax-free buildup of cash values, and would give them very adequate returns with a great deal of safety. They were amazed by how much cash would accumulate over the years. However, since at that time it was more important to have an adequate amount of coverage with an affordable premium, the planner suggested a term policy of $200,000. They talked about the inadequate disability insurance Henry currently had but determined that he couldn't afford any more at that time.

The next question was what to do with the $30,000 savings. First, the planner recommended that the couple put away an emergency fund that totaled three months' income. Since Henry earned $50,000 a year, that amounted to $4,150 a month, so they agreed to put $12,500 in a money market fund which would be their emergency money. The balance of $17,500 was invested in several conservative growth and growth and income mutual funds. The mutual funds would help to offset inflation by building up their asset base.

Even though they wanted to buy a house, they could not consider such a major purchase at that time. They would not qualify for a home loan based on Henry's income nor could they come up with an adequate down payment. It was advisable for them to stay in their current apartment or move into a three-bedroom apartment when they required more room. Although they were disappointed, the couple understood the financial reality of their situation.

Betty decided that she would get a job the following year, work for two or three years, and then consider having another child. Finally, the planner referred them to a legal service that would help them draft a will at very little expense. Henry was very pleased with the plan and told his cynical friends that he was on his way to becoming a financial wizard.

The Producers don't have to accept their financial status as a dead-end street. Just as Henry found out, there is a plan for everyone. The Producers must transform their high work ethic from working hard to working more effectively. They also have to change their self-image as ineffective money managers into confident, successful money managers. If the Producers continue to expect financial disappointments they won't tap much of their financial potential. If they start out with a belief system that emphasizes what they can't do, that system subsequently signals their money personality to respond in a negative way.

What financial results come out of that scenario? Dismal results. What will the disappointing results do to subsequent endeavors? Chances are they will reinforce the negative beliefs that started the whole chain. People like the Producers, who are frustrated about money and live financially discontented lives, have been without the financial results they desire for so long that they no longer believe they can produce the results. Thus, they do little or nothing to tap their money potential.

Let's look at this from another angle. Let's say the Producers begin with great expectations—as Henry did. Starting with a direct, clear commitment, how much potential will the Producers use? Probably a good deal. What kind of actions will they take? Would they procrastinate and sabotage an opportunity? Of course not. If they have expectations for success, they would charge ahead with tunnel vision and optimism. If the Producers were to put out that kind of focused effort, what sort of results would be generated? Chances are the results would be good. And how would those results affect greater financial results in the future? In this case, financial success would feed on financial success.

MONEY MANAGEMENT STYLE

1. The Producers like whole life insurance more than any of the other nine Moneymax groups. The fact that they like whole life insurance, coupled with the very favorable results that high quality whole life insurance contracts have produced over the years, has made it a good investment for my Producer clients. They can accumulate money sheltered from income taxes, and at the same time protect their families against the untimely death of the breadwinner. And in the case of the Producers, where 59 percent are one-income families, this is particularly important.

2. Government bonds are a preferred investment vehicle for some of the Producers. They perceive this investment as moderate in risk—slightly higher than their savings accounts and lower in risk than their IRAs and Keoghs.

3. Of all the Moneymax groups, the Producers have had the least

experience with most investments. One of the investments that they have used with greater frequency than other groups is commodities. Interestingly, they are tied with the High Rollers for the greatest level of satisfaction with commodities. The Producers and the High Rollers are both motivated to gain a feeling of power with their money, and the highly charged commodities market may satisfy that drive.

4. In addition to whole life, the Producers also like universal/variable life insurance and are second to the Money Masters in high satisfaction with this investment. This vehicle can provide protection as well as serve as an investment tool because of the multiple investment options like stock funds, bond funds, and money market accounts. Producers are familiar with the death benefits of insurance, but they, like most people, are more concerned with living benefits. With the additional investment opportunities, the Producers could find universal/variable life attractive financial tools for their financial security in later years.

5. Producers have dabbled in the stock market, particularly with individual stocks—more so than with mutual funds. They are tied with the Entrepreneurs in highest level of satisfaction with their individual stock ownership and also express an interest in learning more about mutual funds.

FINANCIAL STATEMENT—THE PRODUCERS

The Producers have the strongest belief in the American work ethic—hard work produces financial success. They are motivated to get ahead financially and raise their standard of living, yet they rank ninth in income and are tied for seventh in assets. They have average contentment with their money.

For the most part, the Producers see themselves as an integral part of their financial future. They would like money to bring them more prestige than they currently have. Also, they would like their money to provide a power base, allowing them to exercise more influence and control. They believe money is a tool to get prestige and power. Whereas the Entrepreneurs, the Money Masters, and the Achievers rely more on personal assets and achievements to yield power and

influence, the Producers believe that financial well-being and greater
financial resources will create the power and influence they desire.

They lack confidence and are anxious about making financial decisions. The level of anxiety they experience inhibits and handicaps their
skills. Their self-doubt regarding financial success greatly diminishes
their expectations. Their high anxiety, however, does not translate into
destructive emotional spending as it does in other groups such as the
Hunters. The Producers prefer saving money to spending it. They like
to accumulate money even though they have not been successful in
building an asset base.

Their primary financial objective is greater current income. The
Producers want to be involved in money management even though
they don't trust their skills. They have a great trust in their fellow
man's honesty in dealing with money and they are also altruistic and
believe in helping those who are less fortunate.

The Producers are as much married as they are single. When married, they are very low in two-income families and tend to have dependent children in the home.

13

Optimists

The price of wisdom is above rubies.
—Job 28:18

GUIDELINES
Optimists

. . . Feel quite content with their current financial situation.

. . . Believe that fate plays a significant role in their financial destiny.

. . . Are not very analytical or thorough in the way they approach making financial decisions.

. . . Have little desire to be highly involved in their money management.

. . . Experience little stress and worry when making decisions with their money.

. . . Do not desire money to bring them status or prestige.

. . . Get greater enjoyment in spending their money than in saving it.

As a whole, the Optimists are the oldest Moneymax group (51 percent over sixty years old), have the least number of dependent children, and are the most widowed. On the financial scale, they rank sixth in income, fourth in assets. As for their money attitudes: The Optimists aren't particularly ambitious, don't want to be highly involved with their money, and don't look back to evaluate past decisions. In fact, they are somewhat impulsive decision-makers regarding their money—the least reflective of all nine groups. Yet of all the Moneymax groups, the Optimists are the lowest in anxiety and feel very proud about how they deal with money. Of all nine groups, they are the second-highest in contentment—they have peace of mind with their financial status. How does this detachment from money equate with their peace of mind with money? How do their assets offset their liabilities? If they are so content, should they alter their apathetic money attitudes? The Optimists are truly paradoxical money minds.

There is no emotional trauma caused by the gap of where the Optimists are financially and where they would like to be, so they aren't disappointed with themselves like the Perfectionists and the Producers. They have no burning desire to have greater wealth. Many Optimists represent an older generation that does not use money as the only symbol of one's value in society. Those Optimists grew up in an era that did not promote or glorify self-aggrandizement and ostentatious wealth.

While the Moneymax Profiles are determined by grouping people according to their common financial traits, the demographic facts about the Optimists support the analysis of their trait scores. For example, the Moneymax Profile with the least desire for prestige and status with their money, the Optimists, is also the oldest group and the group with the least number of people under thirty. They have very little need for money power, unlike today's younger generation, which thrives on career advancement and status symbols. The Optimists would rather use money to buy them peace of mind than use it as a tool to garner respect and recognition. They certainly are a product of their generation and have reached a stage in life when it is time to stop worrying about money and begin learning to enjoy it. The same as the Money Masters in low emotionality, the Optimists do not let their feelings guide their money. They enjoy spending it rather than saving it but don't destructively act out their emotions with money like the Hunters and the High Rollers.

Because 51 percent of this group are over sixty years old and another 15 percent are between the ages of fifty to fifty-nine, more emphasis in this chapter is placed on how age relates to the Optimists' money personality than is emphasized with other Moneymax groups. However, as mentioned throughout this book, the Moneymax groups are determined solely by attitudes, and not by any demographic factors. A twenty-five-year-old Optimist has the same money attitudes as a sixty-five-year-old Optimist, and 34 percent of the Optimist group are under the age of fifty.

This profile is one of contentment. In fact, the Optimists are very satisfied with their money, surpassed only by the Money Masters. It is interesting to note that these two profiles, the Optimists and the Money Masters, are also very similar in other financial traits: a lack of interest in status and prestige, little emotion invested in money, lowest anxiety in making financial decisions, low risk-seeking tendencies, and high trust in their fellow man's honesty in dealing with money. The Optimists and the Money Masters are the two oldest Moneymax groups—the average age of the Optimists is fifty-two years old and the average age of the Money Masters is fifty.

Yet, the groups are quite dissimilar in other traits. The Money Masters seek the highest level of involvement with money while the Optimists seek the least involvement. Of all nine groups, the Money Masters profess the highest belief that the work ethic brings financial success while the Optimists score the second lowest position in work ethic. Regarding self-determination: the Money Masters are the most self-determined (tied with the Achievers), believing that they are responsible for their financial destiny, and the Optimists are low in self-determination, believing that financial success is somewhat due to good luck. Finally, the Money Masters are one of the highest-scoring groups in reflectivity—thinking about past financial decisions when making current ones—while the Optimists are the least reflective of all the groups and tend to have an impulsive financial decision-making style.

What impact do the differences in these two Moneymax personality styles have upon money and its use? The Money Masters earn and accumulate significantly more money than the Optimists. Yet both groups are quite content with the money they have and are satisfied with their financial status. Both have confidence in themselves and in how they have handled money in their personal lives. The Money Masters have a lot more experience in managing money than the Optimists, and thus have a better chance of ensuring their future security and freedom. The Optimists' blind spot may be their overly confident style with money; they may not be as realistic as they should be.

The Optimists want to live out their remaining years comfortably, without worry and stress from money-related issues. However, they do need to stay away from debt and to keep abreast of any economic and tax changes that affect them. Their lack of money involvement and their preference for spending over saving could be potentially troublesome areas.

It's fascinating to note that the Optimists enjoy their money and are just as content and worry-free as the Money Masters. It proves the point that mental wealth is not how much money you have but how much you enjoy the money you do have. We all know people who are continually driven to acquire more money and possessions, more than they ever will need or be able to use. While some of the Optimists don't have enough assets to be considered rich, they are wealthy in spirit. Not only do they feel content, but they are not plagued by self-doubt or worry about money matters. They don't feel like financial failures and are, in fact, the most proud of all the groups except for the Achievers, Money Masters, and Entrepreneurs. Despite the fact that they don't become highly involved with their money or learn to build an asset base like the Money Masters, the Optimists have reached a stage in their lives where they are at peace with their money.

Many have enough money to spend to enjoy themselves and build a nest egg for retirement years. They are a lot more optimistic about their ability to handle their money and make it work for them than other Moneymax groups. They don't seem to be concerned about surviving a long retirement or any financial calamity that might deplete their savings. The Optimists have no reason to believe that they will have to endure any financial hardship. They have a positive sense of themselves and a positive spirit which trusts that the financial future will be protected.

A significant percentage of this group (20 percent) are widows. In fact, the Optimists have the highest percentage of widows of all the profiles. It is likely that these women were not primary income earners or investment managers; they outlived their husbands and were the beneficiaries of family assets. It is difficult to know whether this segment of widows is optimistic and realistic or whether positive thinking comes from having what they think is a sufficient amount of money. While this happens to be the group with the largest number of widows, this in no way implies that all widows would fall into the Optimist profile.

Shirley was an Optimist who recently had become a widow. Her husband was a fireman who worked for nearly thirty-five years before retiring. Shirley never worked until both her children had married and left home. Then she took a job in a local manufacturing plant.

As a couple, Shirley and her husband, Ken, did very little together. Ken was a homebody and never liked to go on vacation or participate in social activities. They did, however, frequently visit their daughter, who lived about fifty miles from their home. Usually, they took the train because Ken's failing eyesight made it difficult for him to drive at night and Shirley had never gotten a driver's license. When their son, who lived in California, got married, Shirley and Ken splurged and took a month's vacation.

When her husband died, Shirley seriously considered moving in with her daughter, but she wanted to keep her job and remain close to her friends and church activities. Also, she worried about being a burden to her daughter, who was married, had two children, and had a full-time job. On the other hand, if she lived alone, Shirley would always have to ask friends to drive her around town; but at least she was already in a car pool at work. After much deliberation, she decided to live alone because she didn't want to be dependent on her daughter and intrude on her daughter's life.

When her personal life stabilized, Shirley decided it was time to get her finances in order and gathered together all the paperwork—bank statements, income tax returns, insurance policy, Ken's retirement plan, the deed to the house. Shirley was overwhelmed by the stack of paper since Ken had always taken care of their money. She did know that the house was paid for and that all of her money was in a local bank. There was about $30,000, which she and Ken had saved, and another $200,000 from her husband's life insurance policies.

While Shirley felt relatively secure, her family urged her to get some financial help. She took their advice and made an appointment with the accountant who had been handling her income taxes for years. Unfortunately, he wasn't able to give her much help about anything but preparing her income taxes. A little annoyed, she forgot about doing anything with her money until she noticed that a well-known financial planning company had opened a branch office next door to her local bank. After being assured by the bank manager that the firm was reputable, Shirley made an appointment.

When she met with the financial planner, she told him that she had been thinking about retiring from her job but didn't know if she could afford to quit. She thought she was doing all right financially but she wasn't sure how long her money would last, especially if she lost the income from her job. Together they reviewed her finances: She had $230,000 in the bank, $200,000 from her husband's life insurance policies and the $30,000 in savings that she had when Ken died. She was receiving $1,000 a month from her husband's pension, $600 a month from Social Security, which totaled $1,600 a month, plus $1,376 from her salary at the plant. The grand total of her monthly income was $2,976 or approximately $36,000 a year between Social Security, Ken's pension, and her job.

Shirley's house was paid for, but she wanted to move into a retirement village where she could own her own condominium and wouldn't have to worry about home maintenance and repairwork. Also, she had friends who lived in the retirement village and the shuttle service at the village would alleviate all of her driving problems. The condominium she wanted to buy was priced at $47,000 and she figured that her house would sell for around $55,000.

While she did have $230,000 to invest, her income would shrink to $1,600 when she retired. If she wanted to increase her monthly income, Shirley would have to consider some new investments. The financial planner recommended that she put $100,000 in a tax-free municipal bond fund, $40,000 in a Ginnie Mae fund, and another $40,000 in a corporate bond mutual fund. She could keep the balance of $50,000 in a CD. She would receive $7,650 a year (on the average) from the $80,000 invested in Ginnie Maes and the corporate bond fund, $3,500 from the CD, which was paying 7 percent, and $7,250 from the tax-free bond fund, which was paying 7.25 percent. Since she would receive $18,400 a year from this investment strategy, Shirley agreed to go ahead with the investments. The financial planner cautioned her that even though her new investment plan would allow her to retire and have more after-tax income compared with her income before retirement, she needed to be aware that inflation would undoubtedly lessen the buying power of her money and that in the future she would have to make adjustments for inflation. Nonetheless, Shirley had considerably less concern about her financial future and looked forward to leaving her job and moving into the retirement community, which would make her life simpler and more enjoyable.

The Optimists, by nature, are not risk-oriented investors. They are split between desiring greater current income and desiring safety for their money. They prefer to keep their money liquid, but they should be careful as to the amount they keep in savings accounts because savings accounts don't help them keep pace with inflation. If they would use other investment vehicles, they could reap greater returns on their money and still maintain safety. Besides their savings accounts, Optimists are also very satisfied with government bonds, but they might consider, as other Optimists have, investments such as government securities, mutual funds, and real estate partnerships, which can provide good income and the safety that they seek.

Optimists have a high preference for and use other safety-oriented vehicles like annuities and whole life insurance. They also prefer money market accounts, and IRAs and Keoghs. Their IRAs and Keoghs are probably invested in a bank or a savings and loan institution.

AVERSION TO RETIREMENT

Warren was retiring after being a salesman for most of his life. He started selling newspapers when he was ten years old, then sold used furniture on weekends when he was in high school. After graduation, he became a used car salesman, then at thirty he started to sell new cars. He did so well that he bought a percentage of a dealership when he was in his late forties. Warren was divorced with two children from his first marriage and had been married to his second wife Karen for eleven years. Karen had also been married before and had three children. She had just retired from a newspaper company where she had worked as an administrative assistant.

Karen had always been very active socially as well as professionally. Warren, on the other hand, put in long, hard hours at his job and came home every night and crashed in front of the TV. He never developed any hobbies except fishing, a sport which Karen deplored. In fact, Warren and Karen didn't have any activities they enjoyed doing together.

Working six or seven days a week became so much a part of his lifestyle that Warren was having a difficult time making a decision about retirement. Yet, at age sixty-five, he had high blood pressure, and Karen kept urging him to retire and buy a home in Florida where he could fish year round and they could be close to her only daughter, who lived there with her family. Warren had been resisting for years, insisting that he was needed in his business. However, that excuse was wearing thin because the dealership was quite profitable and there were other partners who were capable of managing it.

Even his partners were concerned about his health, but Warren ignored their advice, saying that his health was fine and there was no need for him to slow down. The truth was: the thought of not working was very frightening to Warren. He didn't know what he would do with himself. He worried about it so much that he began to wake up at four and five o'clock in the morning. What should he do? He had no desire to move to Florida and retire. He loved his stepdaughter and grandchildren but he could not envision himself accompanying his wife around all day on shopping trips and visits with friends. Sure, he could go fishing, but he couldn't do that every day.

Warren's dilemma was not easily solved. He was a man without hobbies or any personal goals. He didn't communicate well with his wife, had few friends to talk to, no one to confide in, and was wrestling with what to do with the rest of his life. He felt alone and confused. He had no money complaints, loved his business, and had every reason to believe that his financial future was secure. He just wasn't ready to construct a new life when he didn't want to let go of the old one.

Warren needed to talk to someone and finally chose his oldest son, Alan. While Alan was very sympathetic and understanding, he said he knew nothing about planning for retirement—financial or psychological. However, Alan gave Warren my business card and told his father about financial psychology. As a matter of fact, Alan had been a client because he needed some advice to solve some money problems in his marriage.

Warren was a very interesting man because so much of what he allowed others to see was hiding what was brewing beneath the surface. He was a highly creative man who didn't tap into that part of himself. In fact, he had lots of ideas for retirement but never let himself fully evaluate the possibilities. As soon as an idea surfaced, he quickly rejected it if he thought it was beyond his financial means.

When Warren took the Moneymax Profile and learned that he was an Optimist, he became skeptical. If he was so optimistic, why was he having such a hard time planning his future? After all, a true optimist would throw caution to the wind and do something.

That was a fair observation, but Warren was missing the point. He was, indeed, an "optimist," but one who had compartmentalized his life so rigidly that he had devoted all of his time and energy to his work. In that area, he was highly optimistic, responsible, assertive, and dedicated—so dedicated that he neglected his wife, his family, and a social life with friends. He didn't know how to expect pleasure from a new lifestyle that was completely foreign to him. When he was forced to revamp his old game plan because of his health and family, Warren knew he had to make some big changes.

Some Moneymax Optimists never confront the issues that Warren had to face. But any person who has enjoyed a full and satisfying career can partly understand Warren's personal struggle. Some people are handicapped by their own rigid styles more than others. Warren was able to get away with his rigid style for a long time, but now he was being forced to see how the rest of the world looked and how he would fit into it.

Warren was a man who either took full responsibility and control or none at all. He never took a halfway approach. One of the reasons he loved his work was because he called all the shots. Since he was the veteran car salesman, his partners looked to him for advice. He was usually right and never delayed when an important decision had to be made. Warren was respected and admired by his partners and employees and felt productive and valuable. He didn't know how he was going to capture that same sense of himself in retirement.

Warren was searching for a way to replicate the lifestyle that he had without allowing himself to think more expansively and consider new options. He had always been creative and analytical in his business but needed to transfer those talents to a new set of circumstances—retirement. After seven weeks of discussing a myriad of options, Warren had a game plan that suited his personal style and his money style.

First he sold his share of the car dealership for $85,000 and then he sold his home for $72,000. He and Karen moved to Florida, bought a mobile home, and invested the rest of their money in a small marina. Warren ran the marina with the help of one part-time employee, and his wife did all the bookkeeping and was in charge of the marina's supplies store. Since Warren was such a good salesman, he rented out all of the boat slips and handled all of the customers. Warren viewed the mobile home as temporary, an intermediate step before buying a house. The mobile home was close to the marina and didn't require much capital; he wanted to have some cash in the bank in case of an emergency.

Two years after Warren made the move to Florida, the emergency fund was still intact. In fact, his health had improved and the marina business was doing quite well. All of the boat slips were rented, and Warren was constructing a small addition to the supplies store. The marina was so small that it practically ran itself, so Warren had ample time to go fishing.

Warren bought a business with a positive cash flow, two small buildings that were in excellent condition, and enough expansion room to add more boat slips whenever he so desired. Eventually, he plans to buy a few small fishing boats and operate a rental business from the marina—that is part of phase two of the business plan.

If Warren had remained in the car dealership and continued working for a few more years, it is likely that he would have remained content with his life. However, it is hard to predict what effect the job would have had on his health and his family life. Also, he certainly would not have learned to play and work at the same time, as he was doing in Florida. Finally, he would never have considered going into business with his wife. While Warren and Karen had run a household together and raised two sets of children, Warren never thought he and Karen had enough in common to make a business work. He gained a lot of respect for his wife, who was very adept at managing the supplies store and juggling a number of other responsibilities at the same time. Also, he was feeling a lot less guilty about all the years that he had neglected his wife.

Karen discovered a side of Warren that was usually hidden—a Warren who could have a good time and be relaxed. She realized that her husband was not the type of man to retire completely and devote himself to fishing five days a week. At least he was enjoying the excitement of running his own business again, but this time he didn't have any partners to account to or any sales goals to meet. Karen's only complaint was about housing; she didn't like living in the mobile home. However, since the business was doing so well, Warren agreed with her that it was time to start looking for a house to buy or rent.

Retirement is an issue that some people confront more successfully than others. While some people have enough money to assure a problem-free retirement, others may think they have planned adequately but find themselves coming up short if they outlive their money. Warren did not want to spend his retirement years solely on leisure activities. He didn't work because he needed the money, but because that's all he knew how to do. While he was happy with his life, his family was not happy with him. Because he loved his family and because he knew that stress on the job was affecting his health, Warren was forced to consider new alternatives.

Warren's retirement plan was designed not so much to match his ambitious drive but to allow him to ease into retirement. He had never done any serious thinking about retirement because he couldn't imagine a future without his car dealership and his full-time commitment to work. Since he never had that much discretionary income, Warren chose to ignore the fact that he didn't have a pension plan or any kind of financial strategy to steer him through his retirement years. Luckily, he was able to face all of the necessary issues and design a new life that put him in control of his personal, social, and financial life.

RETIREMENT YEARS—BOOM OR BUST?

When it comes to contemplating retirement, this profile has good reason to be optimistic. Today, Americans over sixty-five are the second-richest age group in America (behind the fifty-five to sixty-four age bracket). According to the U.S. Bureau of the Census, the average household income of those sixty-five and over is $18,279, compared with a national average of $27,464. However, if you divide that income by the number of household members (those over sixty-five have few, if any, dependents), the income per family member is $10,316—above the national average income of $10,207. The statistics on net worth are similarly impressive. In 1984 the average net worth of the over-sixty-five household was $60,266 as opposed to the net worth of the average American household—$32,677.

In the 1950s about 35 percent of the elderly fell below the poverty line; today the rate has dropped to below 13 percent. If benefits such as food stamps, subsidized public housing, and medical reimbursements were considered part of income, the poverty rate for those over sixty-five would drop to 3 percent. Twenty years ago an older person was much more likely to be living near or below the poverty line than a child. Today a child is six times more likely to be poor than an older person.

How did this older generation manage to do so well for themselves? A large part of the answer lies in pension plans, Social Security benefits, and other federal spending plans. Approximately 37 percent of today's retirees have a pension plan that pays average benefits of $5,315 a year. The average monthly Social Security check is $467 ($5,604 a year), but for those who earned more and paid more into the system, the average monthly benefit can be as high as $792 ($9,504 a year). Today's senior citizens group, which comprises 12 percent of the population, is the primary recipient of government social spending. In 1986 approximately $350 billion in government funds were spent on the aged—more than the defense budget. Also, retired Americans tend to have a lower cost of living: most of them have paid off their home mortgages; most have no dependent children; most spend less on basic needs like transportation and clothing. Also, senior citizen incomes usually fall in low income tax brackets. And finally, a 1983 Social Security bulletin estimated that older Americans may be earning more than they report to the IRS, that as much as 41 percent of the group may underreport their incomes because they fear the loss of Social Security benefits.

The major snag in this rosy financial picture is medical bills. Because Medicare does not cover catastrophic illness or long-term health care in nursing homes, many older Americans can lose everything they have accumulated in a very short period of time. The average monthly charge at a nursing home is more than $1,800. One recent study estimates that more than 1,000 Americans a year use up all of the medical insurance benefits and are forced to deplete their personal assets. Regardless of physical health or illness, the financial picture can change for those who live past eighty. According to one report, those people over eighty-five are the poorest in American society; more than one in five are near or below the poverty line.

The recent trend in corporate restructuring—mergers, acquisitions, layoffs—has forced many employees into early retirement. Added to that is the fact that Americans do not tend to stay with one company for a working lifetime: the average American works for ten different employers, keeps each job for 3.6 years, and makes three career changes before retirement. All the above add up to the fact that many employees are not around long enough to accumulate significant pension assets. The Employee Benefit Research Institute reports that people who change jobs—whether they choose to or are forced to because of corporate restructuring—take their lump-sum retirement benefits and spend 70 percent, save 30 percent. The great majority of the money is spent on cars, vacations, and other symbols of the good life. In addition, for those who work for many years for one company, the rules of the pension game often change. When a pension plan is reorganized, workers in their fifties often have to pay in additional money in order to eventually receive the benefits they expect. Finally, 50 percent of the American work force is covered by some kind of pension plan, which still leaves half of all Americans with no such retirement benefits.

Whether we save money to plow into a pension plan or save it via other investments, the question remains: Are Americans good at saving? Unfortunately, the answer is a resounding no. The personal savings rate in 1987 fell to 3.6 percent, the lowest level since 1947, when the rate was 3.1 percent. During World War II, when there were few consumer goods to buy, Americans saved more than 20 percent of their incomes; in the 1960s we were able to put away 8 percent. Today, however, Americans, especially the younger generation, those from twenty-one to forty-five, like to spend and don't worry about the future. According to a spokesperson for the American Association of Retired Persons, "Younger people are setting themselves up for the risk of falling into poverty in old age or living far below their current standards."

What will happen when the baby boomers, born in the decade and a half after World War II, reach retirement age? This group now makes up almost one third of the nation's population. According to government statistics, the number of people sixty-five and older will double by the year 2020. Most retirement planners say that a retiree should have enough pension earnings, investment income, and Social Security benefits to total 64 percent of preretirement income. And when estimating the amount of money needed for retirement, it is necessary to take into account the rising life expectancy rates: by 1990 women will live an average of seventy-nine years and men will live to be seventy-two. If the younger generation cannot manage to save the necessary money, will government plans step in to bail them out?

Both the Medicare and Social Security systems are in serious financial trouble. Some economic experts predict that Medicare funds could go bust in less than ten years. What about Social Security? Today's retiree collects what he paid into the system in about five years; tomorrow's retiree (age forty-one today) will have to collect benefits for ten years in order to recoup her investment.

To make matters worse, Social Security is almost certain to be bankrupt by the time the baby boomers arrive at the retirement door. While Congress has not taken any serious strides to reform the system, the federal government sends out periodic assurances that all is well with Social Security. One report projected that the system will be in balance for the next seventy years. However, that conclusion was based on the following presumptions: inflation can never be higher than 4 percent; by 2010 the birthrate has to rise by 10 percent; economic growth must average 2 or 3 percent a year; there can be no more economic recessions; the unemployment rate cannot rise above 6 percent after 1993; life expectancy cannot increase significantly until 2060; wages, adjusted for inflation, must double by 2037. Even the most financially unsophisticated have a hard time buying into that fantasy.

Fifty-one percent of the Moneymax Optimists are over sixty years of age; another 15 percent are between fifty and fifty-nine. For those who are retired or near retirement, financial security looks promising and there seems to be good reason to claim high contentment and low anxiety when discussing feelings about money. On the other hand, the remaining 34 percent of the Optimists, those who are under fifty years of age, may have to tighten their money belts and reassess their positive outlooks. If the economy worsens and the federal subsidy programs are severely cut back, there may be a lot less optimism around.

In other words, if the Moneymax national survey were repeated thirty years from now, the Optimists profile might disappear.

MONEY MANAGEMENT STYLE

1. They are the number-one investors of all nine groups in annuities, which makes sense because of their overall age. As with most individuals, but especially this group, a diversified approach combining growth to offset inflation, and future income to maintain their standard of living, combined with safety for preservation of capital, is well advised by financial professionals. Frequently, however, these investors are not conscious of the effects of inflation and the importance of providing for the increased cost of living in the later years of their life. The average age of this group is fifty-four and, therefore, they should be concerned with and plan for at least another twenty-five years. Professionals advocate that the plan should consider taxes, inflation, and rates of return and should be viewed in the following way: If you are in a 25 percent tax bracket and the average long-term rate of inflation is 6 percent, you have to earn an 8 percent return on your money just to break even (8 percent less 2 percent in taxes, less 6 percent inflation = 0). If inflation is only 4 percent, you will have to make 5.3 percent on your money to break even, but at an inflation rate of 8 percent, you'll have to get a return of 10.7 percent. Remember these rates of return just bring you even (zero return) and if you aren't willing to settle for making nothing or only making a profit of 2 to 3 percent on your money, then it will be necessary for you to place your money in opportunities that can bring you an annualized return of at least 11 to 13 percent during times of low inflation. Investments that Optimists might consider are well-established conservative growth mutual funds and some public real estate limited partnerships. These partnerships should have very low risk factors, quarterly cash flow on an increasing basis, and equity participation in the increasing value of the properties. They should, of course, have a track record of having made good returns for their investors.

The above recommendations were made by an experienced investment adviser after reviewing the Optimists' money personality. The advice is designed to help the Optimists have a realistic chance of achieving their goals. Considerable expansion of their comfort zone is necessary to implement these suggestions and an educational process, before a decision is made, is critical.

2. The Optimists are most satisfied with annuities probably because of their perceived safety. They will never outlive the income stream if the income option of the annuity is well chosen, so annuities represent safety, which is a large concern for them.

3. The Optimists also use, and like, money market accounts, IRAs and Keoghs, and government bonds.

4. The investments which are least satisfactory are futures contracts, commodities, and individual common stocks.

5. They are more satisfied with common stock mutual funds than individual common stocks, probably because of the higher perceived safety and the professional management of mutual funds.

FINANCIAL STATEMENT—THE OPTIMISTS

The oldest of the Moneymax groups—average age of fifty-four—the Optimists also have the highest percentage of people over sixty years old. They rank sixth in income and fourth in assets. Most of them are married, own their own home, and have no dependent children. This Moneymax Profile also has the highest percentage of widows (20 percent).

Of all the Moneymax groups, the Optimists are the lowest (tied with the Money Masters) in emotionality, anxiety, and power, and are second to the Money Masters in contentment with money. They also have high pride in how they have managed their money and trust that other people are honest when dealing with money. Although their trait scores often parallel those of the Money Masters, the Optimists differ from the Money Masters in three significant areas: involvement, reflectivity, and self-determination. While the Money Masters score very high in those three traits, the Optimists score very low. That may account for the difference in income and assets between the groups.

The Optimists would rather spend money than save it. This group has the highest number of retired people who feel secure about their finances and thus feel more comfortable spending money. They have worked hard to prepare for retirement and are not prone to money worries. The Optimists are not risk-takers and choose current income as their number-one financial goal, followed closely by safety.

14

————⊃⊷⊂————

Summary of Profile and Trait Relationships

Throughout this book, each of the Moneymax groups has been defined by the thirteen financial personality traits. Each of the traits combines with the others to produce a particular set of money attitudes and behaviors. Following is a summary of how the traits interrelate. In addition, a graphic depiction of each trait will show you the following: 1. The rank order—from highest to lowest—of the scores that the Moneymax groups have on a particular trait; 2. The relative scores—high, average, low—of each Moneymax group for a particular trait. If two or more groups appear on the same line then the groups had identical, or very similar, scores on that particular trait.

INVOLVEMENT

The degree you desire to be personally responsible and involved in managing and investing your money.

High desire for involvement with your money management usually is coupled with low anxiety and a high level of pride and contentment. This trait is most important to the Money Masters and Achievers, who desire the most involvement of all nine groups, while groups like the Safety Players and the Optimists avoid getting actively involved.

INVOLVEMENT

HIGH	AVERAGE	LOW
Money Masters	Entrepreneurs	Safety Players
Achievers	Perfectionists	Optimists
	Producers	
	High Rollers	
	Hunters	

PRIDE

An index of the personal satisfaction you have attained in the way you have handled your money.

The Achievers and Money Masters feel the most proud of the way they have managed their money. Your sense of pride is obviously influenced by the degree of success you have attained in your money management, and these two groups have accumulated the most assets of all the Moneymax Profiles. In contrast, the Perfectionists, who have accumulated the least amount of assets, have the lowest pride. Your sense of pride certainly has a significant impact on your financial contentment and sense of well-being.

PRIDE

HIGH	AVERAGE	LOW
Achievers/Money Masters	Safety Players	Hunters
Entrepreneurs		Producers
Optimists		High Rollers
		Perfectionists

EMOTIONALITY

The degree of emotion you feel in dealing with your money.

The Hunters are significantly higher than any other profile in emotionality while the Money Masters and the Optimists are the lowest. Your peace of mind and well-being are obviously affected by the degree of emotion that is projected onto your money.

EMOTIONALITY

HIGH	AVERAGE	LOW
Hunters	Producers	Entrepreneurs
High Rollers		Safety Players/Perfectionists
		Achievers
		Money Masters/Optimists

ALTRUISM

The extent to which you believe in the financial generosity of others.

Although altruistic feelings are not directly related to your financial success, they are nonetheless very much related to your financial attitudes and behaviors. There is no apparent relationship between the amount of money you make and your altruistic tendencies. The Perfectionists, the lowest in assets and among the lowest income earners, have the greatest belief in altruism.

ALTRUISM

HIGH	AVERAGE	LOW
Perfectionists	Entrepreneurs	Achievers
Producers	Hunters	Safety Players
Money Masters	Optimists	
	High Rollers	

ANXIETY

The degree of anxiety you feel in making financial decisions.

Confidence in your decision-making skills is developed through involvement and practice. Usually those profiles low in anxiety are also high in involvement, contentment, and pride. As you become more involved, confidence and pride evolve. The Achievers and Money Masters have the least anxiety in dealing with money management and are the most involved, whereas profiles such as the Hunters—who remain more detached—experience more anxiety. The Optimists are an exception: they do not desire high involvement, yet do not worry about their money and have peace of mind with their financial security. Your drive for power and your propensity for risk are also related to your level of anxiety.

ANXIETY

HIGH	AVERAGE	LOW
Producers		Safety Players/Achievers
Perfectionists/High Rollers		Entrepreneurs
Hunters		Money Masters/Optimists

POWER

The extent that the desire for power drives your behavior.

Your desire for power and prestige with money appears related to your sense of pride, level of anxiety, and the degree of emotion that money conjures up for you. Those profiles with a high power drive experience more anxiety and more emotion in their money management and feel less proud of the way they deal with their money management in general. The High Rollers, the Producers, and the Hunters seek the most power of all nine groups and also experience high anxiety, higher emotionality, and less pride than the other groups.

POWER

HIGH	AVERAGE	LOW
High Rollers	Entrepreneurs/Perfectionists	Safety Players
Producers		Achievers
Hunters		Optimists/Money Masters

WORK ETHIC

Your views of how the work ethic relates to your financial success.

In general, the higher your belief in the work ethic, the more financially successful you are and the more proud you are of your financial accomplishments. The Producers are the only exception to this rule.

WORK ETHIC

HIGH	AVERAGE	LOW
Money Masters/Producers	Hunters/High Rollers	Perfectionists
Achievers/Entrepreneurs		Optimists
		Safety Players

CONTENTMENT

The degree of personal happiness that money contributes to your life.

Generally the more involved you are in your money management, the more confident you feel, the more proud you are of your financial accomplishments, and the more contentment your money brings to you.

CONTENTMENT

HIGH	AVERAGE	LOW
Money Masters	Entrepreneurs	Safety Players
Optimists	Producers	Hunters
Achievers		High Rollers
		Perfectionists

RISK-TAKING

The level of comfort you feel in taking risks with your money.

Overall, more calculated risk-takers are more reflective in decision-making and ultimately more content. Impulsive risk-taking, when it exceeds your comfort level, results in low feelings of pride in money management abilities and skills.

RISK TAKING

HIGH	AVERAGE	LOW
High Rollers		Producers
Entrepreneurs		Safety Players/Perfectionists
		Optimists/Hunters
		Money Masters
		Achievers

SELF-DETERMINATION

The extent to which you feel in control of your financial destiny.

The more responsible you feel for your financial success, the greater the link you perceive between your efforts and your financial success. People with high self-determination have a greater likelihood of accumulating wealth. The Achievers and Money Masters, the highest scorers in self-determination, are also the groups with the most assets.

SELF-DETERMINATION

HIGH	AVERAGE	LOW
Achievers/Money Masters	Hunters/High Rollers	Optimists
Perfectionists	Entrepreneurs	Safety Players
Producers		

SPENDING

Reflects your attitudes for spending versus saving your money.

Those groups who enjoy spending their money, instead of saving it, are the groups who desire and assume the least involvement in their money management. In addition, those groups who score the lowest in spending are the highest scorers in altruism except for the Achievers.

SPENDING

HIGH	AVERAGE	LOW
Hunters/Optimists/	Entrepreneurs	Producers/Achievers/
Safety Players		Money Masters
High Rollers		Perfectionists

REFLECTIVITY

The extent to which you reflect upon past financial decisions while making current decisions regarding your money.

In general, those groups who are conservative with risk are also the most reflective decision-makers. The Achievers are the most reflective and the least likely to assume high risk.

REFLECTIVITY

HIGH	AVERAGE	LOW
Achievers	Producers	Safety Players
Money Masters/Perfectionists	Entrepreneurs	Optimists
	High Rollers	
	Hunters	

TRUST

The level of honesty you believe people have in dealing with money.

In general, the higher your level of confidence (low anxiety) in your own financial decision-making skills and money management, the more likely you are to trust that other people are honest with money. Exceptions are the Achievers and the Safety Players as well as the Producers. (The Producers have a high trust of others, yet lack confidence in their own financial decision-making skills.)

TRUST

HIGH	AVERAGE	LOW
Producers/Money Masters	Entrepreneurs	High Rollers/Hunters
Optimists		Perfectionists
		Achievers
		Safety Players

	INVOLVE-MENT	PRIDE	EMOTION-ALITY	ALTRUISM	ANXIETY	POWER	WORK ETHIC	CONTENT-MENT	RISK-TAKING	SELF-DETER-MINATION	SPENDING	REFLEC-TIVITY	TRUST
ENTREPRENEURS	Average	High	Low	Average	Low	Average	High	Average	High	Average	Average	Average	Average
HUNTERS	Average	Low	High	Average	High	High	Average	Low	Low	Average	High	Average	Low
HIGH ROLLERS	Average	Low	High	Average	High	High	Average	Low	High	Average	High	Average	Low
SAFETY PLAYERS	Low	Average	Low	Low	Low	Low	Low	Low	Low	Low	High	Low	Low
ACHIEVERS	High	High	Low	High	Low	Low	High	High	Low	High	Low	High	Low
PERFECTIONISTS	Average	Low	Low	High	High	Average	Low	Low	Low	High	Low	High	Low
MONEY MASTERS	High	High	Low	High	Low	High	High	High	Low	High	Low	High	High
PRODUCERS	Average	Low	Average	High	High	High	High	Average	Low	High	Low	Average	High
OPTIMISTS	Low	High	Low	Average	Low	Low	Low	High	Low	Low	High	Low	High

PART THREE

ATTAINING
MENTAL WEALTH

15

⋯◆⋯

Profiles of Mental Wealth
Exploring Wealthy Attitudes

Mental wealth is much more than earning a large income and having an abundance of financial assets. To achieve a state of mental wealth you must understand your money personality so that money can be properly integrated within your life and can be in harmony with who you are and what you want out of life. Money should not only provide you with life's necessities but it should also be a source of security, freedom, and enjoyment. You experience mental wealth when your money serves you. As someone once said, "Money is a good servant but a bad master."

The people in this section typify the most exemplary scores on the traits in the Moneymax Profile. They all embody those Moneymax traits which lead to both financial success and contentment with money: confidence in making financial decisions in their business and personal lives (low anxiety); a high work ethic, which they attribute to their extraordinary financial success; high self-determination; a desire for involvement in their personal and business money management; feelings of pride and respect for the way they have handled their money; peace of mind in the way they integrate money into their lives.

In the nine profile chapters the cases presented have sometimes illustrated extreme examples of the traits in order to help you easily distinguish one personality from another. Here, the traits will be viewed within the context of the everyday lives of successful men and women. You will see the possible variations of the traits and how individualistically they can be expressed and characterized by different people.

Most people learn new money behaviors efficiently and effectively by modeling exemplary behavior—watching and listening to those who have maximized their money personalities and financial traits to reach a position where their money is utilized to their best advantage, both emotionally and financially. These interviews are presented as ideal models of the thirteen financial traits. Each of these people has managed not only to accumulate wealth, but to gain a healthy perspective of money and use it optimally for business and enjoyment. Each of them, in his or her own unique way, has achieved a state of "mental wealth."

EUGENE LANG

On June 25, 1981, entrepreneur and multimillionaire Eugene Lang addressed a group of sixty-one sixth-graders during commencement exercises at P.S. 121, an elementary school in Harlem. It was the school that Lang had attended when he was a boy, and his speech was filled with encouragement about dreams and goals and the importance of education. In the middle of what he says was a boring, rehearsed speech, Lang was inspired to make a bold, dramatic promise: "If you stay in school, I will give each of you a college scholarship." Later he sent each of the students a letter in which he wrote, "Keep this letter. It is my bond."

The promise to the students of P.S. 121 became the "I Have a Dream Foundation." In Harlem, where the school dropout rate can exceed 75 percent, the promise was much more than verbal motivation. In addition to monetary support, Lang spent his Saturdays giving his students advice in his midtown Manhattan office. So far more than half of Lang's students were eventually accepted at colleges and other institutions of learning. The "I Have a Dream" project has been so successful that it has gone nationwide, and more than a dozen cities are in the process of inaugurating similar programs.

Founder of REFAC Technology Development Corporation, Eugene Lang grew up in an East Harlem tenement building. The son of a machinist and a schoolteacher, Lang graduated from high school when he was fourteen, attended Swarthmore College on a full scholarship, and earned a master's degree in business from Columbia University. After World War II, he invented the heli-coil, a fastening system for airplanes and cars, and started REFAC to export his product. Today REFAC is a very successful high tech licensing company.

At sixty-eight, Lang enjoys talking about his past—his early jobs as a dishwasher and shipping clerk, growing up during the Depression, the values and beliefs he obtained from his parents. A man who has given away more than $25 million to colleges, hospitals, and scholarship programs, he has a private foundation which he manages with the help of his family—a wife and three children—who are trustees of the foundation. A successful businessman, humanitarian, and philanthropist, Lang says, "I would really like to measure my life in such a way that the day I die, I will have given away my last dollar."

MONEYMAX PROFILE

Eugene Lang has a very strong work ethic and believes that everyone needs to take responsibility for his or her life in order to gain both financial and personal success. According to him, creative energy and dedication to goals are great assets and the source of much personal fulfillment.

He is highly self-deterministic and believes that he controls his own financial destiny. In addition, he believes that it is important always to be prepared to take advantage of opportunities; he especially holds education in high regard.

Lang does not believe in excessive spending and prefers to use his money in philanthropic endeavors. He is highly altruistic because giving to others brings him a great sense of joy and satisfaction.

INTERVIEW

KG: You seem to represent the antithesis of what's happening in the United States with how people are using money and their attitudes and feelings about money. You've managed to stay close to the environment from which you came and you didn't use money to isolate yourself or turn your back on that environment. You are giving back very much. Isn't that unusual?

EL: Let's say that there's a fascination for people with money. Most people would like to give, but at the same time money is capital, and many people find it impossible to resist the temptation of using money to move to the next echelon of fortune, because in this country the level of fortune in many minds is associated with individual status and recognition. It's obviously a false value and it doesn't apply universally. While one can highly regard people who are not rich, the fact of great wealth usually imputes a value that social or ethical criteria may not justify. I find that most people who have money retreat to the objective of accumulating more because they don't really know how to use what they have except to earn more. Many wealthy people don't know how to give and don't really know the satisfaction, the total return that can be associated with giving.

KG: Did you feel this way as you were making your money?

EL: Once I reached a level where I felt that my family was secure, and I don't mean assured comfort for the rest of our lives, but once I felt that I had reached the point where the best possible education for my children was assured, I never really worried about security. I always figured that I could take care of myself and my responsibilities. I had no sense of inadequacy about earning enough money to support whatever desires I have. But then my desires never really were elevated in proportion to my growing resources, my income. I never really felt a great need to accumulate the more ostentatious appurtenances of wealth, whether a boat or a chauffeured car or dining in fancy places. I always worked too hard, I guess, to have the time to waste money on things that were meaningless to me.

You see, I feel giving is an enormous luxury. It's the ultimate you can do for yourself. There is not much that I want to spend money on, as long as I comfortably satisfy—for me and my family—the basic requirements of food, shelter, clothing, education, and the cultural niceties of living. I've found that there's nothing that gives me the return, the sheer joy, the sheer satisfaction of giving money and associating myself with the process.

KG: You're very unusual that way.

EL: I'm only unusual in the sense that I guess I learned that a long time ago.

KG: Do you know how you learned it?

EL: In the first place, my family was poor but we did believe in sharing. We genuinely believed in giving within our means, even if there was nothing to give other than words of encouragement. That's really among the greatest values I think my parents passed on to me. They instilled in me a lust for education and a very strong work ethic. I never was persuaded that I'm in this world primarily to enjoy myself, but rather to get the satisfactions and pleasures that come with the fulfillment of creative purposes. And I believe that my purpose on earth is really a creative one. The justification of my life has got to be what I've done with it, not how I've enjoyed it. At the same time, I find that enjoyment becomes coordinate with the creation. I've been what they call an entrepreneur. I've created new businesses and new ventures, put new ideas into the economy, all of which has given me satisfaction.

KG: What have you been trying to teach the children from P.S. 121 about money?

EL: I don't teach them anything about money. Money doesn't enter into it. Their ambitions and their dreams are what count, and money is essentially a consequence. What's important to these children is not the scholarship. Although they may not perceive it, it's not money or a job. The root value is a dream, that these kids each have a dream, a goal, that they will work toward. They must have the satisfaction of accomplishment along the way or the ultimate prospect of reaching their individual goals. That's the important thing. It goes with self-esteem.

KG: Do you see any differences between yourself growing up in that environment and these children today?

EL: Certainly, but I find that my role is an inspirational one and when the youngsters accept it, the hook sinks pretty deep. Once you develop your sense of purpose, and you relate that purpose to your sense of values—to your self-esteem and to your hopes—then you have created an internal dynamic which becomes part of the human spirit. Then everything else can follow.

You know, a long time ago my philosophy in this respect was shaped by a Swarthmore classmate, who became a very well-known economist. I'm referring to Kermit Gordon, who was the chairman of the Council of Economic Advisers under Lyndon Johnson and subsequently the Director of the Budget. He was a brilliant person and one of the most extraordinary people I have ever known.

We were both honor students at Swarthmore and took a seminar titled, "Social Economics." For the final written examination, we were asked just one question. The question we had was: "What do you regard as the biggest economic problem in the country and why?" To me, the answer was immediately crystal clear. And I think the same answer was almost automatically accepted by many others who were taking the examination. I said "inequality". There were too many people living below the poverty line and our primary purpose should be to bring about greater equality. And I was able to elaborate on that answer in terms of the social impact of inequality, its injustice, the economic cost, and so forth. I wrote an entire answer in this vein. I remember when the exam was over, Kermit and I left together and I couldn't wait to ask him how he had answered the question. I was absolutely sure he would agree with my answer. I thought so much of him and was ready to place his judgment ahead of my own. He was a very socially minded person. I could hardly wait for him to say, "That's what I answered." So I asked, "Kermit, how did you answer the question? Did you also say, inequality?" He said, "No," and it was like getting a kick in the stomach. So I asked, "What did you say?" He said, "Well, I put down raising the national dividend." That means increasing the gross national income. He went on to say, "It makes no sense to just shift things around. What you have to do is make a bigger pie. We have to become more productive, more efficient, use capital more effectively, and increase the total pot so that there's a bigger share for everybody. It doesn't necessarily have to be equal. There has to be enough to go around." And immediately I knew he was right. I had given the Band-Aid answer. To take from you and give to me. To raise your taxes and lower mine. That's not a cure. It provides no fundamental answer. But to do those things that will increase the total pie for everybody and to do the things that help individuals become more productive—like education—that's the better answer. I kicked myself all the way back to the dormitory.

I never forgot that episode. And to me, it tells what the "I Have a Dream" program is all about. I have addressed the root problem, which starts at the time when the youngsters are beginning to grow. And it works. I have sowed seeds of ambition, of dreams. It's legitimate for a poor kid, for a minority kid, to have a dream and to have some credible expectation that it can happen. But even more, by establishing the kind of seminal and fulfilling relationship that develops in our program between me as a sponsor and the children, I have inspired many others like myself to do the same thing. And that, you see, is especially satisfying, not only because I've done something creative with the kids, but I have also done something inspirational for my peers. As a result, my efforts and the project itself has multiplied enormously and continues to grow. So the same philosophy, the same motivation, the same habit of thought that has related to my business life has carried over into my nonbusiness life, my extracurricular life. Someday, I would love to write a book, *The Joys of Giving*. It seems corny and hearts and flowers, but I tell you this: there's no greater thrill than to see a child suddenly blossom where before there had been no hope. I get a thrill when I see a prominent banker playing knock hockey with kids and getting those kids to believe that they too can be good bankers. These kids are becoming members of the total community even though it's harder for them to develop their opportunity because they're starting from minus.

KG: Did you give your children the same sense of inspiration when they were growing up?

EL: My children have built careers of their own. I gave them a good education. Two of them had the very best because they went to Swarthmore College, but they all have elected to follow their own careers, and I have encouraged them to do that. None of them are in my business.

KG: That was their choice?

EL: Any one of them could have come into my business. I would have loved to have them. But, on the other hand, it would have been a selfish thing. I got the thrill out of starting my business and saying, "I did it." That may seem selfish and ignoble, but I found a tremendous satisfaction in that. I did it. And my kids can say the same thing—that whatever they've done, they've done on their own.

KG: I understand that your children will not inherit your estate?

EL: That's right. At least they accept my philosophy. I would not blame them if in their hearts, they wished I would give them some millions of dollars. But they know it's not going to happen; on the other hand, they don't need it. And furthermore, each one is deliberately self-reliant. Each one can honestly say, "I did it. I picked my goal and I'm developing it and building my life on it." And they are, and I'm very proud of them.

KG: Are they resentful?

EL: Not at all. As a matter of fact, we have an extraordinary family life. All of us are very, very close. There's not only love, but a tremendous mutual respect. They get a real thrill out of the good things that happen to me. They get a real thrill out of the good things that happen to their mother, who has her own agenda of commitment. And my children also have their individual commitments, which go beyond their occupations. All of them are involved. And I am so proud of what they do and they are very proud of what I do. We're a very supportive family and we have a common philosophy. That doesn't mean we agree on everything. They all are trustees of the foundation that I've established. Each one of them is involved in certain areas of social activity. And the foundation supports the things in which they themselves are involved.

KG: Do your children have the same views about using their money as you do?

EL: Well, I think probably their standards of expectation are a little different than mine. But that's a consequence of the times. I grew up in a depression. I grew up when nickel hot dogs were a standard. My children's needs, and the levels at which they satisfy them, seem to me almost outrageous in relation to my own experience. They do a lot more vacationing than I do and in a more expensive way. I don't want to do that; I can't adjust to their expectations as my norm. They grew up in a different world with different urgencies.

I couldn't travel first class if I were a billionaire. I'd have to say— even as a billionaire—I don't have enough money to do all the things that need doing, and that need money. Maybe it tickles me to say that I travel on buses and not in taxis. Maybe it tickles me to say that I travel tourist and not first class. I guess I do. But to me, if I see how much it costs to go from here to Los Angeles by first class, I could say to myself, "No problem; I can afford it. I'd never miss it." On the other hand, that extra amount of money for maybe four or five hours of dubious comfort that I don't miss could be used for two weeks of camp for some kids. So, those are the equations that I have in my mind, that I grew up with. But I can't hang that on my children, and I wouldn't try to. Nevertheless, we are philosophically together, and we live with it and support it among ourselves and really rejoice in each other's accomplishments.

Getting back to the point you originally raised about giving money; I think you probably underestimate society when you point to me as perhaps an exception. I'm really no different from almost any other human being and you have to accept that the chemistry of human beings has common elements. Most of us basically are willing to respond to issues of humanity. The problem is, how do we activate that willingness? I've had an extraordinary opportunity to develop a quick release, largely because of the values and inspiration I got from my parents, not from wealth but from values.

One of the reasons my program—and I don't really even like to call "I Have a Dream" my program because it's gone far beyond me—has been so successful in attracting support isn't because we made over the attitudes and the philanthropic instincts of people. We didn't make people more generous than they were before. What we've done is show people there is a way that they can spend their money to get reward, satisfaction, and accomplishment beyond what they could have believed possible. The program has unleashed the capacity of a great many people to do the good that they want to do but who couldn't before find the avenue for doing it effectively.

KG: What's the difference between you and the people that can't find the avenue? Is it because of your background, your parents?

EL: I don't know. Things happen and there is no way of rationalizing how all the strands of fate come together to make something happen. It just happened. You can take all the elements that have made up my life and try to get some formula out of it, but I don't think that's the answer, because each life has its own formula. Maybe I was never housebroken. I was always independent and I did things I felt were "right" even though they might not be popular or they might defy conventional wisdom. I was always confident that I could survive the consequences of whatever I did—even my mistakes. Now, maybe I had more courage and self-confidence than a lot of people.

I feel, in a way, that I have assets that were denied to a lot of my contemporaries. I had a father and a mother who believed in education. My father insisted that I learn how to use tools. From the time I began to walk, I had hammers and screwdrivers. My father would drill holes and I would have to put the screws in them. He felt that no matter what, if I was able to do things with my hands, I would always be able to take care of myself. And I grew up feeling that I could always take care of myself. Having that serenity of self-confidence and sense of survival are important. Many people don't have it. I never felt that my security had to be tied to my bank account. And, bear in mind, there was no Social Security, and there were no IRAs, and there were no pension plans—none of that stuff. Today, you have all those things and still people are scared.

KG: So money was really just the means? It was never a measure of your success? It just came as a consequence of your being successful?

EL: I am personally convinced that I could be the richest man in the world, if I were to address my talents to becoming that. I'm very well off, compared to most, and I know that the people who amass these enormous fortunes by trading paper are not any smarter than I am. But I think their values are different.

My views may be archaic but economic value is not created by trading paper. I don't mean to be looking down my nose at anybody. But I think there is something morally wrong about the acquisition binge that is converting our nation's equity into debt. We're squandering our capital unproductively. Why? To sustain or indulge a top management set who have thrived on a country club existence, unearned profits, and golden parachutes and to provide investment bankers and lawyers with exorbitant fees for their ingenuity. And look how the process of creating paper fortunes tends to corrupt perhaps a new generation of our most gifted young executives.

This is not what our society is all about. I see all of this as degrading our free enterprise economy. Economies grow on productivity, not on paper illusions fashioned by greed and surviving on borrowed time.

I think you have the essence of my philosophy. My biggest personal problem is that I don't know the number of days I have yet to live, because I would really like to measure my life in such a way that the day I die, I will have reached a new peak of accomplishment and given away my last dollar. Of course, it's not going to happen that way. It doesn't matter, because my children will carry on with the same philosophy. I'm confident of that. They will do different things, but that's fine. I don't have all the answers and besides, I couldn't do everything I'd like to do anyway. There's more than enough for all of us to do.

KG: Success to you is being able to give?

EL: When I attended that seminar on Social Economics, I remember one thing I read, and I don't even know where I read it anymore. But it always stuck in my mind. I was tremendously impressed by the values of the natives of the Trobriand Islands. I read that in the Trobriand Islands merit is measured by the amount, the capacity, to give things to others. You know, I've always remembered that as an outstanding measure of humanity and civilization.

I've raised an awful lot of money and I get a lot of people to do things because I do them myself. It really is quite evident that I get an enormous reward out of it. To anyone that would buy a boat for a quarter of a million dollars, or half a million dollars, and spend whatever it takes to maintain it, I just say—you can't love a boat and a boat can't love you.

When youngsters I didn't know six years ago come to me, crossing the boundary lines of their ghetto community, and talk to me about their problems, I feel as though society has won a victory and I was instrumental in achieving that victory. And when a kid called me up and said, "Mr. Lang, I want you to be my valentine," I really got a lift. Youngsters have great ways of showing you that they care.

Things have a way of networking in one's life and if I look for an explanation of my situation in life, it would be the values that I grew up with. It sure wasn't the affluence of my parents, because we had nothing. It was the values that I got, the sense of dignity of the individual, the worth of the individual, the importance of sharing and giving, the work ethic, being encouraged to say what you think and do what you believe.

When my father came to this country, he didn't speak the language and had never finished grammar school. He was apprenticed out to a Budapest machinist at the age of ten, because my grandfather's farm in Hungary could not support all my grandfather's children. By the time he died, my father could speak six languages. He read a lot, and his reading diet would have been a proud agenda for a Ph.D. candidate in philosophy. He became a learned man and worked very hard all of his life, even during the Depression when there were no jobs for machinists. I remember he was a man of uncompromising principle and enormous courage.

I remember one time back in 1934, I guess it was, when Hitler had taken power in Germany, and I was living on the fringes of Yorkville, East Harlem. My father and I went to a movie one night, on Eighty-sixth Street, which was the heart of the German-American territory. It was ten cents admission for each of us. At that time, the Fox Movietone News was a regular part of the theater program. And in Yorkville the news was always slanted to emphasize what Hitler was doing in Germany. When we went to the theater that night, the news showed Hitler giving one of his speeches. The audience applauded like it was the greatest thing. And my father stood up and shouted, "How dare you applaud that God-damned devil?" And he said it in German. There was momentary silence and then reactions like "sit down, Jew." My father could have been lynched. Some of those people walked around in storm trooper uniforms in Manhattan. But he stood up and nothing happened. I guess I was about thirteen. At the time I didn't think anything of it, because I knew my father and his capacity for principled outrage. The newsreel passed and things settled down as though it had never happened, but it had. I will always remember the episode and the strength of character it reflected. My father didn't have to do it, and maybe it did no good. But I think maybe it did some good. He always believed—and I believe—that if the emperor isn't wearing clothes, you say so.

VENITA VANCASPEL

Chosen as "Certified Financial Planner of the Year" in 1982 by the Institute of Certified Financial Planners and voted number-one financial planner in a 1984 survey by *The Digest of Financial Planning Ideas,* Venita VanCaspel has been dubbed "a master of finance" by her peers in the financial industry.

Born in Oklahoma, VanCaspel attended Duke University and the University of Colorado where she was often the only female in her upper-level courses in business and finance. After graduation, she moved to Houston where her husband had taken a job in advertising. When he was killed in an airplane crash, she was forced to rethink and restructure her life. At that time she was working as an executive secretary but decided to move into the world of finance. Then, in the early 1960s, female stockbrokers and financial planners were a scarce commodity.

After obtaining her broker's license, VanCaspel started to conduct investment seminars with the goal of teaching people how to become financially independent. Her philosophy: "Anybody can become financially independent if you have the ability to earn, a little discipline to save, sufficient time, and reasonable intelligence." She began by addressing local women's groups in the Houston area. The popularity of her seminars was so great that they had to be moved from small conference rooms to large auditoriums. Known as "the woman who can strip the mystique from high finance," VanCaspel has been interviewed extensively on television and radio and has written articles on financial planning for numerous magazines. In addition, she is the author of six books, which have sold more than a million copies in hard cover. Her most recent book is *Money Dynamics for the 1990s.*

She is president and founder of VanCaspel & Co., Inc., Stockbrokers; VanCaspel Wealth Management, Inc.; and VanCaspel Planning Services. The editor of a newsletter, *Money Dynamics Letter,* she is also the moderator of "The MoneyMakers," a national PBS show. Active in church, civic, and community affairs, VanCaspel continues to conduct financial planning seminars and frequently appears as a speaker before major national and international financial conferences. Everywhere she goes, VanCaspel stresses the importance of financial planning. As she says: "Most people spend more time planning a two-week vacation than they do their whole financial lives. You've got to have financial options. That's all money ever gives you. It will not buy you happiness, but neither will poverty. Money gives you options in life that you don't have without it."

MONEYMAX PROFILE

Venita VanCaspel endorses a high degree of involvement in money management and financial planning. Having options in life has always been very important to her, and she maintains that the accumulation of wealth for financial security and independence ultimately provides more options in life. She believes that everyone has the potential to achieve financial independence if he or she becomes involved in his or her own money management and starts a financial planning program.

VanCaspel prefers saving money to spending it and feels it is more enjoyable to watch her money multiply than watch it disappear by spending it. Status and prestige—having big cars and big homes—are not important to her; her style is understated, yet comfortable.

Through her books and seminars on financial planning, she aims to demystify the financial planning process so people will not be anxious or fearful of becoming more active in money matters.

INTERVIEW

KG: Did you find that when you started doing your seminars that people really knew what they wanted?

VV: They don't know what they want. We have raised a nation of financial illiterates. Today, they're a little sharper than they used to be. I think the thing that's made them more aware than anything else is IRAs. They've heard enough about them and know they need to set aside $2,000. Then all the advertising about IRAs made people think, "I better look at my options." The other thing that made people more knowledgeable about money is money market funds. Before people always just kept money at the bank in a passbook savings account, or if they were a bit more sophisticated—a CD, and a few of them jumbo CDs. But a lot of people didn't qualify for the jumbo CDs and when the money market funds came out, people started moving their money out of the bank. You used to see ads—back before the money market funds—saying that if you had $100,000, you could get 12 percent on your CDs. The average person could only get 5½ to 5¼ percent. That's when the mutual funds started the money market funds and gathered together all these people and made the million dollars that got the jumbo CD rates. But it took a while for people to really accept the fact that it was all right to put their money in a money market fund.

KG: Why do you think we are raising a nation of financial illiterates?

VV: We don't teach it in school. When high schools did have business education weeks, I'd often go and make a speech. In one school there was a social science teacher conducting it, and I sat down to chat with her one day, and she hadn't the vaguest idea about money herself. So how could she teach it? We don't even teach children the simple percentages. Then we thrust young people out into the most sophisticated money world we've ever known—with no preparation at all. I've done many talk shows, and after one of them I had a young cameraman come up to me afterwards and say, "I've put $10,000 in a CD and it's due in six months and the rate is 8 percent; how much money will I have?"

KG: Are there any overall differences between men and women and how they approach financial planning and view their money?

VV: It really varies from person to person. Women are slightly more conservative than men, but that is not always true. But on the whole, women stick more with quality and have a tendency to choose stocks they are familiar with. Actually women are pretty good investors because they pick some pretty good stocks. For instance, Kellogg's has been around a long time and it's going to be here a long time. A woman who just bought Kellogg's Cornflakes will say that Kellogg's is a good investment. And she's right. Now, you can carry that too far, because then you only invest in things that other people invest in.

A lot of people want glamor stocks. They want to be able to talk about their stocks at the golf club: "I bought so and so"—some high tech stock. Those people wouldn't brag about Kellogg's, even if it is a good investment.

KG: You're a woman who has become extremely successful in a male-dominated profession. You deliberately chose economics and finance. Can you tell me about that choice and why you have become so successful?

VV: It's hard to tell how things get planted in your mind. But I have thought about that. When I was growing up, I had no money at all. I was raised in the dust bowl. So I had a very healthy respect for money. I analyzed "how do you get it?" and "what do you do with it when you do get it?"

KG: Tell me about your parents. Were they good role models with money? Did they teach you the value of money?

VV: They didn't have any. I was the only one of the three children who went to college. But I was curious about what made things tick in the business world. I couldn't go to college when I first got out of high school, so I saved enough money and went to business school. I worked and saved a little money from working in Washington; then I studied economics and business at Duke. When I got to Colorado, the curriculums were separate, so I chose economics over business, though I would have loved to have had the two of them together. I did some graduate work in business afterwards. But economics is a good background. It gives you the ability to stand back and analyze.

KG: Then you went into stock brokerage?

VV: No, I married while I was in college. My husband's first job was in Houston, so that's how I got there. But I didn't get into finance until after he was killed in an accident.

I received a little bit of insurance money and even though I had a degree in economics and finance, nobody had taught me what to do with money. They teach you about the federal reserve system and the kind of stuff that you can never use.

I went back to college and did nothing but study investments, trying to figure out what to do with the money. It was then that I heard these statistics: Out of every 100 people reaching sixty-five, only 2 percent were financially independent. Back in 1961 that was the case, but it's not today; 23 percent had to continue working, and 75 percent depended upon friends, charity, or relatives. There I was searching for what to do with my life. I had no children and I had lost the husband I loved. All I wanted was a home, children, a devoted husband. I had no ambition about setting the world on fire. But I was searching for what to do with my life. I thought, this is something that I could devote my life to—helping people become financially independent. That would be a worthwhile thing to do.

Now, that sounds easy today. But if you were female in Houston, Texas, in 1961 and decided that you wanted to be a stockbroker . . .

No one would hire me. I went from firm to firm to firm. One man said, "We tried a woman once, but it didn't work." Now it's different today. I finally read the rules of the New York Stock Exchange. You know what they said? To become a broker, you had to work for a member firm for six months. It didn't say whether you should scrub floors or what you had to do. So I got myself a job as a clerk in a brokerage house, and I sent off for a study course. I studied the course, and when I'd been there six months, I asked to take the exam. Not thinking I could pass it, they let me, and I did pass, and then they had a problem. They pointed to a desk and said, "There's your desk." I was the farthest away from the peanut gallery. And they said, "We think we'll throw you in the water and see if you can swim. Now let me tell you what that means. We carry men on a draw for a year, but we're not going to give you anything."

So I thought, what do I do? I got a book on selling and there was a chapter on cold calls, and I tried that for a half day. I started with the tallest building in Houston, and I started at the top. By noon I was discouraged. I thought, maybe I could make speeches or do seminars —but I had no speaking experience. I went to the Chamber of Commerce and got a list of all the women's clubs and I prepared a letter— offering me as a speaker—and got my boss to sign it. I literally learned how to make a speech by talking to women's clubs. When I got to the point that I didn't fall off the stage, I started giving little seminars— and they just grew.

KG: Few people in American society do long-range financial planning and set financial goals. You must give people incentive and motivation.

VV: I've tried to tell people that it is not difficult. You just have to figure out the two points—where you are and where you want to go. It's like navigation. When you know the two points, it's not too hard. You just need to sit down with somebody. At least figure out where you are. Anybody can become financially independent, if you have the ability to earn, a little discipline to save, sufficient time, and reasonable intelligence. If you started soon enough and did nothing but set up a bank draft and put it in an average mutual fund, you'd make it. It's that simple.

KG: How would you describe your attitudes about money?

VV: I don't care that much about spending money. It's not that I want to stack it up or anything like that. It's more fun to multiply it than it is to spend it. It's a lot more fun to take one dollar and make two dollars than it is to take one dollar and go out shopping. I think it's good that people want to go shopping but that's not what turns me on. I want to take one dollar and make two dollars, and take two dollars and make four dollars. And I get just as much fun doing it for someone else as I do for myself. It's a game to me to see what you can do with money. Having big homes and big cars—not that I'm not adequately taken care of—is not what turns me on.

KG: Do you notice generational differences between the Depression-era mentality and the baby boomers, the "live for today" generation?

VV: Those who went through the Depression have either one or two reactions and it's black or white. There are not very many shades of gray. Either they clutch the dollar until the eagle screams, or they say, "What can I best do with this money?" A lot of them who went through the Depression do clutch too hard, but some of them have the other reaction. I think my reaction was the other. Not that I would spend it, but "Let's see what we can do with it"—rather than tuck it away some place. That's a hard concept to get across to people.

There are just three things you can do with a dollar—spend, loan, or own. If you spend it, I hope you have fun, but you have cut off our conversation. If you decide you are not going to spend it now, but spend it later, there are only two things you can do with a dollar, loan or own—and it makes a great difference which you choose. That dollar is either going to work for you or for the person to whom you lend it. For whom do you want your dollar to work? If you want it to work for you, you've got to move it over from working for somebody else to working for you. If you lend your dollar, you're only going to get a little sliver of its earning power. After taxes and inflation with the loaned dollar, you've usually lost.

Now, how do you put your money to work? You'll need some liquidity. Keep enough in a guaranteed position to give you peace of mind, for peace of mind is a good investment. But don't keep any more in a "guaranteed" position than it takes to give you this peace of mind. Once you understand how money can work for you, you may not have any peace of mind having it work for others. By the way, all money will ever do for you is give you options. It won't bring you happiness, but neither will poverty.

Any dollar that comes your way comes there for a purpose. You're either going to invest it wisely or you're going to lose. So you have to put money to work. Put it to work where you feel comfortable with it, and if you can't feel comfortable, at least be knowledgeable. But if it's ignorance that makes you uncomfortable, you can overcome it. Ignorance makes a lot of people uncomfortable. It's so important for people to know about money. The only way we'll ever preserve the free enterprise system—and I'm a real believer in the free enterprise system —is for enough people to own a part of it.

People ask me, "Do I have enough money for me to talk to you?" I say, "Of course you do." I say, "You have to be at least willing to have an open mind and consider all these possibilities. You don't have to do any of them." And, when I am doing a financial plan on a piece of paper, I say, "I want you to notice that this is written in pencil and I have an eraser. If it doesn't give you peace of mind, let's talk about it. Let's rearrange these things. They are not written in stone."

KG: You think peace of mind is very important?

VV: The client must have peace of mind. When I take a look at what you have, I know what you ought to do to maximize your return. But if you can't have peace of mind with my suggestions, then it would be the wrong investment for you. If you can only have peace of mind in a money market fund, that's where your money should be until you can emotionally move it. If I were to persuade you to invest it in anything else, you would be unhappy.

So many people forget that they aren't actually spending the money when they invest it, that they are just repositioning it so it can work for them. When they make an investment, some people say, "Boy, you've had me spend so much of my money." I say, "No, I've suggested that you reposition your money so it can work for you instead of the bank or the savings and loan."

KG: What are some of the first questions that people ask about investments?

VV: People don't know how to ask the right questions about an investment. They will ask, "How much does it pay?" That's not the right question. What you want to know is the total return. People get mixed up about that. Something can pay out 7 percent and have no growth. But if it pays out 3 percent and has 7 percent growth, then that's 10 percent. You need to think in terms of total return rather than what something pays. People have been conditioned to a CD that pays so and so, or a savings and loan that pays so and so, or a bond that pays so and so. That's not what you should ask about. You want to know about the total return. You can spend gains just as well as you can spend dividends. People don't understand growth. Growth of capital. And, of course, the market does fluctuate, which bothers a lot of people. I've tried to get them over that.

And you have to learn to do different things with your money at different times. You invest it differently if we have inflation at an increasing rate than if we have inflation at a decreasing rate. The financial planner in your life should be able to stand back and observe where we are in the cycle. Most people are too close to their money to make rational decisions about it. The role of a financial planner is to stand back and figure out where demand will be greater than supply.

You learn that in basic economics—just put your money where demand is greater than supply. Nobody's been able to repeal that law, not even the communist countries. So accept the fact that it will never be repealed. Now the question is, "Where is demand greater than supply?" That's the role of the financial planner in your life. If you are busy with your vocation, how can you be out there studying all the new investment programs coming on the market every month?

Investing is not an exact art and science. Even if you're a pro, you may only be a part-time pro, and you're not going to beat the full-time pros. For example, many people want to self-direct their IRA. Well, how are you going to self-direct $2,000? Not very easily. Now a lot of people have a little bit more than that in IRAs but it's still hard to do. At least, put part of that money under professional management and then see if you can beat the pros. If you do better than they do, take the money away from them. If they do better than you, then give them some more money.

You need to stick to quality things and when the tax laws change, then you change what you do. This new tax law has completely changed how you approach money management. There's no way the average person can know what products will now be offered and how they will fit into the new tax bill, unless you are spending your full time studying it. We have trouble ourselves.

KG: Do people like to believe that things stay the same?

VV: Yes, but things change all the time, and you've got to be able to change. That's why the word "dynamics" is in the title of each of my books. You can't make investments and say, "There, I'm done; I've made my investments." There is no investment for all seasons, but there is an investment for every season. I like my profession because every day I get up, it's a new day. You've got to look around you and see where you should change.

WILLIE DAVIS

Called the "all-pro entrepreneur," Willie Davis has conquered the business field in much the same way that he conquered the football field. When he retired from the NFL in 1969, Davis, a six-time All-Pro, had six divisional championships and five world championships to his credit. He had played for two years for the Cleveland Browns and ten years for the Green Bay Packers, where he was coached by the legendary Vince Lombardi. The end of one career, however, only signaled the beginning of another for the 6 foot, 3 inch, 240-pound defensive end.

Today Willie Davis is ranked as one of the top twenty-five black businessmen in America. Owner and operator of West Coast Beverage Company, the largest beer distributorship on the West Coast, Davis also owns All-Pro Broadcasting, which operates five radio stations throughout the United States. He serves on the board of directors of five major corporations and is involved with many community and civic organizations in Los Angeles. Among the many distinguished awards he has received are the Byron "Whizzer" White Award, given to "the athlete who contributes the most to his country, his community, and his team," the NAACP Man of the Year Award, and the NFL Man of the Year Award. In addition, Davis was inducted into the Pro Football Hall of Fame in 1981.

Married and the father of two children, Davis attended a small, segregated high school in Texarkana, Arkansas, where he was voted "the least likely to succeed." When he graduated from Grambling State University, he became the only student from his high school class to obtain a college degree. In the off season, while he played for the Packers, Davis earned an MBA from the University of Chicago.

George P. Shultz, U.S. Secretary of State and former dean of the University of Chicago's business school, says of Davis: "I'm not an expert on pro football, but I'm sure nobody captains a successful football team except a guy who is looked up to by his teammates. In whatever setting you place Willie Davis, he'll be a leader. People pay attention to him."

MONEYMAX PROFILE

Willie Davis is a calculated risk-taker. He always hedges his bets by having other options and alternate game plans, a strategy he learned when he was a professional athlete. While he was playing pro football, he was studying for his MBA so that he could start a business career when his football career ended.

He is a highly analytical thinker and believes in thoroughly researching all possible outcomes in any situation or task. Preparation is extremely important to him, and he doesn't understand how to conduct business any other way. His decisions, whether financial or business, are never impulsive ones.

Self-determination is one of Davis' strong suits. He believes that everyone has the potential to realize his or her dreams. He advocates action, not passivity; positive thinking and motivation instead of anxiety; and pride in achievement, not avoidance of failure. He believes that hard work will be rewarded, both financially and personally. For Davis the reward is not the prestige or status that money can bring, but the sense of achievement that comes in meeting the challenge and walking away victorious.

INTERVIEW

KG: Do you attribute a lot of your business success to what you learned when you played football?

WD: I think it was at that point that many of the things that governed, that were key factors in my life, were put into place. You have to look at growing up as a learning process. People try to build up the learning blocks along the way, and hopefully you grow into that person your parents want you to become.

In business you might start a plan for something in January and maybe wait twelve months or longer to see whether the plan worked. You are planning and developing something you want to see become a success. To me, athletics almost gives you a short version of that kind of planning process. In fact, in athletics, you have a moment, or a split second, to make a decision—and a lifetime to remember it. You get pushed into quick, reactive decisions that have long-lasting consequences. If you watch a basketball game, you can see what a couple of mistakes can do in the course of seven or eight seconds.

When you go through the athletic process for a number of years, you know how to competitively position yourself so that you can deal with the peaks and valleys. You can deal with the highs and lows, and you can deal with them with a sense of confidence. When I was in football, I took pride in the fact that I really didn't want any surprises in a football game. So how did I avoid surprises in a football game? I spent a lot of time during the week looking at films, studying the opposition, trying to determine, "In this situation, what is the likelihood of this or that happening?" By the time I actually got on the field, I expected very little to unfold in front of me that would be a total surprise. In short, I would say that I prepared myself to be able to handle both the expected and the unexpected.

Today that is probably more critical for me than it was in athletics. Because in business many times you are really looking at a situation that—if it blindsides you and comes as a big surprise—it could wipe you out. It's almost the same as getting an injury that ends your career. So part of my business strategy is to plan ahead and consider what I feel are the hazards, the ups and the downsides, the worst cases. Almost as if I were preparing a game plan to walk on the football field. In many ways, my life is one of drawing parables or comparisons to athletic situations. However, it's a little more complex than that.

It's always been very interesting to me that many of the great football coaches have been war-type strategists. Lombardi, in particular, almost talked to his players as if we were a military force. In many ways Lombardi is well thought of in corporate America because what

Lombardi talked to us about, what he advocated to the world, were things that are very applicable today in business.

KG: Could you give me an example?

WD: I imagine any professional person can be a certain type of Lombardi person—in terms of discipline, organization, and attitude. I believe strongly that at least 60 percent of winning is your mental attitude. It's how you feel about things, how you approach situations, and how involved you get. Everything is structured in attitude. In athletics a lot of times you hear "That guy really came to play." Well, in business, I think it's a larger version of the same thing. I go to the office prepared to win. I go to the office prepared to do whatever it takes to be successful. How do you develop these things? They are partly learned, and they are partly formed through habit. The thing I critique myself by, more than any other thing, is discipline. At the heart of what has managed my energy and my will is my discipline. When my discipline starts to fall apart, I find that I get in trouble.

KG: Where did you get this discipline?

WD: Lombardi left me with a good, basic approach to football and a good, basic approach to life. Much of the approach is in discipline; much of it is in commitment. If you get a person who is pretty disciplined and you get him committed, then you tend to have somebody who won't be denied. That stick-to-it-ness and that toughness is what wins. I know that I can persevere in a tough situation. I know I can walk in the face of adversity, knowing it's going to be tough, but I know that ultimately, I'm going to get the job done.

My mother was a very driving force in my life. I look at her picture today and I can still feel the energy and the forcefulness of this woman. She had a way to just "will" things. She wanted so much for the three of us kids, and I think she just lived through us in some ways. Not pushing, but encouraging and explaining why we ought to be prepared to move to the next level. That was extremely important. The coaches, the teachers, and the people who impacted my life in all the formative stages—all believed that to be extremely important.

People grow and learn out of some very basic things. Everything starts with honesty, with openness, with integrity. You need to be honest and credible with yourself. Whether you can lie down at night and get a good night's sleep or spend half the night wrestling with a problem has a lot to do with what's inside you; whether you can look in the mirror and feel that honesty and integrity are within you. I don't sit around and worry about whether or not I've been fair to other people. I don't sit around and worry whether I gave it my best effort. I don't sit around and wonder whether or not I approach something with stereotypes and predetermined judgments. I can clear my conscience very quickly. And that's important to me.

Sure, I have had some tough moments. I'm a guy who thinks positively and wants to make everything work out. When things don't work out, I'm able to do an introspection, and—if I'm partly to blame —think it through and get the guilt out real quick. But, for the most part, I feel as if I've been able to look in the mirror every day of my life and not find a lot of bothersome past experiences. I grew up with an awful lot of missing pieces in my life. And I say, "When I didn't have this, what did I do?" I'd never want to put my kids through some of the same dreadful experiences I went through, but I think that part of dealing with real life is to have to deal with some of the low moments.

In business today, I've seen people who have been so sheltered that the least little thing sends them off in disarray. And I truly equate that to a lack of having been in the arena, in the real world. In this country and in this system, we all tend to accentuate the positive. America is the land of opportunity, the great reward place to be in. In truth, and in a pure form, we really have more of a system of elimination than one of inclusion. When you get in the business arena, there are more things pushing you out of the business than pushing you in.

KG: Football is one of the best places to learn the true sense of competition and winning. Yet why do so few people do what you have done? Leave the athletic arena and make an impact in business?

WD: In this country we tend to treat athletics almost as a novelty, like the toy department rather than something essential and substantial. That's how we relate to it; it's a leisure activity. We look at athletics as something that we relax with, that takes us away from the real nitty-gritty things in life. And because it's been positioned that way, those of us that walk out of athletics are viewed many times as some kind of specialized exceptions rather than people who need to fit into the whole process. Because the public views you that way, there is something that disrupts your transition from sports to business.

The greatest thing that ever happened to me as an athlete is that I never got carried away with being an athlete. I was almost as practical as an athlete as I am as a businessman. So there was no real change in many ways. My lifestyle didn't change a lot.

KG: You didn't get caught up with status?

WD: No. The problem really occurs if you get trapped into believing that athletics is something uniquely structured in your life. When you have to come out of it and go back into a different world, you might not have prepared yourself. Many people that have had a problem with the transition became somewhat possessed by being an athlete. It's like there is a normal human being track over here, and a track set aside over there for athletes. When you're sitting over here, you can build self-confidence, but once you're thrown back on the average person track, you become a kind of misfit. And it shouldn't be that way. No one felt greater about being in athletics—no one appreciated athletics—more than Willie Davis. But during the whole process, I don't believe football ever changed me. I still appreciate the fact that everything I have done in my life, I had to earn by working hard.

I never got absorbed into being just an athlete. I held on to being a real person. When the athletic part dropped out, I wasn't scrambling over to the other track of people. Obviously, at that time, other entrepreneurs or businessmen already had a quantum leap of experience over me. That was one of the reasons why I went back to graduate school. I knew I had to do something that would help me leap over part of the process. I didn't want that void to handicap me, and I felt one of the ways to leapfrog over some of those years of experience was to be equally, or better, trained.

KG: Did you have a master plan? Did you say, "I want to be a businessman when I leave football, so I better go to school and get trained?"

WD: I had a very definite idea that was structured in my mind and maybe in my soul—about how I wanted to be able to walk away from athletics. I did have that. Even if I didn't make it in athletics, I needed to know what else I could do. I was fortunate enough to do well in athletics, but I kept treating sports as something that enabled me to enhance the whole process of living and working. When the day came that I had to leave athletics, I was able to walk out and basically change hats.

I used to say to myself, "How in the world could I have ever expected, when I was in Texarkana, that one day I would be a pro-football player walking out to practice in this type of setting?" And I would literally feel the adrenaline flowing from that excitement and the feeling of how great it was. And yet I would also say, "But you know, the important thing I did when I was at Grambling was to get my degree so that if I didn't make it in pro football, at least I would be teaching school or coaching or something else."

Someone once said, "Few people get what they want; most people get what they expect." And I guess that kind of characterizes my life in a way. I spent a lot of my life pursuing what I wanted, but I also spent much of it pursuing what I expected to occur. Pursuing what I expected many times enabled me to be somewhere in between what I wanted and what I expected.

KG: Did you want to be a financial success as well as a business success? Was that important to you?

WD: What I wanted, more than anything, was to be able to measure success in my life—in some way. I really don't feel that money is my hot button. The progression of moving from A to B, with B being greater than A, is how I measure it. I heard Merlin Olsen, a former Ram, speak recently about motivation and a winning attitude. Merlin talked specifically about our system rewarding the doers. If you set your sights high in athletics or business, if it's in the direction of winning, then the financial reward usually goes along with it.

You always hear about athletes playing in a championship game and what they are going to be paid per player. In the Super Bowl somebody might mention the ring you get, but mostly people talk about the paycheck. With me, the ring has always been a very meaningful, symbolic statement. You take the money and spend it or invest it, and it quickly fades from sight. But the ring, and all the other symbols—they linger on. I look at my Super Bowl ring and I think about the game, the excitement, all the feelings. . . .

KG: I understand that you really don't like to talk about making money?

WD: No, I don't. Earlier this year a group approached me and they wanted me to speak at this event they were putting together. I listened with great interest. The concept seemed to be about achievements, about how to get things done in life. I agreed to show up on a Sunday and be part of the group. A day or two before the event was to occur, someone asked me if I was going to the "millionaires" networking event on Sunday. For the first time I learned that the whole thrust of the event was to listen to millionaires talk about how they made their money. As the time grew nearer, I knew that there was no way I was going to go to that event. It was out of character for me to be there. If they were going to talk about winning, if they were going to talk about achieving, if they were going to talk about something like that—then I would have gone.

But when they put the dollar sign up, it just changed everything. It made me feel uncomfortable because I never felt it was important to have dollar-sign recognition. Talking about winning or achieving turns me on. If you talk about money, that's not my way of measuring myself.

I also feel that the Yuppie identity in this country has done us a disservice. It has people consciously striving to show off their financial means in a way that I feel has no real value. I've seen people with great wealth, and I almost think it's unfortunate that some of them have it. You have to look at how they got it, and more importantly, how they are using it. Sometimes I see very few values derived from it all. I think this country has a money crazy quality of life that does very little to improve the quality of life or anything else that, to me, is much more important. So I guess I work hard and I expect to be well rewarded, but I don't display my achievements in dollar signs.

KG: How do parents with money instill a good value system in their children?

WD: Money can misdirect how you bring up your children. I sometimes think that all of us are guilty of it. We give our kids everything, yet we turn around and say, "Why is there no motivation?" Having to dig in and work hard, combined with the uncertainty in my life, clearly made me very committed to achievement. Sometimes it was almost like fear motivation.

When you've experienced fear, you understand fear. When people explain fear, you sense what they mean but you really don't understand fear. Not like the kind of fear that you've lived through. I look at my children and think, "Thank goodness they don't have to experience the fear and the rough times." But, on the other hand, maybe it's unfortunate that they didn't experience just a little bit of it.

KG: How much harder is it for a minority to succeed in business?

WD: When you are a minority in this country, the system doesn't shut itself off in total denial, but it doesn't open up completely. You've got to step over taller hurdles and I guess that is part of the mental preparation that I advocate. I have been fortunate to be elected to some corporate boards and I've looked at the essence of the economic and the power structure in this country. When you really look at it, you realize we all are survivors. But some can play the game better than others. We are segmented into minorities and everything else, but when you really throw us into the game, we are all survivors, working our way through the process. And the process is one of elimination. And that's why minorities tend to deny themselves an equal chance in the game. They deny themselves many times, through education, the preparation and the attitudes necessary to get in and actually play the game.

There is a lack of role modeling and a lack of identity. The average white kid can have some expectations almost at any level. Most minorities, who don't have examples to follow, tend to think, "I can never be at that level." When I've walked into different boardrooms, I've seen very talented people, but all of them aren't supermen or superwomen. They are people who have insecurities, who have the doubts and fears of average people. The problem is that we have painted these people into some super category, when in truth they were smart enough to be survivors; they were bright enough to play in the game. And I don't mean that as a negative observation. But I say it to show that minorities lack the exposure to understand the system and how it works. A homogenous existence tends to promote homogenous continuation.

KG: What motivates Willie Davis?

WD: The thing that drives Willie Davis is the challenge to get up every day and say, "I can." To me that's really the essence of my life—that I can get things done.

MILES SEIFERT

Born in Australia, Miles Seifert came to the United States when he was twelve years old; his father was American, his mother a New Zealander. His family relocated so that the children would be educated in the United States. Seifert has been working since he was thirteen, and a combination of summer jobs, scholarships, and loans put him through college. A liberal arts major, he is a graduate of Princeton University.

After working in investment management for twenty years, Seifert started his own company, Gray, Seifert & Co., in New York in 1980. At that time he and his partner, Edward Gray, didn't have a single account. Today Gray, Seifert & Co. manages more than $700 million and the firm is consistently ranked among the top ten investment advisers on Wall Street. The company's accounts are primarily wealthy individuals and family groups; Gray, Seifert & Co. averages a 23 percent return on investments.

Competitive, hard-working, and independent, Seifert does not allow money to enter into his definition of success. According to him: "I never had any concern with money, and I don't want to start now. I always believed that I could make money, so money never became important. The most important thing for me is being respected by other people. I'd rather have that than any amount of money."

MONEYMAX PROFILE

For Miles Seifert, hard work is more than an essential ingredient for success—it is the core of his money personality. He is proud of his business and financial accomplishments, both for his clients as well as for himself. His own internal standards of excellence in his work, as well as his reputation among his peers, are what motivate him and refuel his high drive and work ethic.

Seifert has tremendous confidence in his ability to make sound financial decisions, and a high level of involvement and consistency of focus are evident in his money management style. His altruistic attitudes and behaviors are also a source of great satisfaction for him. He enjoys helping people he believes in professionally and personally.

INTERVIEW

KG: How did you get into the investment business?

MS: When I got out of college, I was looking for a job. And I walked into an insurance company and they wanted me to sell insurance, but I really wasn't interested in selling insurance. And they said, "Well, there's a job open in the investment department."

I didn't know anything about investments. My father never owned any stocks. In college, I was strictly liberal arts—a history and religion major—so I had nothing to do with the financial side of the world. Anyway, I had an interview in the investment department and they hired me. The interviewer said, "You're an analyst," and I learned the job while I was there. That's how I started back in 1958, and I've been managing other people's money ever since.

KG: Has your philosophy about managing money changed over the years?

MS: In this business, everybody grows; you don't stay the same. I know a lot more today than I knew twenty-five years ago. How have I evolved? I think the confidence factor is very important in what I do. If you believe in yourself, chances are you are going to be successful. If you have self-doubt, it's going to be harder to be successful.

KG: How does self-doubt get in the way—in terms of your business?

MS: Our business changes all the time. You've got to continually view the change in this business. You can't stay with one idea, and you've got to be flexible. You've got to be willing to listen to new ideas. You've got to be willing to adjust to new thinking. I've always had the same investment philosophy, but I've changed in application many times in the last twenty-five years. I've been in every possible type of stock. I try to adjust myself to what's happening now, not guess what's going to happen in the future.

There's a certain amount of intuition that's involved, but I would rather use the word "experience." I think it's ridiculous to compare somebody who's been in this business five years with somebody who's been in it for twenty-six years. There's just no comparison. First of all, the person who's been in it for five years has not had the exposure to that many markets. The more exposure you get, the better you are.

You have to believe in yourself. I know I'm going to make mistakes, but I'm not going to be blown away by mistakes. Not every stock you buy goes up. How you view your losers, what effect they have on you —that's important.

KG: You take it in stride?

MS: Just take it in stride. I read the paper every day, and look for the ones showing the best earnings. That's a good starting point. That's how I invest. I invest on current earnings, not projected earnings. Current, reported earnings.

KG: You stay with what's happening now and don't deviate?

MS: I don't deviate. If I see something bad is happening in the company, I just sell it. I don't hold on to it. My discipline is to keep the things that are showing good earnings, and when they stop showing good earnings, we sell. We don't fall in love with a company and wait for it to turn around. You don't make excuses; you sell and go on to something that *is* showing earnings. That practice has paid off over a long period of time.

KG: How would you define success for yourself?

MS: Most people define success by how much money they make. The most important thing for me is being respected by other people— my peers, by people in this business. I'd rather have that than any amount of money. I'd rather have them say, "Miles Seifert does a good job." Our business is very competitive, and there are a lot of very smart people in this business. To have people put me at the top is very rewarding.

KG: How does money enter into your definition of success? Did you use money as a barometer as you were going along?

MS: I never had any concern with money, and I don't want to start now. I always believed that I could make money, so money never became important. I never worried about it. I'm making a lot of money and I'm worth a lot of money. I'd rather be rich than poor, but I don't spend five seconds balancing my checkbook.

KG: You obviously have a very strong work ethic.

MS: You develop a confidence in yourself because you have an ability to do something, which is very important to recycle. You've got to have an ability; you've got to believe in yourself.

There's got to be a work ethic; there's got to be something you *do*. It's important to wake up every morning and say, "By God, I've got something I'm going to have to do. I'm not going to just lie in bed. I'm not going to just relax. I'm not going to think about ways of spending money. I want to go out and do something."

People ask me what I'm going to do when I retire. I'm not going to retire. This is what I like to do. Sit around and read a newspaper in Florida? That's awful. No, I'm perfectly happy to go right here at this desk. And I'll go when I'm looking at this machine.

KG: What motivated you to start up your own company?

MS: I've always enjoyed what I've done, but I've had periods where I haven't enjoyed working with some people. I'm not a good corporation person because I have no patience at all. I've always managed to work—when I worked in companies—for somebody who always wanted to take credit for something I did. And those people don't put anything on the table themselves. The best thing I ever did was to set up my own company in 1980. I didn't have to work for anybody anymore.

KG: What financial accomplishments are you most proud of?

MS: The nice thing about this business is that you're measured against your peers. Obviously, I'm proud because we're at the top.

KG: Would you say you're a pretty competitive person?

MS: Sure, absolutely. I don't do things if there's no competition. I play tennis because I'm playing against somebody.

KG: Did you get that message from your parents? Did they condition you to win?

MS: My father opened the first silk weaving mill in Australia. He was very successful. But he came back to the United States—he was an American—because he wanted his children to be educated in the United States. When he returned to this country, he went into the textile business, but he didn't enjoy what he did. So I grew up in an atmosphere where my father went to work every day but didn't enjoy what he did—which had an effect on me.

It motivated me to make sure that I got myself into something that I enjoyed, instead of being forced into something that I didn't like. And I was lucky. I feel most fortunate that I landed on my feet. And into something that has worked out to my advantage.

KG: You learned responsibility at an early age?

MS: When I was thirteen, I started working summer jobs and made my own money. I got scholarships in school and borrowed money to get though college. It was a wonderful opportunity because it gave me the confidence to believe in myself.

KG: How much does luck enter into financial success?

MS: I've never met a good money manager who's done it by luck. I've met many good money managers who have done it by hard work. Sure, luck might be a part of it. I've looked in the paper and come up with earnings for a company and said, "I haven't had that happen in a long time." Now, was it lucky that I caught it in the paper, or is it luck that I read the paper every day to look at the earnings to see if I'm going to come up with a company that's going to pay? I really believe that you work at what you do. The harder you work at it, the more success you're going to have.

KG: Are you a person who continually sets goals?

MS: I have no goals. I've never had a goal. Obviously, I wanted to succeed, but my concept of success is how I am viewed by others. When I leave this life, I'd like to be remembered for what I put into this business and that includes helping people get jobs, and a lot of things that have nothing to do with managing money. Introducing people, making things fit. Being a good guy. Putting something back.

Would I have succeeded in another business? Probably. As long as I didn't have to work for corporations. I don't have the patience to play. It's not a game I enjoy. I like to be independent and do my own thing.

KG: How has money contributed to your sense of well-being?

MS: Well, not having to worry about it certainly is good. Once I was out of work for a very brief time and that's probably the only time I ever really thought about money. And then I went and got a job.

A lot of people say money is a means of keeping score in our business. I don't subscribe to that, but I suppose it has some validity. I'm very fortunate that I've found an industry and a business that's allowed me to be independent, that's allowed me to develop, that's allowed me to succeed. My own way. I probably couldn't find another area that would give me as much freedom as this does.

KG: Are you much of a spender?

MS: I'm not a spender. I drive American cars. What is a car? My friends have Jaguars and I make more money than they do. I'll drive my American car and people will say, "How do you like your car?" I tell them it's a very comfortable car, it's not fancy, and it runs. I am not a fancy person. I have no interest in status, whatsoever. I have no time for the social world. I don't like parties, but I do like to go out and have fun. I do not like to stand around at cocktail parties where people are lying through their teeth. I don't mind talking about my business, but I certainly don't want to stand around and talk nonsense at cocktail parties.

KG: Have there been turning points in your life?

MS: When I came to this country, I had a terrible time speaking because of my Australian accent—and I had a very heavy one when I came here. It was very much like a cockney accent, and most of the kids at school had never heard an Australian accent and they made fun of me. The teachers used to enjoy having me get up and talk, but it was rather painful because I couldn't speak like the other kids. Finally, I developed a terrible stammer, and when I went away to private school, I could hardly speak at all. When I was fourteen, I decided to try out for the school play. The drama coach decided that he'd give me a leading part in the play, even though I couldn't even get through the rehearsals without stammering. And the first night I went on the stage—it was a comedy role—the audience laughed at the first line I had, and I never stammered again. The drama coach had faith in me, and I guess I had the nerve to get up there and do it. That turned my life around. It gave me a sense of accomplishment that I didn't have before. And I've never looked back. Fortunately, I'll never have to.

KG: Would you comment on the insider trading scandals, the greed that's going on, on Wall Street?

MS: I certainly can. I think there is no penalty severe enough for these people who take public trust and throw it away. I think Mr. Boesky is as much a criminal as we have ever had. What he has done to a business that's given him a livelihood, far beyond his wildest estimation, is just disgusting. And if they said, "Come and get him and throw away the key for a million years," I'd be for it. And people that take suitcases of money like that Siegel person—I have no sympathy, no pity for him at all. I think that the Justice Department in this country is not strong enough. I think that this is a great profession that I'm in. It's taken good care of me, and I'm very proud of what I do.

STEPHEN SOLMS

Stephen Solms is founder and chairman of Historic Landmarks for Living, the largest residential developer of historical properties in the United States. A pioneer in the field, Solms purchases run-down, abandoned industrial properties and converts them into luxury apartments. His inventory of properties includes former warehouses, schools, hospitals, factories, and department stores. Renovated with innovative design and artistic touches, the buildings are transformed into stylish apartments complete with amenities—including high, beamed ceilings; fireplaces; winding staircases; gourmet kitchens; large glass windows; exposed brick walls.

Based in Philadelphia, Solms is known as the man who saved the city from the wrecker's ball. A dominant force in the city's real estate scene, Solms has been praised and honored by city officials for bringing new life into Philadelphia's housing market and for preserving and revitalizing the city's historic areas. As one rival developer says, "Steve has the ability to single-handedly bring back a neighborhood."

Described as candid, unconventional, creative, irrepressible, individualistic, and a genius, Solms and Historic Landmarks control more than 1,600 apartment units in Philadelphia alone and have projects completed or under construction in more than fifteen cities in the United States. His enthusiasm for business is only equaled by his addiction to basketball—the Philadelphia '76ers in particular. A man who consistently beats the odds, Solms attributes his business success "to the fact that people have confidence in me, they like me, and they trust me."

MONEYMAX PROFILE

Steve Solms describes himself as a confident risk-taker. Risk-taking and meeting a challenge head-on are what motivate him in business.

He has great confidence in his money management skills. Now that he has successfully built his business, he knows he could do it all over again if he had to. His money does not bring him as much contentment as does the knowledge that he is in charge of his life; he has found his own comfortable niche.

Solms avoids flash and pretense and abhors the use of money to manipulate others. Trust is an important component of his money style and is evident in his financial transactions and business dealings. He goes out of his way to play it straight and aboveboard and expects the same treatment in return.

INTERVIEW

KG: You are one of the pioneers in the historical redevelopment business. How did you get started?

SS: I was a developer of new construction before I had my own business—mainly multifamily apartments and motels and theaters and condominiums. I had a partner, and we were doing about two or three creative projects a year. That was back as far as 1969, and we did projects better than the next guy—more amenities, a unique design, nice landscaping. We were what you would call quality-oriented and creative in whatever we brought to the public.

In 1977 we both decided: "It's just too much—fourteen hours a day, five to six days a week. Let's close up shop and not do any more development." So we just stopped. I was about thirty-eight years old then. I had six months, or eight months, off, and I didn't have to worry about anything financially, because the business had been successful and I was financially secure. But I'm the kind of guy that likes to work hard and play hard. At the same time, my wife was working in her own career, and I would get up in the morning and make hardboiled eggs and pick up the paper. Then I'd sit out in the park and read the sports section—I'm an avid '76ers fan. And I was having a good time for a while.

Then a guy who did a lot of developments for me called me on the phone and said, "Steve, you are a creative person. You can't retire. You're too young. You have to get back out there." He said, "I ran into a guy who used to go to high school with you and he's doing syndications where you take historic buildings and fix them up. Why don't you meet with this guy?"

About two weeks later I called the guy and went down to his office, which was in Philadelphia's Old City, like Soho fifteen years ago. I saw all these old buildings that were architecturally magnificent, and I thought, "I have to get myself into this. This is a way that I can live out my dreams." So I shook hands with the guy, and I bought a couple of properties, small properties, and all of a sudden, I was started.

I said to myself, "There are all these buildings I could buy for five dollars a foot, all of them are downtown, all of them are in great locations. All you need is a brain to make this work." No conventional apartments had been built in Philadelphia since about 1967. No one had really built apartments in the last twenty years to any great degree. I went to the bank and said that I wanted to buy 3 million square feet of inventory. So I went from doing twenty or thirty units in my brain to doing thousands.

KG: That didn't seem like too great a risk for you?

SS: It really didn't. I used to take the bank people into the buildings and they would say to me, "Are you crazy?" They had no vision. Finally, I convinced them to lend me the money. Once I did three or four deals, it started to get easier.

We're averaging $65 to $70 million a year for the last two years, and our volume has gone from 300 units to 500 units to 800 units, and we are now capable of doing 1,500 a year. Then we went from three cities to five cities to ten cities, fifteen cities. We started off with 8 to 10 people, and now we have 300 people.

KG: You think expansively and don't mind taking risks. Were you always that way, or was it something that you acquired?

SS: No, I always had confidence. People always think that people with money only think about money. I went into the business because in the back of my mind I thought, "I'm going to figure out a way to make this work. The banks have confidence in me and I'll figure out a way to make it work." I always believed that if you give somebody a unique product, a quality product, they're going to rent it or buy it. And if you know that you are better than the other person . . .

KG: What has driven you?

SS: Somewhere along the line I must have wanted to take risks. I always forced myself to be on the borderline of disaster. In other words, for some reason I was never satisfied with just doing one thing.

I would always say, "If we made this work here, why don't we go to another city?" Or, "Why don't we do more volume?" There was always a next level. I must have had something in mind; for some reason I must have wanted to form my own organization. I have always been creative financially, and I have always been a good judge of people— what people are really like and what kind of character they have.

KG: What about the combination of values and ethics with business?

SS: If someone lies to me, that's it. Everything is over because I can't deal with lying.

And I don't back down. Once I believe in something, I follow through. My value system is strong and I bend over backwards to make a deal work for the other person. In my business approach, I like to bring everything out in the open and hold no cards back. Here's the deal, this is what's there. If people take that as a sign of weakness, then they are fools.

KG: Do many people take that as a sign of weakness?

SS: Absolutely.

KG: Why?

SS: Because they are not very smart. With those people I start wondering about their defense mechanisms, how secure they are, and where their integrity is.

KG: Some people must find your style very unique?

SS: I guess some people aren't used to people like me. I have a lot of enthusiasm, I like to bring everyone out and not make the negotiations boring. I like to deal on a personal level. That might cause some conflict. Some people seem to like you because they would like to be entrepreneurs themselves, but they might really despise you because you are out there doing it and they aren't.

KG: Did you always want to be in business for yourself?

SS: I worked for someone else in the real estate business, and for years I thought I was a failure. My boss threw me out and said, "Lease shopping center space." I would go into these small towns, where they had never seen a shopping center, where people were paying only $100 a month rent. And I would have to sell them on the idea of paying ten times more rent. At twenty-four or twenty-five years old, I wasn't too sophisticated, and it was two years until I made my first lease. I was working for $125 a week, and I thought I was a failure. I used to make eight or ten cold calls a day and finally I must have caught on to what these people needed to hear. Then the next year I made 100 leases and the year after that—150 leases. One morning I looked in the mirror—I was twenty-nine years old—and I laughed and said, "I'll never be intimidated by anything as long as I live. I'll never take no for an answer and I can get whatever I want with perseverance."

When I was thirty, I decided to go out on my own. So I went in with another guy who was a lawyer and we put a deal together. I didn't know one thing about construction. And we went out there and learned the business. I lived it—starting every day at seven in the morning. I'm totally untechnical; I can't even turn a key in the door. But I went out and I learned what it takes to get a job up and running.

KG: You obviously love a challenge?

SS: A friend of mine relates a lot of what I do in real life with basketball—the fine machine, the mental toughness that you need to work as a team and excel. I must like the challenge of taking on a challenge. I also know that down deep it really doesn't matter. Because if you are working with people who respect you and you respect them, then the whole process is working. If the world caved in tomorrow, I know that I can still go out and make a living. Once you know that you are good, you never really worry about money or not being able to start over again. You know in the back of your mind that you can always come back, you will always be able to start all over the next day. You wouldn't want to do it all again, but you could.

KG: How do you feel now about your business versus how you felt when you were putting it together?

SS: I can be as involved as much as I want to be now, or as little as I want to be. That's how I have the company structured. Before I probably enjoyed the excitement and the challenge of walking the fine line between failure and success. In those days I was involved in the day to day battles. Today I oversee the business and I'm not in the trenches. Not that I want to go back in the trenches, but I think I enjoy the trenches more.

For some reason, I was never afraid of taking risks. Some of my friends would say, "You've built this deal; you've built that deal; you're doing this; you're doing that. Slow down." These guys were slowing down too much; they weren't doing anything. They were almost dead. And I was thinking, "What else am I going to do?" I had enough money to live on, and I was never worried about being secure. I love this business, and I love learning how to structure each new level.

KG: In high school you were voted "least likely to succeed." What were you like in high school?

SS: I had bad vision when I was growing up. I had weak muscles in my eyes and I had problems reading. Probably I overcompensated in trying to be liked, even though I always had a great personality. I was funny—had a good sense of humor. My parents acted like they were disciplinarians but basically they figured, "We don't know what this kid is going to do; he's not interested in money; he just wants to have a good time; let's hope he goes to college."

KG: You have always been a maverick?

SS: Oh, definitely. I think about friends of mine who were going to Yale and Harvard—some of them could barely talk. I used to think they were so boring, and they used to think they were so smart. I just knew I was smarter in knowing how to live life.

If I'm able to enjoy myself every day and be an adventurer, I ought to just continue going about my life. I have never worried about what everyone else thinks. Some of my friends are still trying to find out who they are and what has been happening to them for the last twenty years. Why don't they just go out and be themselves and find their own niche?

KG: Somehow you must have gotten the message that it was all right to be yourself. Where did that come from?

SS: I really wasn't good in school; I was sort of rebellious. I did have a lot of love at home. But I was never programmed about money —that was not very important.

My parents were pretty low key about money. My father was a successful mortgage broker, president of the company. I used to look at him and think, "I'll never be a president of anything; I'll be lucky if I can get a job in a store." He used to tell me, "You can't go on like this, making sixty dollars a week, whatever you're doing." When I first started out, I worked for my uncle and worked seventy to eighty hours a week selling luggage. I kept telling my dad, "This is great; I love selling; I meet wonderful people." He said, "You're a schmuck. One day you will understand that if you want the nice things in life, you better wake up and get out there."

I thought our family was comfortable, a little bit upper middle class. Most people like to look at a successful guy and say he got his money from his father or that other people helped him. Some people who want to make a lot of money, like to think about money. They add it up all the time, and talk about ways to make money. At least from my own experience, I never went through that process. I threw the balls up in the air and I figured they would come down. I never sat around and said, "I'm going to make $50,000 this year or $80,000 next year."

KG: What does money mean to you? Do you enjoy your money?

SS: I actually do. I go on vacations, have a little home in Maine, but I'm pretty low key. I hardly ever talk about money. At parties or even in business, I'll have a three-hour conversation with somebody and maybe ten minutes of it is about business. I have always lived the same way. I lived either in a nice house or nice apartment, but I was never flashy. I was always embarrassed by being showy. I'm a casual dresser.

KG: You don't flaunt money?

SS: I don't like people who are snobs. I have down to earth values. Sometimes you meet people who are impressed by your money. And, at the same time, you meet people who are real intellectuals and they are irritated that guys like me are successful. You can close a deal in thirty seconds and some of these guys spend an hour talking around one sentence. That irritates me. It's not that complicated.

I'm the kind of person who likes to go out at night, have a good time, and share experiences with other people. Before the basketball games, I bring together people from all walks of life and we all go out to dinner—once or twice a week. Usually there are ten or fifteen people—one guy works in the parking lot, another guy is a banker. We all go to the game and we have something in common to talk about. It's all very social and there's a certain warmth to it.

KG: What advice would you give to someone who wanted to start up a business?

SS: You have to learn to be yourself, be an individual. Go in with a confident attitude, be consistent, and be willing to hang in there at any cost. You have to concentrate on dealing with obstacles, not just positive things, so you are able to move quickly to cover any negatives in a deal. One of the most important things is your integrity, and you should let people get to know you as a human being. I don't think that business is a superficial world. All of my successes have been based on the fact that people have confidence in me, they like me, and they trust me. I don't think you have to be mean or tough. You have to be smart enough to give the other guy the benefit of the doubt. At least from my own experience, I've always gained more from being generous than not being generous.

16

---◦►◄◦---

Maximizing
Your Money Personality

The purpose of this book has been to provide insight into your money personality and Moneymax Profile so you can become more successful in the use and enjoyment of your money. For some of you, that may mean not altering your money personality at all but just accepting who you are and now being able to act with greater insight and understanding, as well as acceptance. Others may choose to take more control, plan for the future, and institute better money management systems on a daily basis. And still for others, learning how to enjoy money has been the main benefit extracted from knowing their profile tendencies and traits.

If you are not content with your money personality, you can certainly make changes. Many of my clients started out in life with traits that needed to be changed if they were going to achieve their goals. Many of you will have identified traits within yourself that you would like to change. Most people are rarely satisfied with their money behaviors. There is always something you can find to improve. The important thing to keep in mind is that you can change your money life.

If a particular Moneymax Profile interests and motivates you, then study its traits, contrast them with your own, and then formulate a game plan for how you are going to make the necessary changes. Since pioneering the field of financial psychology, I have concluded that most of my clients lack control over their money and resources more than they lack money and resources.

When working with clients and others I have met through seminars, speeches, and workshops, I have focused on short-term counseling whenever possible. In order to change your money personality traits, it is not necessary to dredge up deep-seated negative experiences and relive them again. Rather, I believe that producing more effective results begins with creating a new model for the process of change. Through modeling techniques based on the financial personalities of the Moneymax Profile, my clients have been able to make significant and rapid changes to help them achieve their financial goals and desires. For most, there was a gap, a real distinction, between where they were and where they wanted to be. They wanted to change their money styles for a great variety of reasons: to earn more money, to solve marital and family disputes, to change jobs, to make better investments, to become more adept at financial negotiations, to provide for future security, to get out of debt or bankruptcy, or get more enjoyment from hard-earned money.

If you want to change your money style, you have to alter the internal ways you represent money—your personal financial traits—by changing negative attitudes and behaviors into positive ones. If a certain Moneymax Profile produces financial, personal, or social results that you would like to model, you need to review how that profile thinks and feels about money, how they manage money, and perhaps how they got that way. There are a number of Moneymax Profiles worthy of emulation. Choosing a style is a very individual decision, which requires an assessment of your values, lifestyle, and financial goals.

You have learned about your money personality by reading about the lives of anonymous people and how they have conducted their financial lives, according to their personal financial traits, and how the traits have influenced their money management styles. In some cases the traits served as assets and in others they were liabilities which blocked financial success and/or contentment. Also, in the previous chapter, "Profiles of Mental Wealth," you read about people whose financial traits and money personalities have served them well in achieving financial security as well as a high degree of contentment with their money.

These stories and interviews have been presented so that the Moneymax Profiles and the thirteen financial traits would come alive in real people and real situations. Although it has been mentioned before, it is important to point out once again that the nine Moneymax groups were formed according to money attitudes and nothing else—not age or sex or financial status. While I have reported the interesting demographic findings of the Moneymax national survey, those factors should not influence your perception of any group's personality. For instance, even though the Optimists have the largest percentage of widows, many of the other Moneymax Profiles have widows, and twice as many married people as widows comprise the Optimist profile. Likewise, there are many self-employed people who do not score as a Moneymax Entrepreneur; just as there are people who do not work for themselves that do score as an Entrepreneur.

Future Moneymax national surveys may find different clusterings. For example, there may be fewer female Hunters as women become more integrally involved with careers and money management. The male-dominated Entrepreneur group is certain to change as more women learn to think and behave like the Entrepreneurs. Attitudes drive behavior, and behavior drives attitudes, causing a reciprocal effect. So as more women enter the business world, learn to take more risks, develop dreams and visions that require independent and creative effort, their money personalities will have a good chance of changing accordingly.

Because of the current changes in the tax law, as well as the recent scandals on Wall Street and the stock market crash of October 1987, consumers will become more vigilant about their money, more scrutinizing about what they do with it and who they allow to handle it. This may well become the age of the enlightened financial consumer. As consumers take on more responsibility and play an active role in their money management, they will think less like the Producers and Safety Players and more like the Achievers and Money Masters.

As a society, our thinking has changed substantially from believing that money is the root of all evil to the lack of money being the root of all evil. Once an understated culture in terms of displaying wealth, we now flaunt our newfound money in a way which is considered vulgar by some critics. Thus, the Moneymax Profiles that are driven to achieve varying degrees of power, prestige, and status with their money—like the High Rollers, the Entrepreneurs, and the Hunters—will probably continue to flourish. Also, since we are in the fast-lane society of high stimulation, the High Rollers look like they are here to stay.

In my business, I meet many people who complain about not being able to stay on top of their money because of time constraints and all of life's other demands. With the baby boomer generation at its prime and many two-income families at the peak of their earning power, there is more discretionary income to invest than ever before. This high percentage of potential investors, as well as the peaked money motivation of our culture, makes it essential that more people understand how their money attitudes affect their money behavior.

The Moneymax Profile allows the world of finance to be viewed from a very personal point of view. It's time to consider the investor as an integral part of the investing equation. This does not mean that financial professionals have not been considering the individual investor; it means that they have had to rely on information investors offered voluntarily or in response to their questions. Since money is the last taboo and not easy to talk about for most people, the task of professional financial advisers has not been an easy one. Up to now, financial professionals have been expected to be genies with a crystal ball, trying to predict investor satisfaction with a particular investment based on the investor's temperament—i.e., how much risk could be tolerated.

Now that you are equipped with information about your money personality, you can relate to your money with a greater awareness of your attitudes. This awareness can be transferred into your everyday money management style and into the world of investing, if you so desire. Financial psychology and the Moneymax Profile concept help to build a more enlightened relationship between the consumer and the financial professional.

HOW YOUR MONEY PERSONALITY AFFECTS MONEY MANAGEMENT

We are a nation of naïve investors because we have had very little money education and few role models to emulate. The financial planning industry is growing by leaps and bounds, yet consumers are unaware of what the industry has to offer, and they are often too fearful to get involved. If you are one of those people, you are not alone. I have talked with people throughout the country—with many different financial and personal situations—who feel that they don't manage their money as well as they could or should. Yet most of them have not sought out help for various reasons: not enough money, embarrassment about their current financial situation, desire for privacy, not enough interest or drive to become involved, other conflicting demands which have taken priority.

Some of us feel quite confident about managing our own money, using a financial consultant or broker merely to execute our financial transactions. The rest of us, however, hang back and wait for someone, anyone, to take us by the hand and tell us exactly what must be done with our money and how to do it.

The extent to which we participate in money decisions can forecast how successful or unsuccessful we are in handling our money on a daily basis. There are people, for example, who refuse to budget. They have numerous excuses like "I can't stand to know how much money I don't have" or "I am terrible at math" or "I might make a mistake and lose money." Other "sensible" reasons are "You have to have a lot of money before you need a budget" or "Only people who have very little money need to make a budget."

These thoughts and excuses are self-defeating and prevent people from assuming control over their money. Everyone needs a budget because a budget is nothing more than a money plan. It's been said that a budget even allows spendthrifts to become better spendthrifts if that's what they want to become. Many people, especially those in the Moneymax Profile called the Hunters, prefer a "spending plan" to a budget. A spending plan helps people to prioritize how they are going to spend their money; "budget" has assumed a negative meaning because it implies a restriction of money, a cutting back of expenditures. Some people are investors but defer all investment decisions to professional money managers. Some people enjoy active participation in the financial arena and carefully select their investments and execute their own trades. Other people are too fearful to trust their money to anyone else or to any place other than the bank or a shoe box.

Are you not making investments because you are not interested in having more money? Very few people would answer, "Yes." Then what is the reason? Because you don't understand investments? Because you are too poor? Because investing is your spouse's responsibility? Whatever the reason, we have to face the fact that we have the ability to participate whether we deal with our money alone or have someone else manage it for us.

Are you an investor who has the knowledge and emotional fortitude necessary to make profitable financial decisions? Or would you prefer to rely on the skills of a professional money manager? Even when there is a desire to have a financial expert intervene in money matters, there is often a reluctance to seek out advice. The reasons that prevent people from hiring a professional include lack of trust, need for control, a desire to be personally involved.

Choose an investment, any investment—stocks, bonds, real estate— and ask yourself these questions: How active do you want to be in making the investment decision and in managing the investment? Do you want to be the primary decision-maker or leave the major responsibility to someone else? How much control do you want, and need, over your money to give you a sense of comfort and peace of mind?

Some of us like to follow market trends, read the stock reports, decipher the tax laws, and be in a position to manage our money intelligently. Others do not want to take the time to get a financial education and would like to give the responsibility to someone who earns a living by understanding the economy. If we choose to work with a financial professional, there are different ways of interacting with that person. We can give the professional total control over our money, or we can give control but always ask for final approval, or we can insist on a variety of investment options so we can be participatory decision-makers. The style of interacting as well as the choice of investment vehicles depend on the characteristics of the investments as well as the money personality of the investor.

One key idea to keep in mind about money management and investing: whatever you do not invest for profit, you forfeit. Anyone can invest; not everyone will. Money management programs often fail because people are thrown into a sea of financial terms and plans and neither the investor nor the financial professional takes into account the psychological attitudes toward money.

What's your perfect investment? "One that makes a bundle of money," might be the expected answer. But that is not always the case. Why not?

The perfect investment for you is not determined solely by the characteristics of the investment—your psychological needs and your personality are important, too. When your personality and sound judgment are in sync, chances are you'll have better results.

Most people think of risk tolerance when they think of matching personality characteristics to investments. An "I can't stand taking big chances" might lead to an investment portfolio of high grade municipal and corporate bonds and government securities. If, however, this risk-avoider winds up with a portfolio of stock in emerging growth companies, commodity futures contracts, and similar speculative investments, all he or she has bought is a period of sleepless nights and nail-biting days—or worse—no matter how much profit is made.

Investing is the process of giving up something now in order to receive something (preferably more) in the future. Taking risks in investments refers to giving up something known now without always being certain of what your return will be in the future. Often, the possibility exists that what you get will be less than your investment. Your risk tolerance is your ability to make decisions, trading the known for the unknown, and to be comfortable with the decision once it is made.

But risk tolerance is only one of the financial traits to consider before you create an investment portfolio that will make you feel comfortable. There are other traits, which have been examined in this book, that need to be considered when matching your investments and money management style to your money personality. The kinds of investments you'll feel comfortable with will depend on the dominance and configuration of your personal financial traits.

Before you can begin to understand how to use money, what it is, or how it works, you've got to know where you are in relation to money. What are your attitudes, good or bad, right or wrong, toward money?

How are you using money now? What fears and insecurities do you have about money? In what ways do you handle money well?

You have developed a money style just as you have developed a style of interacting socially and a style of thinking and learning. Your money style defines the amount of money you will continue to make until you change your patterns. Whenever you learn a new process, you have to determine your current skill level. After you become aware of your present behavior and thinking patterns about money, you can then begin to develop a new money management strategy.

Before you can learn to manage money successfully, you need to reprogram your money life so that you can gain insight into how you can make life pay off for you. You need to get control—alter your thinking and behavior patterns so that you are aligned emotionally and intellectually with the attitudes and behaviors that lead to financial gain. Getting the most out of money depends entirely on you—who you are, what you want, and how far you are from where you want to be.

Successful money management skills encompass three areas:

1. Self-awareness—what is really happening in your money life. Not what you wish would happen, like to see happen, or don't want to admit is happening.

2. An awareness and sensitivity to other people—being able to anticipate how others will act in a given money situation. Not how you would like them to act, hope they will act, or fear they will act.

3. An understanding of how money works—being able to predict how money will flow in transactions between yourself and other people.

It is important to take a hard look at how you perceive money. Successful investors are usually in control of their emotions and make decisions based on facts, not feelings. Psychological research tells us that behavior shapes attitudes just as attitudes shape behavior. If your behaviors are positive and productive, then your attitudes will be positive. Positive attitudes will, in turn, affect further productive behavior. Obviously, negative and counterproductive attitudes and behavior also follow the same cycle. When it comes to money, investing is an interaction between individuals and their money, and you can't leave the individual out of the equation.

REPROGRAMMING YOUR
MONEY PERSONALITY

The basic concept behind reprogramming is to identify the barriers which prevent better self-expression with money. For a lifetime, we have reinforced what we think is "right" about our money, so there is a good chance that there will be a lot of resistance in giving up a particular attitude or behavior. Our desire to be right about money often keeps us stuck in a money rut until we can identify money truths for ourselves. If we cheat with our money, we will always feel cheated.

What would you have to give up to make your money work better for you? Perhaps you would have to curb your spending habits or learn to abide by a budget. Maybe you would have to give up some of your leisure time in order to attend a few financial planning seminars. It might be time to stop complaining about a comfortable, but low-paying job, and begin a search for a new position. Many people are not motivated to take the necessary steps to streamline their financial affairs because they don't see an immediate payoff. You might ask yourself why you would like to have more money. What would be your personal rewards? Would you perhaps feel more in control of your life? Would you use money to enjoy your life more freely?

Americans have been conditioned to worry about money; it's part of our capitalistic birthright. Money problems are an accepted part of the price we pay for living in a competitive, free-enterprise society. There is, however, a big difference between money problems and money worries, and most of our money thoughts fall into the latter category. Regardless of income, most people don't feel particularly good about their financial status. But "worrying about money" is never a solution to a money problem. Could it be that worrying about money gives you an acceptable excuse not to risk a plan of action that would force you into taking control of your money?

There are many psychological barriers you face when confronting your money: guilt, indifference, anxiety, envy, a feeling that you're not smart enough to have money, a feeling that people will think less of you if you appear to hunger after money. These barriers have to be recognized, analyzed, discussed, and conquered. You must either take responsibility for your money attitudes or let them victimize you. If you take charge of your money, you will be in control; if you choose to play a money victim role, then your power lessens and someone else gains the upper hand. Accepting and taking responsibility for your money barriers are the first steps in making them disappear.

The starting position for reprogramming should be viewed as a process of re-creating, not change. Thinking about "change," might cause more anxiety than necessary. Instead, think of shifting your money problems and issues from a place of frustration to a place of opportunity. You have a much greater likelihood of switching your money perspective if you don't dwell on all your past financial mistakes, blaming yourself for each and every error in judgment. Take an inventory of your money beliefs; on one side list your money attitudes that you think are self-defeating and unproductive, and on the other side list those that you believe have been beneficial in your financial life.

After creating a personal attitude balance sheet, determine which traits are acting as barriers to a healthier, more productive money life. Next, create a game plan—I call it a Money Action Plan with my clients—to change your money liabilities into money assets. Start by listing moderately difficult goals—goals that will make you stretch and alter your money behavior, yet will not be too high and set you up for failure. Your Money Action Plan can be designed in modules with varying degrees of difficulty. With my clients, I set up modules in six-week segments, each module with specific goals to accomplish. The goals are more manageable that way, changes are cumulative, and you have the opportunity to restructure them as you go along.

My clients find that after the first six weeks, awareness of their money behavior is heightened and they have been able to observe some definite changes. For some clients, it is the first time they have been able to learn more about who they are—by observing themselves through their actions with money. Never before had they questioned why they were doing what they were doing with their money—and if they wanted to be doing it. In addition, they found that their attitudes and behaviors were definitely linked to the way they earned money, spent it, saved it, and invested it. Finally, they were able to gain insight into how their money actions affected both their personal and business relationships.

The only way your money situation will improve is if you improve your self-awareness. The major stumbling block to a better financial future is you. Most people continue working hard to make a living, instead of working smart to earn financial freedom and more time to enjoy the fruits of their labor. In other words, most people work hard on the job but not on the economic future. Hard work alone never buys financial security; it comes from being a proficient financial planner. Financial dreams and aspirations do not become reality because of wishes and fantasies. For your money to change, you have to change. You must first believe that you deserve money, and then act with conviction and trust to get it. Only if you believe you are entitled to have what you want will you take advantage of opportunities to reach your goals. There is nothing wrong with asking yourself to provide yourself with a more secure financial future. Asking is the beginning of receiving because it kicks off the process. Wealth accumulation starts with the desire, then conviction, then commitment. Someone once said that wealth is 20 percent knowledge, 80 percent strategy.

How do you begin to re-create?

It takes self-knowledge, self-discipline, self-motivation, self-assertion, self-rehearsal, and the nurturing of the whole process with a lot of self-respect. If you keep trying to blame your financial situation on your parents, your spouse or ex-spouse, the economy, or the world—wishing that life were more equitable—sooner or later you will realize that even if outside factors are partly to blame, you can't do much to change them. You can, however, re-create for yourself a new money outlook.

You can design your life so that you wear what you want, drive what you want, live where you want, and generally use money to your benefit. If you don't take action now, it will be too easy to let your financial life deteriorate, and your money will only serve as a means of "just getting by." It is easy to fall into the trap of financial mediocrity. Is your current bank account balance a true indicator of your personal worth? If not, you need to review the reasons why you should re-create your money life. Those reasons will drive you to find the answers to how to begin a new relationship with money.

Wealth accumulation takes planning and diligence as well as inspiration. You will need short-term strategies as well as long-term goals. An action plan, coupled with commitment and discipline, will ensure a great likelihood of success. As you design your Money Action Plan, list the personal strengths as well as personal barriers to attaining your goals. You won't always like what you have to learn to re-create a new money self and life, but the financial and emotional payoff will make the effort worthwhile.

IN PERSPECTIVE: MONEYMAX STRATEGIES

Each of the Moneymax groups has a personality distinct from all the other groups; each has its own particular set of money attitudes and behaviors. I am often asked by clients and participants in Moneymax seminars to encapsulate the essence of each personality—in particular, to focus on the traits that need to be placed under scrutiny and perhaps changed. Thus, let's take a final look at each of the nine profiles:

ENTREPRENEURS

You earn the most of all the Moneymax groups yet don't often consider yourself as financially successful as you would like to be. Why? Because having contentment with your money might mean that you have "made it." If that were true, you might not have a reason for the high drive and ambition that keep you pushing ahead in life. You are not motivated by money as a primary goal; rather money is a by-product of your drive to succeed in whatever you do.

A word of caution: you might sometimes mislead yourself into thinking that money is more important to you than it really is. As a Moneymax Entrepreneur, you need to recognize that your drive to excel, to be the best, is most important. You are most content when you are accomplishing your goals, so those goals should always be clearly delineated. While your goals may always be higher than anyone else's, your expectations are also higher. Your willingness to work hard and your high degree of confidence will always be valuable assets.

Since money is so closely intertwined with your sense of achievement, you may never experience the high contentment of the Money Masters or the Optimists. Security and peace of mind with your financial status is not as important to you as it is to many of the other Moneymax groups. You are willing to sacrifice a total sense of financial well-being for the excitement and the challenge of attaining a goal and then moving on to a new and bigger goal. This willingness to challenge the forces, to tempt fate, can be your blind spot. When calculating how much risk to assume with your money, your internal barometer can sometimes fool you. You may convince yourself that a particular risk is reasonable when in reality it could be higher than you think; you may already be too stretched. You tend to believe that good luck will be on your side, and it often is because you usually position yourself so that you have as much working for you as possible. However, it is wise to acknowledge that fate doesn't always cooperate.

Your highly positive attitude can appear cavalier to many a friend and even a spouse. Some people may accuse you of winging it, being unprepared or unconcerned. They don't know that you just appear as calm as a duck on top of the water. No one really knows the energy that is expended as you think and plan, just as no one really sees how quickly a duck is moving underwater. For the most part, your high optimism is an asset, but keep in mind that your future may slip up on you when you least expect it. Your concentration on the present and your focus on current goals may distract you from more mundane matters like tracking your money and planning for your retirement years. Since money is not your end goal but a scorecard of your achievements, you will never be the type of person who chooses to spend time counting up your money. Just remember that it is important to know how much money you have, where it is, and how it is doing. If you don't want to be the primary money caretaker, make sure you find someone you trust to do that for you. You work hard, are successful, and earn good money, so it makes sense to have someone help you accumulate as much money as you need for future security. You don't need to alter your priorities, but your money might provide an even greater sense of achievement and contentment if you knew that it was working smarter for you.

HUNTERS

You are highly educated, are successful in a professional career, yet you don't always acknowledge your abilities and assets and apply them to your money. Taking charge of your money obviously is an area of conflict for you and one of great frustration. Often you are not consciously aware of your feelings but act out your emotions in the way you express yourself with money. At the same time, you are ambitious and want to get ahead financially, yet your behavior reflects another motive—spending money. To learn about your money attitudes, watch and monitor what you actually do with money instead of rationalizing your money behavior. You can gain insight by making a list of the money habits that disappoint you or sabotage the position you would really like to be in financially. These behaviors will give you clues into those areas that require change. Working through those changes will be frustrating, but you have to admit that you are already frustrated.

Money is important to you because you enjoy expressing yourself and your emotions with it. You have to transform some of those expressions into healthier attitudes and behaviors—ones that allow you a sense of enjoyment but don't sabotage your sense of well-being and self-esteem. As soon as you start to make changes in your money style, you will experience a greater sense of pride with your money and you will find it easier to commit yourself to continuing with those changes.

Currently, you don't reap what you sow. You want to be both financially successful and financially independent, but the goals appeal to you more than the process necessary to attain them. Wealth accumulation is not an instantaneous process for most people. It requires plodding along, delaying gratification, planning for the future as well as monitoring the present. Your style is not working for you because you want your money to provide contentment and peace of mind, yet you haven't found a way to make that happen for you.

First of all, you need to take active charge of your money and be vigilant about it. Take yourself more seriously as a money earner and a money manager. You are very capable of managing your work and can adapt those professional talents into money talents. Since you judge yourself and value yourself by your financial stature, you must treat that part of you more seriously. The real power of money comes from knowing that you can both get it and have it work for you. Your style prevents money from working for you and you fool yourself with how you use it in the short term. You are not content with your financial status and want more of a power edge with money—a greater sense of status and prestige. The power you want to derive from your money will be greatly enhanced when you truly believe that you are capable of earning money, managing it, and accumulating it. Those people who are successful in wealth accumulation are generally content with their money, but don't necessarily want money to bring them the prestige that you desire. Of course, the power derived from money may become less important to you as you become more active and more assertive with your money.

Start by assessing what money really means to you. What is its value and what do you expect it to provide that it isn't already providing? What could you do today to help you realize your financial aspirations? Are you placing too much responsibility for that task outside of yourself? If so, design a plan to put yourself in command. You can certainly get professional assistance along the way, but you have to evaluate all outside advice to see if it is taking you where you want to go. Of course, you have to know where it is you want to be in the money world and how you picture yourself when you get there.

If you don't start taking charge of your money and instead rely on fate, or other people, you will never achieve the sense of confidence and power that you want and you are entitled to have. You certainly are capable of being your own financial power base, but you have to reframe your money picture and begin to see yourself differently; then you can start behaving differently with your money.

HIGH ROLLERS

You enjoy making a statement with your money—expressing yourself and your feelings. In addition, you enjoy and seek stimulation with money. To support your style, you need plenty of reserve capital; however, not all High Rollers have the funds to support their style. Insufficient funds can get you into trouble and reflect on others in your life who are affected by your money style. Your choice of a creative and exciting way to live is fine as long as your financial statement matches up with the way you design your money management style.

You live for the moment. There are many people who could use a little of your ability to enjoy money and test fate by living more freely; their fears often inhibit them from spending money and enjoying it. You have fears as well, but you deny them and distract yourself by acting them out with money instead of confronting them. Facing those fears might cramp your style and prevent you from really "living." Unfortunately, you often choose short-term excitement with your money over the peace of mind that can come from knowing you are financially prosperous and secure.

Altering your money style doesn't mean that your life has to change radically in terms of your values and priorities. It means that you have to remove your emotions from your money and take a good hard look at your current financial situation and your style of dealing with money. You have to fine tune your perceptual skills and use them to get a good view of what is going on inside of you, instead of focusing your energies outside of yourself. Start betting on yourself instead of betting on fate, because betting on yourself will bring a much bigger payoff. You will always be the type of person who wants to be a player and participate in your money life—that is admirable and beneficial as long as you are not hurting yourself or anyone else in the process. Your money style tends to be very frustrating when you stand still long enough to acknowledge it, but you can reach a happy medium without giving up what is important to you.

You have a tremendous amount of untapped power and talent to instill in your money management. Getting focused and applying your talents to winning the money game is a challenge that many a High Roller has taken—and won. I have seen High Rollers turn around their money styles and channel their energies inward to winning at a game that they designed. Then they were not betting on luck, but on themselves. They had to face some of their own emotions, like fear of failing, or even fear of success. But they moved forward and went on to learn that they enjoyed the game even more when they were active participants. In the end it was much more thrilling when they were structuring the rules of the game and had a greater likelihood of being a winner, instead of a loser.

You can get out of a game that you can't seem to win with your present money style and create a new game—one in which you know the rules and are more likely to be able to control the outcome. You can still have excitement, feel challenged, stretch yourself. The payoff may not be as glamorous; however, it will be more assured. This new strategy will get you where you ultimately want to go, but it will take longer and require new attitudes and behaviors. This may feel uncomfortable at first, and you may become bored and somewhat distressed. But, if you can get through the discomfort of change, you will find a new excitement that will last beyond the moment and bring you greater rewards in many areas of your life—your work, your relationships, and also your sense of yourself.

SAFETY PLAYERS

You are not an adventuresome money sailor like the High Roller. In fact, you don't particularly like to captain or steer your money ship. You would rather hope that outside forces keep you and your money safe. However, you are not going to count on outside forces because you basically don't trust anyone else with your money. As a result, you are in a Catch-22 with your money—you are not particularly interested in becoming more active in mastering it, but you really don't want someone else to take control of it. To avoid frustration, you have placed yourself in a sea of indifference about money. If there were a golden ring within reach, you might see it and say, "I believe that is a golden ring, but I bet it is hard to catch; I'm not going to try. I know others have tried, and it's probably impossible to capture. Why frustrate myself?" Thus, you might rationalize away a good opportunity or never see it—even if it was in full view.

Some people, like the Entrepreneurs, are driven toward success. You are motivated to maintain and protect your status quo—which is fine by many people's standards. Because you want to minimize your losses, you don't risk. For you, assuming risk is not worth rocking your money complacency and low anxiety. Because you want to eliminate any kind of money stress in your life, you are more concerned with protecting what you have rather than multiplying it. However, at times, you do find yourself making impulsive financial decisions because you want to avoid getting too involved and too analytical. Your low key, protective style does pay off for you in some ways, so you tend to stay away from projects, people, or ideas that necessitate getting involved beyond your comfort zone.

Your style, while safe and secure, does not bring you very much contentment. Perhaps you haven't thought through how money could bring you more pleasure or reflected on whether or not your money management system has been effective for you. Taking that kind of overview would bring you greater insight and show you how your money could serve you better. You will need to look at how your money attitudes impact the money you earn, how you earn it, and if you use it to improve and enjoy your life. You might find that your attitudes about money involve an inordinate amount of skepticism, which can restrict your optimum use of it.

You have a tendency to disbelieve that your money situation could be much different. You question whether your individual efforts could really make a significant improvement in financial prosperity or your money contentment level. You might portray yourself as more of a money victim and not see the possibility of defining yourself as a Money Master. Remember, your perception of yourself can become the role you play with your money. Other people might see you differently and think you are quite adept at earning and managing money. They might envy the skills and talents that you don't recognize, capitalize on, and reinforce.

Try seeing yourself as having the ability and the insight to turn your money attitudes around—moving away from indifference, status quo, and low contentment. Instead of trying to protect yourself from the potential loss of your money, try trusting yourself and believing that you can achieve whatever money life you design.

Without much involvement or self-determination, you have managed to earn a respectable financial ranking among all the Moneymax groups. That, in itself, is valid proof that you do possess the potential to alter your money situation. If you were to reevaluate your attitudes about money and become more self-assertive and involved in managing your money, then you could not only move up the money ladder but could also enjoy your money more and gain greater peace of mind.

ACHIEVERS

You attribute your financial successes to your skills and abilities and your failures to the fact that you didn't try hard enough. You are confident of your money management skills and don't feel comfortable making any financial decision unless you have thoroughly reviewed all the facts. When you succeed, you know that it has been because of your own talents and not because you were lucky. Likewise, if you experience financial failure, you conclude that you didn't put enough effort into a particular task or decision.

You are at the helm of your money ship. In fact, you rarely let anyone else steer. When it comes to your money, you believe that you are the best at controlling it and are not very confident that others will be as trustworthy. This tenacity to control your money may create some problems for you in relationships if you hold too tight to the purse strings. You feel most comfortable when you are the sole decision-maker. This tendency, of course, becomes troublesome when another person wants to become involved in your financial picture—whether it be personal, business, or social circumstances.

While your high desire for involvement and control with your money can be extremely beneficial and allow you to reap rewards, it can prevent you from maximizing your money gains. You certainly are doing very well by most standards, but you are not as content with your money as the Money Masters, who have greater trust in others when it comes to money. The Money Masters also desire high involvement yet don't tend to worry as much as you do. Your difficulty in delegating any financial responsibility, your strong need to control all money matters, and the high standards you set for yourself can create some anxiety. You might experience less stress and be even more content than you already are if you would take a critical look at your financial concerns and determine if the concerns are well-founded.

If you are dissatisfied with the return on your investments or the money you are accumulating, remember that for you the return always has to be judged against the risk. You are more relaxed and secure when your risks are well calculated and on the low side.

You are more confident and proud than most Moneymax groups. You take charge of your money and don't believe in leaving anything to chance. Those characteristics are very admirable and will continue to generate good results for you unless you squeeze your dollars too tight or stifle your creativity and self-expression in the process.

PERFECTIONISTS

The Achievers make their highly analytical money style pay off for them whereas you allow yours to hold you back. Achievers would feel most comfortable trusting someone else with their money if they could clone that person to be exactly like them. You, however, don't trust the judgment of others, yet you also don't trust your own judgment. Both Perfectionists and Achievers like to handle money decisions alone. This is not necessarily a problem and can certainly be an asset unless it blocks you from missing opportunities to both use your money and enjoy it. You could easily talk yourself out of a good money opportunity because you tend to be too skeptical of a successful outcome. The Achievers are very proud of their successes, yet they are also able to take their setbacks in stride, knowing that they will put forth even more effort the next time to assure success. That kind of attitude keeps Achievers striving for a high level of achievement and gives them a sense of pride in their financial feats. You, on the other hand, have a tendency to block your own flow of energy, even when you are moving in the right direction. You can stop yourself before you even begin and can become your own worst enemy. Your tendency to worry can cause you to look for a reason why a financial decision won't work, fostering a negative way of viewing your money that affects your sense of financial security and your peace of mind.

You have a pent-up desire to relate to your money differently. You want to believe that you can attain financial freedom without struggle. Changing your perception of your money glass from half empty to half full certainly is possible. Unfortunately, that change will not just happen to you. You will have to look inward and change the way you react to opportunities in your money life. You have to look at your resistance to being unburdened by anxiety about your money. What are the excuses you use for explaining why money is not working properly for you? What would your money self be like if money were working for you?

Your life doesn't always have to be a struggle with money. The situation can definitely improve, but you have to be willing to give up that part of you that worries and is discontent with money. I've often had Perfectionist clients say that they were afraid to change because they couldn't imagine that their lives could ever really be free from worry and doubt about money. If you have trouble picturing what your life would be like without money struggles, then it's no wonder that you have those struggles in your life. Obviously, there are real problems regarding money in everyone's life, but how you perceive a problem determines whether you can turn a situation from one that is stressful to one that is manageable. Resistance builds barriers that can become immovable and unchangeable. Your resistance and negative perceptions may be so automatic and unconscious that you don't even realize that you are getting in your own way. Perception is a tricky business. One person may view a particular situation as insurmountable while another person sees it as a challenge. Some people never change their money attitudes and the way they relate to money because they can't imagine a more prosperous and content life. You can change the frustration you may be feeling by starting to notice how you perceive different money situations. Make a concerted effort to think of those situations in a more positive manner—concentrating on the bright side instead of the dark side.

MONEY MASTERS

The artist has a gift for knowing how to put things in proper perspective and is an expert at mixing colors, combining oils so that the finished masterpiece depicts the desired image. Whether the painting is realistic or abstract, it is a complete and well-executed expression. A Money Master knows how to blend money throughout life so that it complements and enhances personal fulfillment.

Your style is subtle and you prefer a low key expression of your money. You use your money to complement who you are instead of trying to find yourself in your money. You have been diligent with your money management and have provided amply for your security and well-being. You are in control and have attained tremendous confidence from exercising your money skills. You are certain that your money efforts, when correctly channeled, will continue to bring you financial success.

Your keen sense of yourself can sometimes be misjudged and misinterpreted. You may appear aloof, without vulnerabilities, and therefore threatening to others who have never been able to reach your level of confidence and expertise. You respect people who are self-reliant and self-assertive and sometimes have difficulty understanding why some people can't make money work properly in their lives.

No matter what your age, you are not a person who enjoys living just for the moment but always need to calculate what lies ahead. You have a talent for putting things in proper perspective in order to maximize your financial efforts and are aware of the importance of being rational instead of impulsive with your money. Faced with a financial decision, you know when to hold on and when to let go. You trust that others are basically honest with money and this trust allows you peace of mind when you find it necessary to share or delegate financial responsibility.

You have reached optimum levels of self-regulation and self-expression with your money. You have been a front-runner in all money arenas—earning it, investing it, accumulating it, enjoying it, allowing it to provide personal freedom and contentment. You are truly a master of the money game.

PRODUCERS

You believe in working hard but are disappointed with the financial rewards of your hard work. You never really feel that you have control over your money management. The lack of control is not due to excessive spending habits but because your financial status and earning power don't keep pace with your desired standard of living.

To relieve a great deal of the anxiety you feel about your money, you have to gain a better understanding of the money world—not only how to get more money but also what to do with it once you get it. There are many people who, like you, believe that hard work is, or should be, the key to accumulating money and achieving financial freedom. Unfortunately, hard work is not the sole criterion for financial success. People like the Money Masters have accumulated wealth because they have a more expansive perspective on money. Like you, the Money Masters have a strong work ethic, but they also have a solid knowledge and understanding of the business world and the investment world.

You have to make a commitment to yourself to fill the gap between where you are now and where you want to be. Making that commitment to go after some of your unfulfilled dreams will ultimately pay off not only financially but will also result in a greater sense of confidence and pride.

Be sure to choose your goals wisely and develop a focused game plan so that you can capitalize on the efforts you are going to have to expend. You have the personal stamina necessary to reap greater benefits with your money if you are more deliberate and analytical in going after what it is that you want out of life.

You have a great deal of integrity and an admirable set of personal standards and values. However, you may devote too much time and energy being concerned about what other people think of you, instead of focusing on yourself. Some of the energy that is used to accommodate other people's needs should be redirected into accommodating your own needs and desires.

You do want to be financially successful and secure. You are entitled to a better money life but you must first believe that you are entitled to it. Once you decide to aim for a stronger money style, you will have to work hard, but hard work is one of your strong points. You can feel more valuable to yourself and to others, but you need to believe you are deserving; ask for what you want and be more self-assertive. Once you activate a plan to improve your money life, your admirable work ethic will be the source of greater wealth instead of frustration.

OPTIMISTS

You are complacent with your money but some people may call it a blind bliss. You aren't particularly interested in taking charge of your money but don't experience money anxiety because you feel your financial needs are pretty much satisfied. However, your confidence in your money management style is not a result of diligent planning. Quite the contrary. You do not want to be integrally involved in money or investment decisions. Nonetheless, you are quite proud of the way you handle your financial affairs, and your expectations for future success are high, even though you don't devote much energy to ensuring success.

You would rather spend your time enjoying your money instead of cultivating its growth. You appear to have a low frustration tolerance so you avoid situations that might engender any kind of money stress. This complacent, status quo approach can backfire when a more vigorous approach is required. For instance, if you are at an age when long-range financial planning is necessary, you might jeopardize your future if you neglect to become involved. Since financial planning is not a task that you welcome, you need to be aware that you are likely to opt for impulsive, rather than analytical, decisions.

You like to enjoy your money in a low key fashion and don't need to make other people aware of your financial status. You accept yourself as you are, have no desire to change, and have little to prove with your money—all of which give you a great deal of contentment and peace of mind.

There are, however, two areas that warrant your attention. First, you should take a second look at your lack of involvement in money management. Without a plan to monitor your money, you may come up short some day when you least expect it. Inadequate planning could result in insufficient funds to meet your future needs. Thus, you might consider positioning some of your money in investments that are growth-oriented so you can sustain the lifestyle you enjoy today. Second, since you do like to spend your money rather than save it, you might have a tendency to overspend. Implementing a prioritized spending plan—one which wouldn't cramp your style—is another option you should consider.

You are living proof that it takes more than just having money to enjoy it; it takes the expectation and the inclination to enjoy it. Your money orientation is positive because you are confident, proud, and content. As a result, your money enhances your sense of well-being and happiness in your life—just as it should for everyone.

POSTSCRIPT

Money cannot buy happiness but it can be used constructively, as a tool to improve the quality of life, to increase the options in life, and to provide a sense of security and well-being. A true sense of mental wealth is attained when the following criteria are met:

1. You understand your money personality—how you relate to your money and how your attitudes affect your money behavior.

2. You neither exaggerate or deny the importance of money.

3. Money is not viewed as an end in itself, but as a reward for achievement.

4. You control your money instead of letting it control you.

5. Money provides satisfaction and enjoyment as well as security.

You cannot afford, financially or personally, to take a passive approach to money. Like it or not, money can enhance happiness and posterity or it can destroy security and well-being. No one can drift to the pinnacle of success—you have to climb.

Ambivalent feelings about money are counterproductive. In order to become financially liberated, it is essential to understand who you are in terms of money, who you would like to be, what changes are necessary, and how to make those changes. Our money lives are filled with a lot of emotional baggage which must be discarded before we can reach financial success and peace of mind. Indecision and inactivity only create financial paralysis and chaos.

Ultimately, money success comes from self-validation—as you think about your money self, so you become. Those who are willing to take an honest look at money truths—instead of camouflaging life with money myths and illusions—have a much better chance of achieving mental wealth.

Index

ABOUT THE AUTHOR

Dr. Kathleen Gurney, president of Financial Psychology Corporation, is a Los Angeles-based psychologist and former professor of psychological research and testing at the University of Southern California.

She is solely responsible for pioneering the field of Financial Psychology and has worked with various financial service companies and Fortune 500 companies. In these companies her consulting work has included training of financial professionals in the use of the Moneymax Profile with clients, recruiting and selecting of employees, career development and enhancement, management training, compensation analysis, motivational development, and marketing research.

In addition, she also counsels individuals and couples and conducts seminars and workshops for private groups and public corporations on the psychology of money and related topics. She has been a guest speaker at numerous national conferences and meetings.

Dr. Gurney's work has been discussed in national newspapers and magazines as well as on national television and radio. She writes a monthly column, "In Session," for *Registered Representative* magazine.